Audio Production Basics
with Pro Tools|First

To access online media visit:
www.halleonard.com/mylibrary

3058-7927-1283-4969

Audio Production Basics
with Pro Tools|First

Frank D. Cook
Eric Kuehnl

Hal Leonard Books
An Imprint of Hal Leonard LLC

NextPoint Training, Inc.

Published in 2017 by Hal Leonard Books
An Imprint of Hal Leonard LLC
7777 West Bluemound Road
Milwaukee, WI 53213

Trade Book Division Editorial Offices
33 Plymouth St., Montclair, NJ 07042

Printed in the United States of America

Book design by NextPoint Training, Inc.

Library of Congress Cataloging-in-Publication Data is available upon request.

ISBN 978-1-4950-9558-0

www.halleonardbooks.com

Contents

Acknowledgments

The authors would like to give special thanks to the following individuals who have provided assistance, input, information, material, and other support for this book.

Mark Anderson, Bruce Bennett, Nick Benz, Jon Connolly, Andy Cook, Dave Cotton, Mark Garvey, Michael Flores, Simon Pennington, Connor Sexton, Michael Tanamachi, Ryan Wardell, The Pinder Brothers, Bruce Tambling, Zack Vieira.

Eric would like to thank his wife and children for their support and understanding: Amanda Goodroe, Thom, and Freddie.

Frank would like to thank his wife Beth and sons Colton and Brett for putting up with the long work hours and chaos associated with life as an entrepreneur and small-business owner.

Welcome to the World of Audio

Sounds are all around us. They make our world interesting, informative, and engaging. It's only natural to want to capture these auditory experiences—the sounds we like, the sounds that we want to share, and the sounds we create. That is truly what audio production is all about: capturing and sharing sound.

Pro Tools|First software provides a perfect springboard for learning the basics of audio production and improving the results of all your audio endeavors.

With this book, you're taking the first step toward discovering the power of Pro Tools and unlocking your audio creativity. Whether you've selected this book to use for self-study or have picked it up as the required text for instructor-led classroom training, you will find that it provides essential background information on audio production from the ground up. It also gives you everything you need to know to fully understand the roll of Pro Tools in today's landscape of digital audio workstations (DAWs).

Getting Started in Audio Production

This book teaches the basics of recording, editing, mixing, and processing audio and MIDI using Pro Tools|First software. It also provides plenty of power tips for going beyond the basics to unleash the true power of this award-winning technology. Nearly everything you learn in this book will apply equally to commercial versions of Pro Tools. This means you'll have a solid foundation, should you upgrade in the future or find yourself working in a full Pro Tools studio down the line.

Who Should Read This Book

Although this book is written to support the free Pro Tools|First software, the concepts apply equally to standard Pro Tools software and Pro Tools|HD systems. As such, this book serves as a resource both for Pro Tools|First users and for users of commercial versions of the software. Readers who are running paid or subscription versions of Pro Tools software can use the techniques described in this book, and complete the included exercises, with virtually identical results to those running Pro Tools|First software.

To ensure that the topics covered in this book apply to all versions of Pro Tools, we have included additional details on the differences between platforms where they apply. This book is designed to help new and inexperienced users get started with little or no background knowledge. However, the scope is not limited to novice users who are experimenting with DAWs for the first time.

What Is Pro Tools|First?

Pro Tools|First is a free version of Pro Tools software that is available via download from Avid.com for use by anyone who wishes to create or collaborate on Pro Tools projects. The software is fully compatible with commercial versions of Pro Tools, allowing complete freedom to interchange projects with systems running standard Pro Tools or Pro Tools|HD software.

Pro Tools|First runs on any compatible host computer. It does not require any additional hardware or authorization keys (such as the iLok key that is required for commercial versions). The free software download includes over 20 plug-in processors as well as the Xpand!2 multitimbral virtual instrument.

As you will learn, Pro Tools|First includes nearly all of the audio production features and capabilities found in standard Pro Tools software, limited primarily by a restricted track count, constrained I/O support, and limited storage options.

Pro Tools|First offers a more streamlined user experience and a gentler learning curve than commercial versions of Pro Tools. However, the depth of features that it includes makes it an ideal learning environment and an excellent springboard for advanced Pro Tools use.

About This Book

This book is designed for use in a formal course of study and offers a preview of Avid's official Pro Tools certification courses. This course serves as a natural precursor to the in-depth, hands-on learning experience available by taking classes with one of Avid's authorized training partners. For more information on the classes offered through the Avid Learning Partner program, visit www.avid.com, click on **Learn & Support**, and explore the available topics, or go directly to www.avid.com/education.

Requirements and Prerequisites

This course does not require any specific background knowledge of computer systems, recording technology, or digital audio workstations. However, before starting to work with Pro Tools|First, it definitely helps to have at least a passing familiarity with computer concepts and recording gear. If you consider yourself a novice in these areas, pay special attention to the first four chapters of this book.

To try out the concepts and complete the tutorials in this book, you will need to use a compatible computer and install the Pro Tools|First software (or have access to a commercial version of Pro Tools software). Details on computer requirements are provided in Chapter 1, and installation details for Pro Tools|First are provided in Chapter 2.

If you will be using other connected audio or MIDI hardware, you may need to install device drivers for those components. Consult the documentation that came with your hardware or search the manufacturer's website for details.

Media Files

This book includes exercise tutorials at the end of each chapter that make use of various media files. The media files can be accessed by visiting www.halleonard.com/mylibrary and entering your access code, as printed on the opening page of this book. Instructions for downloading the media files are provided in Exercise 1.

Course Organization and Sequence

This course has been designed to teach you what is required to get the most out of your work with Pro Tools or Pro Tools|First. The material is organized into ten chapters, as follows:

- **Chapter 1. Computer Concepts**—What you need from a computer

- **Chapter 2. DAW Concepts**—What you need from your DAW

- **Chapter 3. Audio Recording Concepts**—What you need to record audio

- **Chapter 4. MIDI Recording Concepts**—What you need to record MIDI

- **Chapter 5. Pro Tools Concepts, Part 1**—What you need to know to get started with Pro Tools|First

- **Chapter 6. Pro Tools Concepts, Part 2**—What you need to know to work with Pro Tools|First

- **Chapter 7. Mixing Concepts**—What you need to know to mix a project

- **Chapter 8. Signal Processing**—What you can do to optimize your audio

- **Chapter 9. Finishing a Project**—What you need to do to create a stereo mixdown

- **Chapter 10. Going Beyond the Basics**—What to explore to become a power user

Users who have experience with computers and other DAWs may wish to skim the first four chapters, focusing mostly on the details that are specific to Pro Tools|First.

Conventions and Symbols Used in This Book

Following are some of the conventions and symbols we've used in this book. We try to use familiar conventions and symbols whose meanings are self-evident.

Keyboard Shortcuts and Modifiers

Menu choices and keyboard commands are typically capitalized and written in bold text. Hierarchy is shown using the greater than symbol (>), keystroke combinations are indicated using the plus sign (+), and mouse-click operations are indicated by hyphenated strings, where needed. Brackets ([ ]) are used to indicate key presses on the numeric keypad.

Convention	Action
File > Save Session	Choose Save Session from the File menu.
Ctrl+N	Hold down the Ctrl key and press the N key.
Command-click (Mac)	Hold down the Command key and click the mouse button.
Right-click	Click with the right mouse button.
Press [1]	Press 1 on the numeric keypad.

Icons

The following icons are used in this book to call attention to tips, shortcuts, listening suggestions, warnings, and reference sources.

Tips provide helpful hints and suggestions, background information, or details on related operations or concepts.

Shortcuts provide useful keyboard, mouse, or modifier-based shortcuts that can help you work more efficiently.

Power Tips provide shortcuts and tips for power users that can dramatically speed up your work but go beyond the scope of the current discussion.

Listening Suggestions refer you to audio examples that illustrate a concept or technique discussed in the text.

Warnings caution you against conditions that may affect audio playback, impact system performance, alter data files, or interrupt hardware connections.

Cross-References alert you to another section, book, or resource that provides additional information on the current topic.

Online References provide links to online resources and downloads related to the current topic.

Chapter 1

Computer Concepts

...What You Need from a Computer...

In this chapter, we introduce you to the basic components of a computer system and the minimum configuration required to run Pro Tools|First software. We also discuss how to configure the hardware for your system and how to configure your computer's software settings for optimal results. Lastly, we take a brief look at how to work within your digital audio workstation, using Pro Tools|First as an example.

✪ Learning Targets for This Chapter

- Understand how to select a computer for your digital audio workstation

- Understand how to navigate your computer's operating system for basic file management purposes

- Understand how to set preferences for your computer and your software

- Understand how to perform basic operations with your digital audio workstation

Selecting the right digital audio workstation (or DAW) involves many considerations: What features do you need? How big will your projects be? What kind of production work do you intend to do? What kind of system can you afford? And so on. Prior to making a purchase, you would be wise to check out a trial version or low-cost (feature-limited) edition of the product you are considering, if available.

Fortunately, for those considering Pro Tools as their DAW of choice, Avid offers Pro Tools|First software completely free of charge. Although Pro Tools|First does have certain limitations, it is remarkably full-featured. Pro Tools|First provides a streamlined user experience and a gentler learning curve than commercial versions of Pro Tools, making it an ideal learning environment for new users.

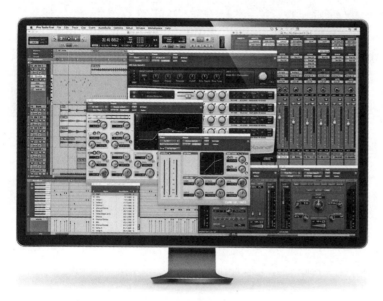

Figure 1.1 Pro Tools|First software with plug-in windows open

Before installing Pro Tools|First (or other DAW software), you'll need to verify that your computer system meets the minimum requirements for the software. Once you've cleared that hurdle and installed the software on a suitable computer, you will want to configure your computer and the software application for optimal performance. This chapter will help steer you in the right direction for these and other considerations to get a system up and running successfully.

Selecting a Computer

In this section, we will look at how to select a computer for use with Pro Tools|First or another digital audio workstation of your choice. We will also look at options for optimizing your computer setup to get the most out of your work environment.

Mac Versus Windows Considerations

One of your first considerations is whether to run your DAW on a Mac-based computer or a Windows-based computer. This decision is primarily one of personal preference, but it may also be based on the kind of system you already own.

If you are purchasing a new system for your DAW, understanding some general characteristics of Macs and Windows machines may help you decide on one platform versus the other.

Mac-Based Computers

One of the big selling points for Macs is how well they interact with other Apple products: iPhones, iPads, AppleTVs, and the AppleWatch. If you have already bought in to the Apple ecosystem, it may make sense to purchase a Mac computer for that reason alone. You will find the user experience on a Mac to be similar to that on other Apple products, in many respects.

Interoperability aside, Macs systems have a reputation for being easy to use and simple to understand. Additionally, Macs are known for high quality construction and attention to detail in their design.

The downside to purchasing a Mac is the higher price you will pay for those conveniences. You will likely spend more for a Mac-based system than you would for a similarly configured Windows-based system.

Windows-Based Computers

Windows-based computers are available from many different manufacturers, giving you an abundance of choices when selecting a system. The competition between manufacturers means it may be easier to find a system that meets your needs at a more affordable price point.

In addition to competitive pricing, Windows computers may also have an advantage in terms of the applications they support. If you use certain Windows-only applications for personal or work-related purposes, you may find that issue to be a deciding factor in your choice of platform.

Whichever platform you choose—Mac or Windows—be sure to purchase a system with adequate RAM, processing power, storage space, and connectivity options to support your needs.

The Importance of RAM

A computer's installed RAM, or random access memory, determines how much data and information can be stored in the computer's memory at any given time. RAM is generally used for temporary storage while an application is running. The RAM allocation is typically measured in Gigabytes (or GB).

Figure 1.2 Illustration of a typical RAM module

Running Windows on a Mac

If you prefer to work on a Mac but need to run Windows for certain applications, several options are available. Modern Mac computers allow you to run a Windows operating system (OS) on your Mac hardware. You can configure a Mac to run Windows 10, for example, using either a separate disk partition or a virtualization software option.

To configure a separate disk partition for Windows 10, you can use the Boot Camp Assistant utility that comes with your Mac. This utility will partition your drive and guide you through the installation process for the Windows software. Using this option, you will need to restart your computer whenever you wish to switch between the Mac OS and the Windows OS.

To run Windows 10 with virtualization software instead, you can purchase and install software such as VMware Fusion or Parallels Desktop. These applications allow you to run a Windows OS on your Mac desktop without rebooting.

With either option, you will need to purchase Windows 10 separately and install it. Factor this in when considering the total budget for your system. The virtualization software (if used) and the Windows OS may also impact the amount of RAM, storage space, and processing power required for the system.

How RAM Is Used

When you select a paragraph of text in a word processor and choose the **EDIT > COPY** command, the text is stored temporarily in RAM. You can then move your cursor to a new location in the document and choose **EDIT > PASTE**. The text stored in RAM gets added to the document at the current cursor location.

Most applications also use RAM to keep track of the work you do in your open documents. As you work, a record of your changes and edits is saved in RAM. This allows you to use the **EDIT > UNDO** command, for example, to reverse any changes you've made.

The code required to run the application is also stored in RAM while the application is running. This allows the computer to work faster than it would if it had to run the application entirely from the hard drive.

Storing data in RAM allows the information to be retrieved and operated on very quickly.

However, once you quit an application or shut down your computer, the information stored in RAM is lost. That is why your changes must be saved to permanent storage first.

Why More RAM Is Better

DAWs such as Pro Tools rely on RAM to work efficiently. Like a word processor, a DAW uses RAM for edit operations. Your DAW will also use RAM to keep track of your changes and undoable actions.

In Pro Tools software, we call the list of user-undoable actions the *Undo Queue*.

The more RAM your computer system has installed, the more memory will be available to your DAW software for temporary storage. This means the application can run more efficiently, you can copy and paste larger amounts of data, and you can maintain a longer list of complex undoable actions.

Symptoms of insufficient RAM can include sluggish behavior, frequent error messages, long pauses (or hangs) when you perform certain actions, and sudden crashes.

DAW manufacturers typically publish minimum RAM specifications required to run the application. They may also suggest that you install more RAM for more efficient operation. For work on very large or complicated projects, you may want to exceed the manufacturer recommendations.

RAM Required for Pro Tools | First

The minimum RAM allocation to run Pro Tools | First on either a Mac or Windows computer is 4 GB, with 8 GB or more recommended. If you plan to run Pro Tools | First at the same time as other applications (iTunes, a web browser, an email client, etc.), you would be wise to target the high side of these numbers.

If you think you might upgrade to a paid version of Pro Tools in the future, you will need a larger RAM allocation. Standard Pro Tools 12.8 software requires a minimum of 8 GB of RAM, with 16 GB or more recommended. Pro Tools | HD 12.8 requires 16 GB, with 32 GB or more recommended.

Installing More RAM

Depending on the model computer you buy, you may be able to add more RAM at a later time, as your needs grow. This can help keep the initial purchase price down. If this is your plan, make sure to do your homework before purchasing a computer. Certain models (especially "budget" options) have RAM chips soldered in place and cannot be upgraded later with more.

Also note that upgrading RAM often requires you to replace all RAM in the computer, rather than simply adding to the existing RAM. Most computers have an even number of memory slots, with RAM assigned in pairs across them.

For example, a laptop may have 4 GB of RAM allocated across two available memory slots. In such a case, each slot will have a 2 GB memory module installed. To upgrade to 8 GB of RAM, you would need to replace each module with a new 4 GB module. (RAM modules should be added in matching pairs.)

Processing Power

The processing power, or how fast a computer runs, is a function of the computer's central processing unit, or CPU. The CPU is responsible for performing all of the processing and calculations required by an application.

Figure 1.3 The computer's central processing unit determines how fast the computer can run.

Processing Speed. The speed of a CPU is based on its clock speed. Clock speeds for modern computers are measured in GHz (Gigahertz), or billions of cycles per second. A 1 GHz processor, for example, can process up to one billion instructions per second. The faster the CPU, the more powerful the computer, and the faster your applications will run.

Processor Cores. Another consideration is the number of processing cores in the computer chip. Many computer chips today offer dual cores, quad cores, or more. This means that the CPU includes multiple processing units within a single chip. The benefit of multiple cores is that the computer can process multiple instructions at one time. This in turn allows modern applications to run faster and more efficiently.

Hyper-Threading

Many CPUs support hyper-threading as an alternative (or supplement) to multiple physical cores. Intel's hyper-threading technology allows a single physical core to perform as two virtual cores. This has the same benefit as adding physical cores, as it doubles the number of instruction threads that the CPU can process at once when running an application.

How Processing Power Affects Your DAW

A host-based DAW like Pro Tools|First relies on the processing power of the host computer for all audio editing, mixing, and processing. A system with insufficient processing power may exhibit sluggish performance, unwanted audio artifacts, and frequent error messages. Projects involving large track counts and heavy use of plug-ins will be more susceptible to issues.

Certain audio processes are especially CPU-intensive. Some examples of common practices that may tax your CPU include the following:

■   Using certain Edit operations that automatically split audio into many smaller pieces

■   Stacking plug-ins on inserts, especially convolution reverbs and analog gear emulations

- Using many virtual instrument plug-ins in a project

- Using real-time Elastic Audio processing

- Configuring complex signal routing for submix groups, headphone outputs, and effects processing

To avoid running into processing limitations as your projects grow in complexity, look for a multi-core CPU that runs at a reasonably high speed.

Processing Requirements for Pro Tools

The minimum CPU requirement for Pro Tools|First is an Intel Core i5 processor running at 2.6 GHz or more. The same minimum CPU requirements apply if you plan to upgrade to standard Pro Tools. However, Pro Tools|HD requires an Intel Core i7 processor or an Intel Xeon processor; these processors generally use four or more cores running at high speeds.

Most computer systems available today meet the minimum CPU requirements to run Pro Tools|First.

 Pro Tools|First supports multithreading, so you will get better performance out of a quad-core processor than you will out of a duo-core, for example.

Always Check Compatibility Before You Buy!

New versions of Pro Tools often have more stringent compatibility requirements than previous versions. Prior to buying a system, be sure to check the compatibility requirements on the Avid website.

Requirements for Pro Tools|First, standard Pro Tools 12, and Pro Tools|HD 12 can be found at the following web addresses, respectively:

- http://avid.force.com/pkb/articles/compatibility/Pro-Tools-First-System-Requirements

- http://avid.force.com/pkb/articles/compatibility/Pro-Tools-12-System-Requirements

- http://avid.force.com/pkb/articles/en_US/Compatibility/Pro-Tools-HD-12-System-Requirements

---

Storage Space

Another important consideration when buying a computer is the amount of storage space the computer provides. This is a function of the computer's installed hard disk drive (HDD) or solid state drive (SSD). The size of the storage drive determines how many applications you can install and how much space you will have for saving files on your system.

Figure 1.4 Illustration of a hard disk drive

Determining How Much Drive Space You Need

When determining storage requirements for your DAW, you will need to consider multiple factors:

- How much space is required to install the DAW software application itself.

- How much space is required to install the plug-ins you intend to use with the DAW.

- How much space you will need for the projects and media files that you create with the DAW.

- How much space you will need for other media files that you may want to use with the DAW (such as sample libraries, loop libraries, and sound effects).

In addition, you may need to consider the impact of other files and applications that you want to use on your computer. For example, if you plan to store your digital photos and your personal music collection on the computer, you will need to allocate addition space for those purposes.

Likewise, if you will use the computer for work in programs such as Microsoft Word, PowerPoint, and Excel, you will need additional space to install each of those applications.

Installation Requirements for Pro Tools|First

To install Pro Tools|First software, you will need a minimum of 15 GB of storage space for the application and the included plug-in options.

 Standard Pro Tools 12.8 and Pro Tools|HD 12.8 software have the same 15 GB installation requirement, although more space may be required for additional plug-in options.

Storage Options

Many storage options are available for today's computer systems. A computer's internal system drive may be either an HDD or an SSD. The internal storage can be supplemented by any number of external drives and storage options. To allow your files to be accessed from anywhere, you can also consider cloud-based storage.

HDD Versus SSD Storage

HDD. Hard disk drives use spinning metal disks to store data. The more disks in the drive, the higher the data capacity. Storage sizes for modern HDDs typically range from around 1 to 4 Terabytes (TB).

The data transfer speed for an HDD is based in part on the speed of the spinning disks, measured in revolutions per minute (or RPM). Common options include 5400 RPM drives and 7200 RPM drives.

Hard disk drives provide greater storage capacity at a lower price than their solid-state counterparts.

SSD. Solid state drives, by comparison, use flash memory for storage instead of spinning metal disks. The storage capacity of an SSD is based on the number and size of memory chips it has. Storage sizes for SSDs typically range from 256 GB to 1 TB.

Solid state drives provide faster access speeds than HDDs, meaning they provide better read/write performance for the computer's functions. This is noticeable in faster start-up times for the computer, faster launch times for applications, and faster file transfers among systems and drives.

Solid state drives also require less power than HDDs. This gives them an advantage for laptop computers and mobile devices. Additionally, SSDs have no moving parts, so they operate silently and are less prone to mechanical failure. These advantages come at the expense of higher cost and lower overall storage capacity.

External Drive Storage

A popular option for supplementing a computer's storage is to use an additional, external drive. External drives are readily available, offering a variety of connection types to match the available ports on your computer. Some common connection types include the following:

- FireWire 400 or 800
- USB 2.0 or 3.0
- USB-C
- eSATA
- Thunderbolt 1, 2, or 3

If you plan to store media files on an external drive for use with your DAW, look for a high-performance drive with a high-speed data connection to your computer. Good drive options would include a 7200 RPM HDD or an SSD. Good data connections would include USB 3.0, USB-C, eSATA, Thunderbolt 2, or Thunderbolt 3. Be sure to match the capabilities of your computer when selecting the connection type.

Cloud Storage

Both the internal system drive of your computer and any connected external drives are considered local storage. Your local storage can be complimented by any number of cloud-based storage options.

Cloud storage utilizes large-capacity storage servers and data centers that you connect to via the Internet. Cloud storage options generally require a subscription. To allow for quick access to your cloud-based content, cloud storage services usually allow you to sync your cloud content to your local storage.

The advantages of using cloud storage are many. For example, cloud storage enables you to keep your files in sync across multiple devices, to easily share files with anyone who has an Internet connection, and to retrieve your files from any computer, anywhere in the world.

Some popular cloud-based storage services include Dropbox, SugarSync, and Google Drive.

Cloud Storage and Pro Tools

Pro Tools|First uses cloud-based storage for your Pro Tools projects and the associated media files. Every Pro Tools|First user gets a 1 GB allocation of Avid cloud storage associated with their Avid Master Account free of charge. This means that your projects are available to you from any computer running Pro Tools|First whenever you log in to your account.

Standard Pro Tools and Pro Tools|HD software also come with 1 GB of Avid cloud storage. These commercial versions of Pro Tools provide the option to work either from your local storage or from your Avid cloud storage allocation (Pro Tools 12.5 and later).

Avid cloud storage can be upgraded for any Pro Tools product to an Avid Cloud Collaboration Premium Plan. These plans boost your cloud storage space for a monthly fee.

Onboard Sound Options (Audio In and Out)

Another aspect to consider when selecting a computer is the onboard sound options that the model offers. Many DAWs, including Pro Tools|First, can utilize the computer's built-in sound options for recording and playback. This allows you to use any built-in microphone inputs on the computer for recording to your project and to use the built-in computer speakers for playing back your project.

While you may not want to use the computer's microphones for any meaningful recording project, having onboard audio will allow you to run your DAW without requiring a connected audio interface. This can save you some money at the outset. It also provides the flexibility to work on the go, especially when using a laptop, without needing to bring along additional hardware.

Although audio inputs are not required, audio outputs are critical. Look for a computer that has built-in speakers and/or a stereo headphone jack for monitoring playback from your DAW.

Other Options to Consider

Aside from the computer hardware itself, you may also want to consider options for peripheral devices. With the right accessories, you can customize your setup for efficiency and/or personal preference.

Mice and Trackballs

Many computer users find the mouse that comes with their computer to be less than ideal for long-term use. Numerous alternatives are available, offering features such as multiple buttons, scroll wheels, trackballs, gesture/touch input, and wireless connection to the computer. Mouse upgrades can range from around $20 to upwards of $100. Be sure to try out any options you are considering while running your DAW (or a similar application) to determine what works best for you.

Trackpads and Touchpads

As an alternative or supplement to a traditional mouse, Apple offers several "Trackpad" options (such as the Magic Trackpad and Magic Trackpad 2). These devices provide touch-based gesture input, similar to that found on many modern laptops. Logitech, Dell, and others offer similar "Touchpad" devices for Windows computers.

Extended Keyboards and Keypad Options

An upgrade option that is well worth the investment is an extended keyboard. If you plan to do any serious work in Pro Tools or Pro Tools|First, an extended keyboard is a must. The extended keyboard provides access to numeric keypad keys on the right-hand side, which are used extensively in Pro Tools.

Figure 1.5 Standard Mac keyboard (top) and extended Mac keyboard (bottom)

If you own or purchase a laptop computer, you can opt for a numeric keypad extension instead. These are available from various manufacturers and can be connected to your laptop wirelessly or via USB cable, depending on the model.

Figure 1.6 Numeric keypad extension option from Cateck

Benefits of an Audio Interface

Many audio interfaces are available that are compatible with Pro Tools|First. Any audio interface that is CoreAudio-compliant (Mac) or ASIO-compliant (Windows) will work with Pro Tools|First.

Some good options include the **Focusrite Scarlett** series or **Focusrite iTrack Solo**. These Focusrite products each come bundled with the **Pro Tools|First – Focurite Creative Pack**, which provides 12 additional Pro Tools plug-ins. (See https://us.focusrite.com/scarlett-pro-tools-first.) Many Focusrite interfaces are also available in **Studio** editions, with microphone and headphones included.

The benefits of using an audio interface can include better sound quality, a greater number of available inputs and outputs (I/O), and access to digital I/O options. For many beginning users, the number of inputs may be the most significant issue. Pro Tools|First supports up to 4 simultaneous inputs, with a compatible interface, meaning that you can record from up to 4 different sources at once. Without an audio interface, you are limited to the input options available on your computer.

Working with Your Computer

Once you have selected an appropriate computer to host the DAW of your choice, you should spend some time to get familiar with basic operations on the system. If you already have experience with computers and the operating system you will be using, you may want to skip or skim this section. The information in this section focuses on navigating among the files, folders, and applications on your computer.

In this section, we cover basic operations such as locating, moving, and organizing files; creating folders; launching applications; and saving files.

File Management

Perhaps the most important thing you should know about your computer is how to navigate among the files and folders using the computer's operating system. On the Mac, you will use the Mac Finder for this purpose. On a Windows computer, you will use File Explorer windows.

Using the Finder (Mac-based OS)

The desktop experience in a Mac-based operating system is defined by the Finder application. The Finder is the first thing you see after you start up a Mac, before you launch any applications or open any files or folders.

Figure 1.7 The Finder icon on a Mac

The Finder includes a menu bar at the top of the screen, the desktop display in the center (background image along with any desktop icons and open Finder windows), and the Dock at the bottom of the screen. The term "Finder" is commonly used interchangeably with the term "desktop" on a Mac.

Figure 1.8 The desktop in the Mac Finder (OS X 10.11 El Capitan)

The Finder Versus the Desktop

Technically speaking, the Finder and the desktop are two different things. The Finder is an application on the Mac that is always running. You can switch to the Finder application at any time, the same way you can switch between other running applications.

The desktop is the default location displayed by the Finder. You can think of the desktop as the background canvas upon which your open folders and applications are displayed. The desktop also provides a location to store folders and files.

The items stored on the desktop are visible from the Finder. They can also be displayed in a Finder window, by opening the Desktop folder.

From the Finder, you can:

- Navigate through the file system on your storage drive(s)

- Open folder locations, and

- Manage files within open folders

To open a new Finder window, choose **FILE > NEW FINDER WINDOW** from the menu bar at the top of the screen (or double-click on a folder on the desktop). You can navigate within an open Finder window by clicking on a location in the sidebar or by double-clicking on a displayed folder in the file list to open it.

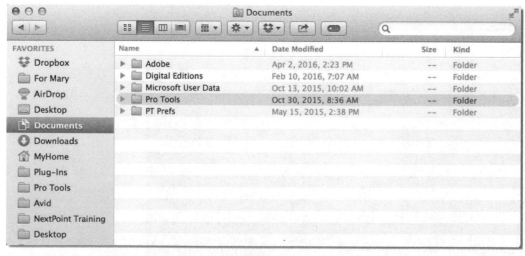

Figure 1.9 An open Finder window (Mac OS X)

Using File Explorer (Windows-based OS)

Windows computers also provide a desktop view (similar to the Mac Finder). However, the desktop might not be the first thing you see upon startup, depending on the operating system you are using. (Windows 8 and Windows 8.1 use the "Metro UI" tile view by default, similar to that on a Windows Phone.)

To open a new File Explorer window, do one of the following:

■ In Windows 7 or Windows 10, click on the yellow File Explorer icon in the taskbar at the bottom of the desktop screen (or double-click any folder on the desktop).

Figure 1.10 Mouse cursor next to the File Explorer icon in the taskbar (Windows 7 shown)

■ In Windows 8 or Windows 8.1, first click the **DESKTOP** tile from the tiled Start screen; then from the desktop, click the File Explorer icon in the taskbar (or double-click any folder on the desktop).

(i) In Windows 8.1, you can also access the File Explorer directly from the tiled Start screen by typing *file explorer* and clicking on the File Explorer icon that appears.

As in the Mac Finder, you can navigate within an open File Explorer window by clicking on a location in the Navigation pane on the left or by double-clicking on a displayed folder in the file list to open it.

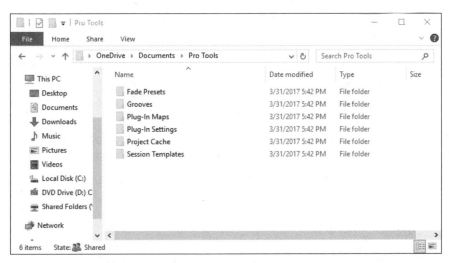

Figure 1.11 The File Explorer window (Windows 10)

Locating, Moving, and Opening Files

Using the locations in the sidebar of a Mac Finder window (or the Navigation pane in File Explorer), you can navigate to different folder locations on your computer. For example, clicking on the DOWNLOADS location will take you to the Downloads folder on your system (for any files you've downloaded from the Internet). Clicking on the DOCUMENTS location will take you to your Documents folder.

You can access the files within a folder at a given location by double-clicking on the folder to open it. On a Mac, you can also click on the triangle next to a folder to expand it and display its contents.

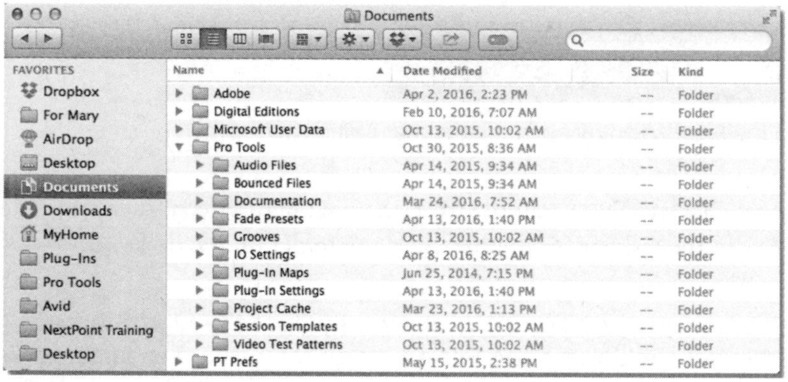

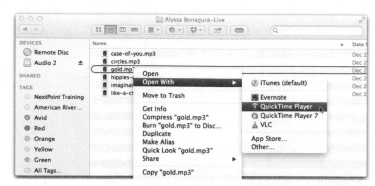

Figure 1.12 Finder window with the Pro Tools folder expanded

Moving Files. To move a file from one location to another, you can drag the file from its current location to any other visible folder within the window or to any location displayed in the sidebar/Navigation pane. You also can drag a file from one open Finder window or File Explorer window to another.

Opening Files. Opening a file from a Finder or File Explorer window is usually as simple as double-clicking on the file. In most cases, the file will open in the application that created it, if available on your computer. If the application is not available—or if your computer cannot determine an appropriate application to use for the file—you can choose a compatible application on your system. On both Mac- and Windows-based systems, you can right-click on a file and select an application to use for the file from the right-click menu.

Figure 1.13 Right-click menu for a file in a Mac Finder window

Accessing Right-Click Functions on a Mac

For users who are new to the Mac, using the mouse can require an adjustment. The Apple mouse doesn't offer separate left- and right-click buttons. Instead, you must rock the mouse to get the desired effect. For a standard left-click, you must click on the *left side* of the mouse, causing the mouse to rock the left. For a right-click, you need to click on the *right side*, causing it to rock to the right.

To improve your results, practice using two fingers on the mouse. Place your index finger on the left side and your middle finger on the right. (Reverse if you are left-handed.) For a left-click, roll your hand to the left and click with your index finger. For a right-click, roll to the right and click with your middle finger.

If you are using a Mac trackpad instead of a mouse, use a two-finger click to access right-click functions.

Creating Folders

On both Windows and Mac, you can easily create a new folder on the desktop or at another desired location. While displaying the desktop or viewing a location in a Finder or File Explorer window, simply right-click with the mouse and select NEW FOLDER (Mac) or choose NEW > FOLDER (Windows) using the pop-up menu. (See Figures 1.14 and 1.15.)

You can also create a new folder by using a menu command (Mac) or Ribbon button (Windows 8 and later) or by using associated keyboard shortcuts: COMMAND+SHIFT+N (Mac) or CTRL+SHIFT+N (Windows).

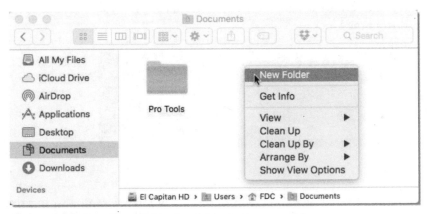

Figure 1.14 Creating a folder by right-clicking on a Mac

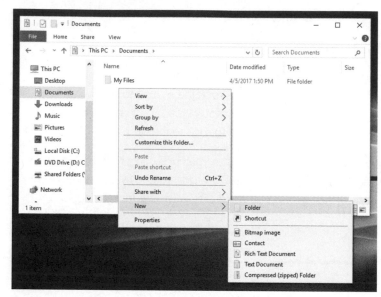

Figure 1.15 Creating a folder by right-clicking on Windows

Launching Applications

To launch an installed application, you can either double-click on the app file in your computer's Applications directory or use one of the shortcut operations provided by your OS.

Mac-Based Systems. The easiest path to opening an application on the Mac is the Dock. The Dock is a bar of icons that sits at the bottom of your Mac screen by default. It provides quick access to your installed apps. To launch an app, simply click on its icon in the Dock.

Figure 1.16 Launching Pro Tools|First from the Dock

Windows-Based Systems. One easy way to launch an application on any Windows system is to use the Search function. Simply press the **START** key (also known as the **WINDOWS** key) and begin typing the name of the application you wish to open. (See Figure 1.17.)

 Pressing the START key followed by any text activates a Start Menu search in Windows 7, a search in a right-hand pane in Windows 8, or a Cortana search in Windows 10.

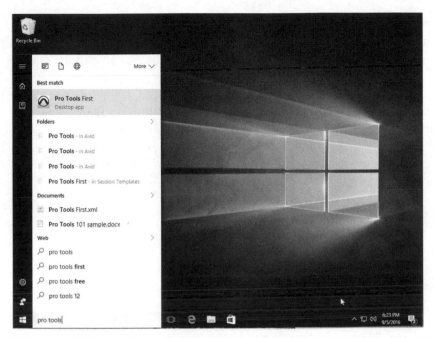

Figure 1.17 Using a Cortana search to locate Pro Tools|First in Windows 10

Launching an App from the Desktop

During the install process, many applications will offer the option to place a shortcut icon, or *alias*, on your desktop. This shortcut links to the application file in your Applications directory.

Figure 1.18 Pro Tools|First shortcut on the Windows 10 desktop

Shortcut icons provide a convenient option for launching an application, as you can simply double-click on the shortcut from the desktop to start the application.

Saving Files

Most applications allow you to start working on a file and save it at a later point, once you've created something worth keeping. The usual process for saving your work is to choose FILE > SAVE using the menus at the top of the application.

Pro Tools|First is somewhat different, in that you must name and save your project *prior* to starting your work. This is partially because you need to configure the project parameters in advance. It is also because Pro Tools|First saves your work using a hierarchy of files and folders that must be available in the storage location prior to audio operations you will be performing.

To accomplish this, Pro Tools|First presents you with the Dashboard when you launch the application. The Dashboard is your starting point for creating a new project (or opening a project you previously created).

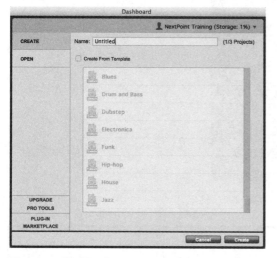

Figure 1.19 The Dashboard in Pro Tools|First

 For details on using the Dashboard to create a project, see Lesson 5 later in this book.

The Pro Tools File Hierarchy

The concept of a file hierarchy is common to all varieties of Pro Tools software. This structure is used to allow the software to reference media files, rather than embedding them inside of the Pro Tools file itself.

For example, any audio files that you record or import into Pro Tools|First will be stored separately within the project hierarchy. The actual Pro Tools|First file simply links to the audio files, keeping the size of the Pro Tools file itself to a minimum.

Once you have created your initial project, you can save the changes you make as you work by using the standard **FILE > SAVE** command.

Working with an Application

With your application up and running, you will be able to begin working on a project—whether that be a slide presentation, a spreadsheet document, or an audio recording project. Most modern applications, including Pro Tools|First, use menus and keyboard shortcuts for accessing their main commands.

Menus

The term *menu* is commonly used in software to denote one of the pull-down lists of commands at the top of the application. On Windows computers, the menu bar is typically anchored to the top of the application window. On Mac computers, the menu bar is typically anchored to the top of the screen.

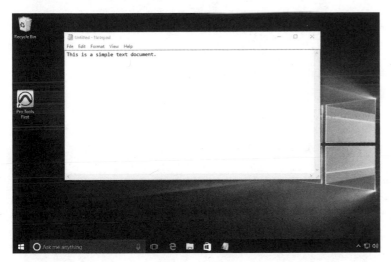

Figure 1.20 Menus in the Notepad app on Windows 10 (top of application window)

Figure 1.21 Menus for the TextEdit app on Mac OS X 10.11 (top of the screen)

To select a command, click on the associated menu name in the menu bar (such as the **FILE** menu) and then click on the desired command from the pull-down menu (such as the **SAVE** command). In some cases, menu items will include a submenu that you can use to select from between multiple choices.

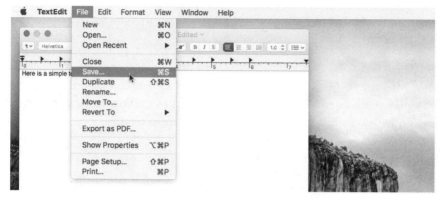

Figure 1.22 Selecting the Save command under the File menu

At times, you may have to distinguish between menus used by different applications or by the operating system (such as the Mac Finder). On a Windows-based system, you will likely find it easy to tell which menus belong to a given application, since the menus are anchored to the application window.

On a Mac-based system, however, you can run into situations where an application's windows are closed, but the application is still active. In these cases, you may see the desktop or another running application on screen, making it less apparent which application is active.

Figure 1.23 Pro Tools|First menus displayed on a Mac with all application windows closed

To determine which application is active on a Mac, look for the application menu on the left side of the menu bar (immediately to the right of the Apple menu). The name of the active application will always display, regardless of whether the application has any windows open.

 Clicking on the desktop screen, an open Finder window, or a background app will make that item active, replacing the menus at the top of the screen.

 You can toggle through open applications by pressing COMMAND+TAB on a Mac or ALT+TAB on Windows.

Keyboard Shortcuts

As an alternative to using the menus to access commands, you may also be able to use keyboard shortcuts. Keyboard shortcuts use one or more modifier keys in combination with a standard key press to activate a command. Common examples include COMMAND+S on the Mac (CTRL+S on Windows) to save the open file or COMMAND+C on the Mac (CTRL+C on Windows) to copy a selection.

Mac and Windows systems each use different modifier keys, but their functions are similar. Table 1.1 shows the modifier keys available on each platform.

Table 1.1 Modifier keys available on Mac and Windows systems

Modifier Keys on Mac-based Computers	Modifier Keys on Windows-based Computers
The COMMAND key (⌘)	The CTRL key
The OPTION key (⌥)	The ALT key
The CONTROL key (^)	The START key (⊞)
The SHIFT key (⇧)	The SHIFT key

The advantages of using keyboard shortcuts include speed and efficiency, as well as reduced dependency on the mouse. This not only makes your work more precise, but it also helps avoid ergonomic problems, including carpal tunnel syndrome.

Often, keyboard shortcuts are listed next to the command names in the pull-down menus. You'll find it worth your time to memorize the shortcuts for some of the commands you use frequently in your DAW. In addition to the shortcuts shown in menus, Pro Tools|First includes numerous other "hidden" keyboard shortcuts. We will be covering many of these in this book.

Review/Discussion Questions

1. What are some reasons for choosing a Mac computer for your DAW? What are some reasons for choosing a Windows computer instead? (See "Mac Versus Windows Considerations" beginning on page 7.)

2. How is RAM used by an application? Is RAM used for permanent storage or temporary storage? (See "How RAM Is Used" beginning on page 8.)

3. What are some indications that a computer system does not have enough installed RAM for the applications you are using? (See "Why More RAM Is Better" beginning on page 8.)

4. What factors affect how much processing power your computer has for running applications? (See "Processing Power" beginning on page 10.)

5. What are some examples of audio processes that can strain the CPU of an underpowered system? (See "How Processing Power Affects Your DAW" beginning on page 10.)

6. What are some things you should consider to determine how much storage space is required for your DAW computer system? (See "Determining How Much Drive Space You Need" beginning on page 12.)

7. What is the difference between an HDD and an SSD for storage? What are some advantages of each? (See "Storage Options" beginning on page 13.)

8. How are built-in sound options on a computer useful for Pro Tools|First? (See "Onboard Sound Options" beginning on page 14.)

9. Why might you want to consider an extended keyboard for your Pro Tools system? (See "Extended Keyboards and Keypad Options" beginning on page 15.)

10. How can you quickly navigate to different folder locations on your computer? (See "Locating, Moving, and Opening Files" beginning on page 20.)

11. What are some ways to create a new folder at the current location on your computer? (See "Creating Folders" beginning on page 21.)

12. What is the Dashboard used for in Pro Tools|First software? (See "Saving Files" beginning on page 23.)

13. How can you select a command in an application such as Pro Tools|First? (See "Menus" beginning on page 25.)

14. What modifier keys are available on Mac computers? What modifiers keys are available on Windows computers? (See "Keyboard Shortcuts" beginning on page 27.)

Exploring Audio on the Computer

🎧 Activity

In this exercise, you will download the media files used for this course and move them to an appropriate storage location on your system. Then you will use your computer to listen to sample files for an excerpt from the song "Overboard" by Sacramento-area band, The Pinder Brothers.

🕐 Duration

This exercise should take approximately 10 minutes to complete.

⊕ Goals/Targets

- Practice file management techniques
- Practice critical listening techniques
- Explore sonic elements that comprise a finished mix

Getting Started

To get started, you will download the media files for this course and locate them in your **Downloads** folder. You will then move the downloaded media files to your **Documents** folder or other appropriate location.

Download the course media files:

1. Launch the browser of your choice on your computer (Safari, Microsoft Edge, Firefox, Chrome, etc.)

2. Point your browser to <u>www.halleonard.com/mylibrary</u> and enter your access code (printed on the opening page of this book).

3. Click the **DOWNLOAD** link next to the APB Media Files listing in your **My Library** page. The ABP Media Files folder will begin downloading to your Downloads folder.

4.   Open the Downloads folder on your system:

   • On Mac, activate the Finder and choose **Go > Downloads**.

   • On Windows, press **Ctrl+J** from within your browser and then click the link labeled **Open Folder, Show in Folder**, or similar.

Move the ABP Media Files folder to a permanent location:

1.   Select the **ABP Media Files** folder in the Downloads folder and drag onto the Documents location displayed in the sidebar/Navigation pane of the Finder or File Explorer window.

2.   Click on the Documents location in the sidebar/Navigation pane to open the Documents folder.

Figure 1.24 APB Media Files folder in the open Documents folder (Windows 10 shown)

Listening to Sample Files

In this part of the exercise, you will locate and play various audio files. In the process, you will practice listening for different musical parts in each file.

Listen to the music mix:

1.   Double-click on the **APB Media Files** folder in the open Finder or File Explorer window to open the folder and display its contents.

2.   Double-click on the **01. Pinder Brothers** folder to open it. You will see the following files in the folder:

   • OverboardMix.wav

   • Stem1.wav

   • Stem2.wav

   • Stem3.wav

   • Stem4.wav

3. Select the OverboardMix.wav file.

4. Do one of the following to listen to the selected file:

    • On a Mac-based system, press the spacebar to begin playback using the QuickLook feature.

    • On a Windows-based system, right-click on the file and select PLAY WITH WINDOWS MEDIA PLAYER.

5. As you listen to the mix, listen for each of the different instruments and sounds that you can hear.

    Write down each part that you hear in the table below. Rate the prominence of the part in the mix on a scale from 1 to 5, with 5 being very prominent/easy to hear and 1 being barely noticeable.

Instrument or Part	Prominence
Lead Vocal	5

Listen to the stem files:

1. Select the Stem1.wav file and listen to it using the same method that you used in Step 4 above.

2. Write down the main part you hear in the stem file, along with a short description, using the table on the next page.

3. Listen for additional parts in the stem file and indicate each different part you hear in the table along with a short description of each.

4. Repeat the process using each of the other stem files (Stem2, Stem3, and Stem4).

    Not all of the stems will have different discernable parts. If you are not accustomed to picking out and describing the different musical sounds you hear, just do your best to make distinctions where something sounds different. This is good ear training regardless of what type of audio production you are interested in.

Some terms you might use in your descriptions include the following: lead vocal, background vocal, vocal harmony, vocal double, rhythm guitar, lead guitar, bass guitar, kick drum (bass drum), snare drum, crash cymbals, hi-hat, ride cymbal, etc.

Stem File	Description of the Instrument or Part
Stem1	Lead vocal – Main vocal melody throughout

Finishing Up

After you've listened to each of the stem files, return to the OverboardMix.wav file and listen through it again. Are you better able to distinguish each part in the mix, now that you've heard them in isolation?

You should now be able to clearly pick out things like the cymbal crashes and vocal harmonies that you may have missed before. You may be able to distinguish subtler details as well. Can you hear what the bass guitar is doing during the lead guitar part? Can you hear individual kick and snare drum hits? Can you tell where the hi-hat is being played and where it switches to the ride cymbal?

 To hear individual drum parts in isolation, check out the audio files in the z-Drum Parts folder. These files will help you learn what each drum piece sounds like and let you know what to listen for in a drum kit.

That completes this exercise. For more practice honing your listening skills, try identifying parts in popular songs that you hear on the radio or Spotify. If you are more interested in post-production applications, listen for different sound elements in your favorite TV program. Examples include dialog, background ambience (birds chirping, waves crashing), Foley (footsteps, character movements, noise from objects being handled), sound effects (telephones ringing, gun shots, laser beams), and background music.

Chapter 2

DAW Concepts

...What You Need from Your Digital Audio Workstation...

This chapter introduces you to the basic concepts of the DAW or Digital Audio Workstation. We begin by looking at some of the popular DAWs in use today. Then we explore the common audio plug-in formats that are used to add both effects and virtual instruments to a DAW. Next we look at the various Pro Tools systems that are available. We conclude this chapter with a brief explanation of some important terminology that you'll need to know to work effectively with Pro Tools|First.

⊕ Learning Targets for This Chapter

- Learn the basic concepts of Digital Audio Workstations

- Gain an understanding of common plug-in formats

- Explore available Pro Tools systems

- Become familiar with important audio terminology

Although this book is written for Pro Tools|First, it is important for you as an audio production enthusiast to have at least a passing familiarity with other digital audio products on the market. Not only are you likely to encounter audio practitioners who favor these platforms, you may end up using some of them yourself from time to time, to supplement your work in Pro Tools|First.

Functions of a DAW

The term DAW stands for Digital Audio Workstation. This term is used generically to refer to any software that can be used to record, edit, and mix audio, although most modern systems can be used for MIDI recording and editing as well.

What Can a DAW Do?

Some DAWs excel at audio editing, while some are primarily known for their MIDI features, but almost every modern DAW can do both to some degree. Pro Tools is generally considered to be a superior platform for working with audio content. However, Pro Tools also provides a robust platform for MIDI work.

In addition to basic recording and editing functions for audio and MIDI, DAWs often provide sound modules (or virtual instruments) for use with MIDI data. Such virtual instruments are commonly available in the form of plug-ins that use MIDI data to trigger sounds.

Most DAWs also use plug-ins for audio processing, to apply effects and polish to audio recordings. Additionally, DAWs typically provide mixing and automation functions, for blending tracks, creating an effective stereo image, and incorporating dynamic changes during playback.

Common DAWs

Many DAWs are available, ranging in price and feature set. Here, we provide an overview of some of the most popular DAWs and highlight some of the differences between them.

Avid Pro Tools and Pro Tools|First

Pro Tools became the first commercially successful DAW in the audio world when it was introduced back in 1991. The original version of Pro Tools could play only four tracks of audio and cost around $6000 for the hardware and software.

Since then, Pro Tools has evolved from a tool built exclusively for audio professionals to the popular entry-level DAW that it is today. The Pro Tools audio editing feature set is still unsurpassed in its power and simplicity, making it the de facto standard in professional music production and audio post-production for film and TV. The introduction of sophisticated control surfaces in the late 1990s furthered its professional evolution, making Pro Tools an extremely powerful mixing tool.

The term mixing-in-the-box was coined to describe the process of mixing complete albums and films inside the computer with only a small amount of external audio hardware.

In the 2000s, Pro Tools made great strides as a MIDI production tool, adding a number of advanced MIDI features as well as the ability to edit using standard music notation. Cross-integration with the Sibelius notation platform has made it easy to interchange MIDI information between Pro Tools and Sibelius, for sophisticated, professional-grade scoring.

Pro Tools|First was released in 2015 as a free option for aspiring audio engineers. The product became a successful entry-level option for audio enthusiasts. With the release of version 12.8, Pro Tools|First was updated to facilitate cloud collaboration workflows and interchange with standard Pro Tools software and Pro Tools|HD systems.

Figure 2.1 A project in Pro Tools First

Apple GarageBand

GarageBand is Apple's entry-level DAW. As an Apple product, it is available only for Mac OS computers and iOS devices, and it won't run on Windows computers or Android devices.

GarageBand makes it easy to get up and running to start making music right away. This DAW includes a nice complement of effects plug-ins including EQ, compression, reverb, and delay, as well as excellent guitar amp and pedal emulations.

The included virtual instrument plug-ins span the gamut from synthesizers to acoustic instruments to an automatic drum pattern generator. GarageBand also features a large selection of Apple Loops, which are professionally-recorded sound files that can be used to build a song very quickly.

The mobile version of GarageBand can run on both iPads and iPhones, making it easy for users to sketch out a song on-the-go, and then transfer the files to a Mac OS computer for further polishing. You can also import GarageBand songs directly into Apple's professional DAW, Logic Pro X.

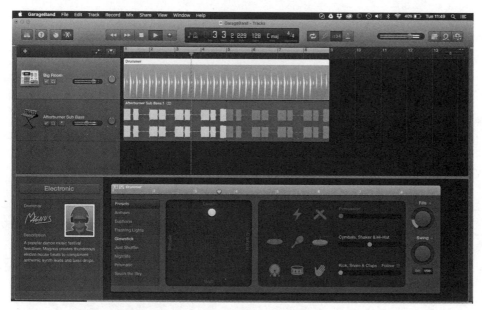

Figure 2.2 The Drummer instrument in Apple GarageBand

Apple Logic Pro X

Logic is GarageBand's big brother. Like GarageBand, Logic runs only on Mac OS and iOS platforms. The product was originally developed by a company called Emagic, which got its start creating MIDI sequencing software for Atari computers.

Logic includes the same core feature set as GarageBand, but it expands upon that to offer a truly professional audio production tool. Logic features a huge number of plug-ins effects including pro-level EQ, dynamics, and modulation effects. It also features a convolution reverb effect that can be used to create ultra-realistic models of real acoustic spaces.

The included virtual instruments in Logic are equally impressive. Logic includes a number of synthesizers, a physical modeling synth, a sampler, several drum instruments, as well as an organ and clavinet. Many MIDI composers and producers select Logic as their go-to DAW due to its robust support for virtual instruments.

Additional power-user features in Logic include Flex Time and Flex Pitch. These features allow users to freely adjust the timing and pitch of recorded audio.

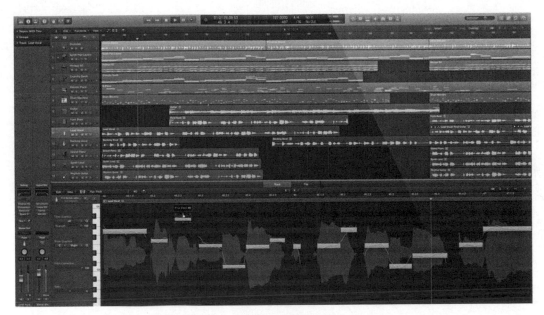

Figure 2.3 Flex Pitch editing in Apple Logic Pro X (APPLE)

 The Elastic Audio feature in Pro Tools and Pro Tools|First provide functionality similar to Logic's Flex Time.

Ableton Live

Ableton's Live is a unique DAW that was created specifically as an electronic music performance tool. It offers a familiar track layout and audio and MIDI editing toolset in its Arrangement view. But where Live really stands out is the revolutionary Session view that took the DAW world by storm back in 2001.

In Session view, audio and MIDI clips are loaded into "slots" that can be triggered, stopped, and looped independently from one another. As a result, complex song arrangements can be performed on-the-fly in a way that isn't really possible with many other DAWs. This has made Live a favorite among live performers, DJs, and electronic musicians.

The inclusion of Cycling 74's MAX software with Ableton Suite (known as "Max for Live") offers another unique feature—the ability to create custom effects and virtual instrument plug-ins without writing any code.

In recent years, Live has probably seen more development of dedicated control surfaces than any other DAW, with Akai's APC series, Novation's Launchpad series, and Ableton's Push devices leading the way.

Figure 2.4 The Session View in Ableton Live

Steinberg Cubase/Nuendo

Steinberg's Cubase is one of the oldest and most respected DAWs on the market. The product began its development in the 1980s as a MIDI sequencer for the Atari ST (like Logic). Cubase has since evolved into a world-class DAW with outstanding MIDI capabilities and solid audio editing.

In particular, Cubase is very popular with hardcore MIDI users (such as film composers). This is due to several innovations that Steinberg introduced, including an ingenious chord track and elegant sampler articulation management. Additionally, the included VST plug-ins are top-notch.

 For information on VST and other plug-in formats, see "Plug-In Formats" later in this chapter.

Steinberg also manufactures another well-known DAW, by the name of Nuendo.

Nuendo is essentially an enhanced version of Cubase with more advanced audio features that target the audio post-production industry. Cubase and Nuendo both run on Mac OS and Windows computers, making either option an excellent choice for users who need to work on Windows or move between the two platforms.

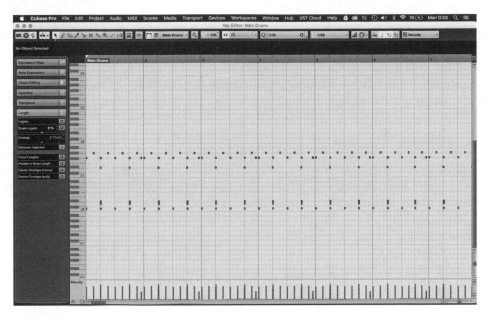

Figure 2.5 The powerful key editor in Steinberg Cubase

And the Rest...

Numerous other DAW options are available, with more coming to market everyday. Some examples of other popular DAWs include the following:

- **Cakewalk Sonar**—Sonar evolved from the original Windows-only Cakewalk application that was a popular early MIDI sequencer. It now offers powerful audio functionality and has recently crossed over to Mac OS.

- **Cockos REAPER**—REAPER is an inexpensive and flexible DAW. Many users are drawn to REAPER for its incredible customization options: REAPER allows users to create complex "actions" to accomplish almost any task. In addition, REAPER can be configured so that its editing features mimic the functionality of another DAW, making it easy to use for "switchers."

- **MOTU Digital Performer**—Digital Performer is another Mac-only DAW that has a loyal following in the film-scoring world. Its credentials include well-known users such as Danny Elfman. Digital Performer offers a number of editing tools that hold particular appeal for classically-trained composers and orchestrators, as well as a deep general toolset for MIDI and audio work.

- **PreSonus Studio One**—Studio One is a relatively young DAW that has garnered a lot of attention in recent years. It offers a nice balance of MIDI and audio tools and is constantly adding innovative new features.

- **Propellerhead Reason**—Reason was once an absolute necessity for any DAW user looking to add a cost-effective bundle of virtual instruments. Reason has since matured into a full-featured MIDI and audio editor. It continues to offer a huge range of virtual instruments with a user-friendly interface.

Plug-In Formats

Most DAWs support plug-ins for both audio processing and MIDI virtual instruments. But not all DAWs support plug-ins in the same format. As a result, a fair amount of confusion surrounds the issue of plug-ins and plug-in formats.

What Is a Plug-In?

A plug-in is a small software program that runs inside of your DAW to extend its functionality. Plug-ins are typically inserted onto a track in the DAW to run in real-time, although some plug-ins can also be used to directly process a selected portion of audio on a track.

Plug-ins fall into two general categories:

- **Effects Plug-ins**—Effects plug-ins offer a range of signal processing effects including equalization (EQ), dynamics processing (such as compressors and limiters), modulation (such as chorus and flange effects), harmonic processing (such as distortion), and time-based effects (such as reverb and delay).

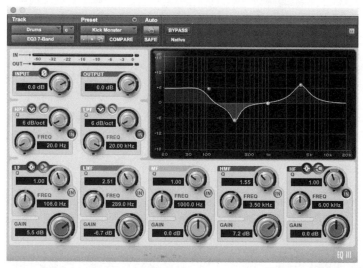

Figure 2.6 Avid's EQ3 7-Band is an example of an effects plug-in

- **Virtual Instrument Plug-ins**—Virtual instrument plug-ins are software emulations of hardware musical instruments. These instruments include synthesizers (both analog emulations and modern digital algorithms), samplers, and drum machines.

Figure 2.7 Xpand!2 by AIR is an example of a virtual instrument plug-in.

Common Plug-In Formats

Some common plug-in formats include the AAX format, developed by Avid for modern Pro Tools systems, and the AU and VST formats developed by Apple and Steinberg, respectively. The RTAS and DSP formats used by older Pro Tools systems are also still common in many audio production facilities.

The following breakdown provides details on each of these formats:

- **AAX Native and AAX DSP**—The Avid Audio eXtensions (AAX) specification is the current plug-in format supported in Pro Tools. This specification supports both AAX Native and AAX DSP formats. AAX plug-ins use 64-bit floating-point math and support sample rates up to 192 kHz. AAX is the only plug-in format supported in Pro Tools 11 and later. One unique feature of this format is that the native and DSP versions are interchangeable, ensuring that Pro Tools sessions will sound exactly the same when moved between host-based and DSP-accelerated systems. AAX plug-ins are not currently supported in any other (non-Avid) DAW.

- **AAX AudioSuite**—The AAX AudioSuite format is Avid's plug-in format for rendered plug-in processing. Most real-time AAX plug-ins also include an AudioSuite version (available under the **AUDIOSUITE** menu in Pro Tools). Certain plug-ins, such as Reverse and Normalize, are available only in AudioSuite format. When AudioSuite processing is applied, a new file is rendered with the effect written in. AudioSuite processing can be undone using the Undo command, but it cannot be changed in real-time like other AAX plug-in processing.

- **AU**—The Audio Units (AU) format is Apple's audio plug-in format. AU plug-ins are used primarily in Logic and GarageBand, but they are also supported in several other DAWs (including Ableton Live) as well as a number of simpler audio applications on Mac OS.

- **VST**—Virtual Studio Technology (VST) is a plug-in format created by Steinberg. It was originally developed for Cubase in the 1990s, but the format was rapidly adopted in most of the other DAWs of that era. VST is easily the most popular format for third-party plug-ins and is supported in every major DAW except for Logic, GarageBand, and Pro Tools.

- **RTAS and TDM**—Real-Time AudioSuite (RTAS) and Time-Division Multiplexing (TDM) are obsolete plug-in formats that were created by Avid (then Digidesign). RTAS plug-ins are host-based processors that run on the computer's CPU, while TDM plug-ins are DSP-based and run on custom Motorola DSP chips included on older, professional-level Pro Tools DSP cards. These plug-in formats are supported through Pro Tools 10; support was discontinued beginning with Pro Tools 11.

Pro Tools Systems

Pro Tools systems typically include a combination of both software and hardware components. With the multitude of options available, it can be difficult to know where to start when building a Pro Tools-based system. The following sections break down some of the choices for you.

Pro Tools Software Options

The Pro Tools software product line includes three options:

- Pro Tools|First

- Pro Tools (often simply called Pro Tools software or standard Pro Tools)

- Pro Tools|HD (required to use Pro Tools|HDX or Pro Tools|HD Native hardware)

Pro Tools|First is the free, feature-limited edition of Pro Tools software. Version 12.8 of Pro Tools|First provides the following capabilities:

- Support for up to four channels of audio input and output (depending on audio hardware)

- Up to a total of 16 audio tracks (mono or stereo)

- Up to 16 Aux Input tracks (mono or stereo)

- Up to four Master Fader tracks (mono or stereo)

- Up to 16 MIDI tracks

- Up to 16 Instrument tracks (mono or stereo)

- 32-bit floating-point audio resolution, at sample rates up to 96 kHz (depending on your hardware)

- Non-destructive, random-access editing and mix automation

- Audio processing with up to ten real-time plug-ins per track (increased from four in earlier versions)

- Up to ten sends per track (increased from four in earlier versions)

- Up to 24 internal mix busses for routing and mixing

Standard Pro Tools software provides higher track counts, greater I/O capacity, support for video, and support for sample rates up to 192 kHz. Pro Tools|HD software increases track counts and I/O capacity further, adds support for Avid HD-series hardware, and includes advanced mixing and automation features.

Table 2.1 provides a feature comparison of basic functionality for the three Pro Tools software options.

Table 2.1 Comparison of Pro Tools software features

FEATURES	Pro Tools|First	Pro Tools	Pro Tools|HD
Input Channels	4	32	192
Output Channels	4	32	192
Audio Tracks	16	128	768
Instrument Tracks	16	512	512
MIDI Tracks	16	512	512
Aux Input Tracks	16	128	512
Busses	24	Unlimited	Unlimited
Video Tracks	None	1	64
Supported Projects/Sessions	3	Unlimited	Unlimited
Maximum Sample Rate	96	192	192
ASIO, Core Audio, EUCON Support	Yes	Yes	Yes
Supported Plug-In Formats	AAX Native, AAX AudioSuite	AAX Native, AAX AudioSuite	AAX DSP (HDX only), AAX Native, AAX AudioSuite
Surround Mixing	No	No	Yes
Advanced Automation	No	No	Yes

Pro Tools Hardware Options

All versions of Pro Tools software support a range of audio hardware. The specific devices supported vary based on the software product you're using:

- **Pro Tools|First**—Pro Tools|First supports any non-HD Avid audio interface, as well as ASIO-compliant (Windows) or Core Audio-compliant (Mac) audio interfaces. These may include your computer's built-in audio hardware or an external interface that connects via USB, FireWire, or Thunderbolt. When considering the purchase of an external interface, it's important to remember that Pro Tools|First supports a maximum of four input and output channels. Although interfaces with more inputs and outputs can be used with Pro Tools|First, you'll only be able to access four inputs and outputs at one time.

Figure 2.8 Focusrite's Scarlett 2i2 is an excellent entry-level interface.

- **Pro Tools**—Like Pro Tools|First, the standard version of Pro Tools software supports any non-HD Avid audio interface, as well as ASIO-compliant (Windows) or Core Audio-compliant (Mac) audio interfaces. However, standard Pro Tools software supports up to a maximum of 32 channels of input and output, so larger interfaces can provide a significant advantage.

Figure 2.9 MOTU's UltraLite Mk3 is an affordable, mid-range interface.

- **Pro Tools|HD**—While Pro Tools|HD software will also work with ASIO and Core Audio interfaces, it is designed to work with one of Avid's professional–level hardware options. These include Pro Tools|HDX, Pro Tools|HD Native, and Pro Tools|HD Native Thunderbolt. Avid's HD hardware options work in conjunction with one or more Avid HD-series audio interfaces: Pro Tools|HD IO, Pro Tools|HD OMNI, Pro Tools|HD MADI, and Pro Tools|MTRX.

Figure 2.10 Avid's Pro Tools|HD OMNI is a professional-level audio interface.

Pro Tools|HDX Versus Pro Tools|HD Native

Avid's professional-level hardware options fall into two basic categories:

- **Pro Tools|HDX**—Pro Tools|HDX systems feature PCIe cards with digital signal processing (DSP) chips for audio processing. The DSP power of an HDX card supplements the computer's CPU, so HDX systems will always be significantly more powerful than a computer alone.

Figure 2.11 Avid Pro Tools|HDX PCIe card

■ **Pro Tools|HD Native**—Pro Tools|HD Native systems come in two varieties: the original Pro Tools HD|Native PCIe card and the newer Pro Tools|HD Native Thunderbolt external interface. Both systems provide high-speed connections to HD-series audio interfaces (like HDX systems), but they do not include DSP chips. As a result, HD Native systems do not provide greater signal processing power than the computer alone.

Figure 2.12 Avid Pro Tools|HD Native PCIe card

Figure 2.13 Avid Pro Tools|HD Native Thunderbolt interface

Downloading and Installing Pro Tools|First

If you are ready to proceed with Pro Tools|First as your DAW of choice, you will need to start by installing the software. Several steps are required to download and install Pro Tools|First. Fortunately, Avid has created a dedicated Pro Tools|First webpage that walks your through all of the steps.

Accessing the Installer

To being the process of downloading Pro Tools|First, direct your browser to the associated web page at https://my.avid.com/protoolsfirstactivation. This page will walk you through the entire process of creating your Avid Master Account (if necessary), creating an iLok account (if necessary), depositing the Pro Tools|First authorization into your iLok account, and downloading the Pro Tools|First installer.

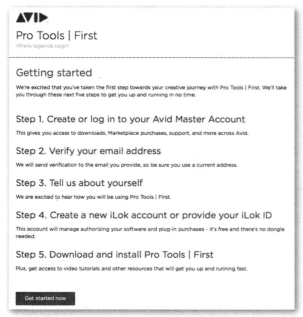

Figure 2.14 Getting started with Pro Tools|First from the associated Avid web page

Installation Steps

To install Pro Tools | First, click the **GET STARTED NOW** button in the Avid web page and follow the steps in the onscreen instructions:

1. **Create or log in to your Avid Master Account**—An Avid Master Account is required to download and activate your Avid products. In this first step, you will log in to your existing Avid account, if you already have one, or create an account for use with Pro Tools|First. (See Figure 2.15.)

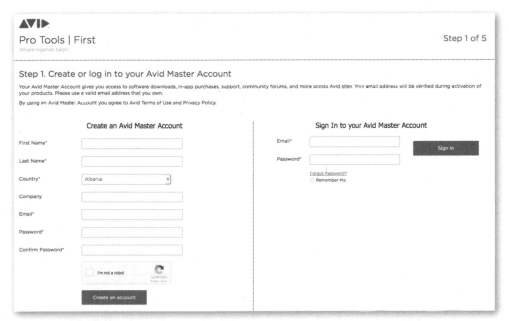

Figure 2.15 Step 1: Create an Avid Master Account or log in to your existing account

2. **Verify your email address**—You will need to validate your email account for verification purposes. Follow the onscreen prompts.

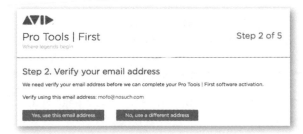

Figure 2.16 Step 2: Verify your email address

3. **Complete a brief survey**—During the process, you may be asked to provide some background information on your level of experience with audio and how you expect to use the software.

4. **Create an iLok account or link to an existing iLok account**—Pro Tools software products are protected using the Pace iLok system. This is a third-party (non-Avid) system. To enable iLok authorization, you'll need an iLok account (in addition to your Avid Master Account).

You can choose to create a new account or link to an existing iLok account, if you already have one. (See Figure 2.17.) Your Pace iLok account is where Avid will deposit your authorization for Pro Tools|First.

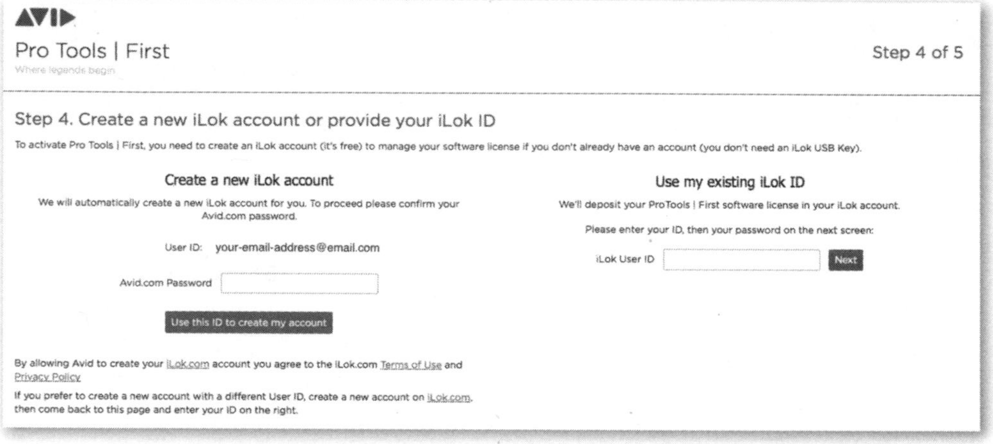

Figure 2.17 Step 4: Create a new iLok account or use an existing iLok ID

About the Pace iLok System

Software products can be protected with a USB smart key device, known as an iLok key. Developed by Pace Anti Piracy, the iLok system is used to authorize Pro Tools as well as many other software products and plug-ins. Using an iLok key allows you to transport licenses for your protected software products and authorize the products on different computer systems.

The Pace system also allows you to authorize Pro Tools|First directly to your computer, once the authorization is in your iLok account. Thus you do not need a physical iLok USB key for Pro Tools|First.

5. **Download and install Pro Tools|First**—Finally! In this last step, you will access a page where you can download the installers for Pro Tools|First. (See Figure 2.18.) You can also link to Avid's support pages, view some video tutorials, and watch installation videos from this location.

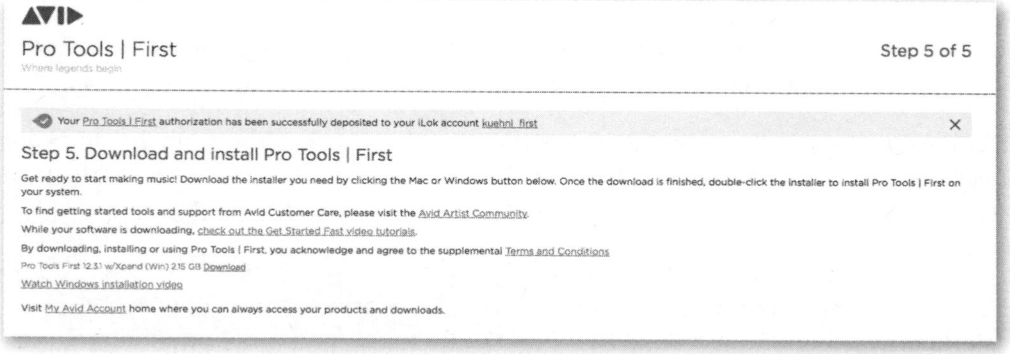

Figure 2.18 Step 5: Download and install Pro Tools|First

The Pro Tools|First Installer

Unlike other versions of Pro Tools, the Pro Tools|First installer includes everything you need to get started working with audio and/or making music. The Pro Tools|First application, AAX effects plug-ins, and the Xpand!2 virtual instrument are combined into a single installer.

Launching Pro Tools|First for the First Time

The first time you launch Pro Tools|First, you will need to specify a few settings. Upon the initial launch, you will be presented with a welcome message that directs you to the Playback Engine dialog box. (See Figure 2.19.) Other options you may want to configure include the drivers for your audio interface and the settings in the Hardware Setup dialog box.

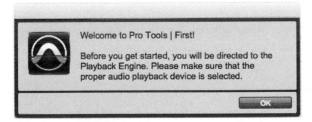

Figure 2.19 Welcome message in Pro Tools|First

- **Playback Engine**—Once Pro Tools|First completes the startup process, it will display the Playback Engine dialog box. (See Figure 2.20 below.) The Playback Engine dialog box is where you can specify the following settings:

  - **Playback Engine**: The Playback Engine selector lets you choose your audio interface. If you don't have an audio interface connected, this will default to the computer's built-in audio. Built-in audio will generally display as **Pro Tools Aggregate I/O** on Mac-based systems or **Windows Audio Device** on Windows-based systems.

  - **Default Output**: The Default Output selector lets you specify the stereo output channels used for your tracks by default. This will automatically be set to the main outputs for your selected audio interface, which is generally what you'll want.

  - **Sample Rate**: When no session is open, you can use the Sample Rate selector to specify the sample rate that will be used for new projects with the current audio interface.

  - **Optimize Engine**: Here you can optimize the audio engine for different tasks. You'll want to choose **RECORD** when you're planning to record audio or play virtual instruments from a connected MIDI keyboard. On the other hand, you'll want to choose **PLAYBACK** to maximize the number of tracks and plug-ins you can use while playing back and mixing your project. You can change this setting at any time while working on a project.

Figure 2.20 The Playback Engine dialog box in Pro Tools|First

(i) **To return to the Playback Engine dialog box during work on a project, choose Setup > Playback Engine.**

■ **Hardware Drivers**—Although not always required, it is a great idea to install the hardware drivers for your audio interface before launching Pro Tools|First. Doing so will allow you to select your desired interface immediately upon launching Pro Tools|First. But don't worry; you can always change the interface selection later if you haven't done this yet.

■ **Hardware Setup**—The Hardware Setup dialog box can be used to configure your audio interface using its associated control panel. To open the Hardware Setup dialog box, choose SETUP > HARDWARE. Pro Tools|First will automatically launch the control panel for the interface you have selected in the Playback Engine dialog box.

(i) **The Hardware Setup dialog box may not be available on some systems.**

Important Concepts in Pro Tools|First

There are a few key DAW concepts that you should master before getting started with audio software such as Pro Tools|First. These include understanding how the software handles audio files for your projects and recognizing the fundamental differences between audio and MIDI data.

Project Files Versus Audio Files

Pro Tools|First manages two main file types: project files and audio files. It is important to recognize the relationship between these file types.

- **Project Files**—The first thing you'll do when you start working with Pro Tools|First is to create a new project. A Pro Tools|First project file contains all of the information about the current audio production. This information includes the number and type of tracks in the project, the position of audio and MIDI data on each track, the plug-in assignments used on each track, the mixer level settings, the project settings, and a whole lot more.

  You will typically create a unique project file for each song or production you work on.

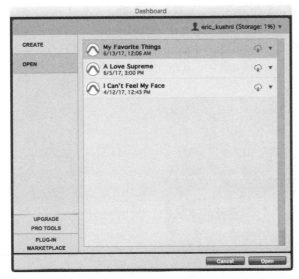

Figure 2.21 The Pro Tools|First Dashboard showing three projects

- **Audio Files**—An audio file represents a single audio recording (or "take") that you've either created directly in your project or imported into the project from a disk location. A typical project will have dozens or even hundreds of audio files associated with it.

  Pro Tools|First stores recorded or imported audio files in a local cache on your computer. This cache is synchronized with your Avid Cloud storage each time you close the project (assuming your computer has Internet access at that time).

  Pro Tools stores audio files as WAV files by default, but many other types of audio files can be imported into your project including AIFF, MP3, QuickTime, Audio CD, and more.

Referencing Versus Copying Imported Audio Files

Unlike standard Pro Tools and Pro Tools|HD software, Pro Tools|First always makes a copy of any file that is imported into a project. It does not offer the option of referencing files in their original location.

Audio Versus MIDI

The differences between audio and MIDI data are very important to understand when you're just starting out in the world of audio production. Audio files represent the audio signal that was recorded when the sound (from a voice, instrument, or other source) was captured using an audio interface. Therefore, the audio file itself actually *contains* the sound information that was captured. Audio files can be played back through the audio interface, allowing the sound to be heard using monitor speakers or headphones.

On the other hand, MIDI data is a series of note and control messages, typically recorded from a MIDI controller (like a keyboard or drum pads). (MIDI data can also be manually entered in Pro Tools | First.) The resulting MIDI file does NOT actually contain any sound information. The MIDI file's note and control messages must be sent to a real or virtual instrument, which can then turn the messages into an audio signal.

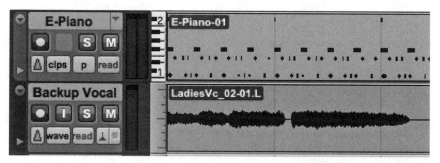

Figure 2.22 An Instrument track with a MIDI clip (top) and an Audio track with an audio clip (bottom)

Review/Discussion Questions

1. What are some tasks that can be completed using a Digital Audio Workstation (DAW)? (See "Functions of a DAW" beginning on page 36.)

2. What are some of the differences between the common DAWs? How are they similar? (See "Common DAWs" beginning on page 36.)

3. What is an audio plug-in? How are plug-ins enabled in a DAW? (See "What Is a Plug-In" beginning on page 42.)

4. What are the two general categories of plug-ins? Give some examples of plug-ins in each category. (See "What Is a Plug-In" beginning on page 42.)

5. Which of the common plug-in formats is/are supported in Pro Tools? (See "What Is a Plug-In" beginning on page 42.)

6. What are the three versions of Pro Tools software? (See "Pro Tools Systems" beginning on page 44.)

7. What are some of the differences between Pro Tools|First and the other versions of Pro Tools software? (See "Pro Tools Systems" beginning on page 44.)

8. What audio interfaces are supported in Pro Tools|First? (See "Pro Tools Hardware Options" beginning on page 45.)

9. What is the maximum number of audio input and output channels supported in Pro Tools|First? (See "Pro Tools Hardware Options" beginning on page 45.)

10. What is an iLok USB key? Is an iLok key required to authorize Pro Tools|First on your computer? (See "Downloading and Installing Pro Tools|First" beginning on page 48.)

11. What are some of the settings you'll need to specify upon first launching Pro Tools|First? (See "Launching Pro Tools|First for the First Time" beginning on page 51.)

12. What are the two primary types of files that Pro Tools|First manages? (See "Important Concepts in Pro Tools|First" beginning on page 52.)

13. What are some of the differences between audio and MIDI information? (See "Audio Versus MIDI" beginning on page 54.)

Setting Up a Multi-Track Project

🎧 Activity

In this exercise, you will create a simple project containing the main parts for the song "Overboard" by Sacramento-area band, The Pinder Brothers. You will then configure the project settings for playback and play through the project.

🕐 Duration

This exercise should take approximately 10 minutes to complete.

◈ Goals/Targets

- Launch Pro Tools|First
- Use the Dashboard to create a blank project document
- Import audio to the project
- Use the Playback Engine to configure the project for playback
- Save your work

Getting Started

To get started, you will launch Pro Tools|First as described in Chapter 1. Then you will use the Dashboard to create a new project.

 Before starting this exercise, Pro Tools|First must be installed on your system. If necessary, complete the Pro Tools|First download and installation steps, as outlined in Chapter 2.

Launch Pro Tools | First and create a project:

1. Launch Pro Tools | First using one of the following options (or another method of your choice):

    - On a Mac-based system, click on the Pro Tools | First icon in the Dock.

    - On a Windows-based system, double-click on the Pro Tools | First shortcut on the Desktop.

2. When prompted, log in to your Avid Master Account with your username and password.

3. When the Pro Tools | First Dashboard appears, click the **CREATE** action in the left sidebar, if not already selected.

4. Using the field at the top of the Dashboard, name your project OverboardTRX-*xxx*, where *xxx* is your initials.

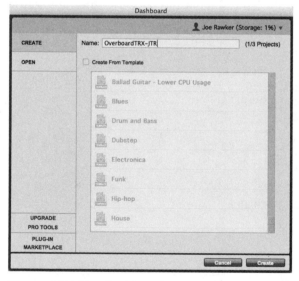

Figure 2.23 The Dashboard configured for the project

5. Click the **CREATE** button at the bottom of the Dashboard to create the project. A new project will be created and will display on screen.

 Basic Pro Tools | First configurations support a maximum of three projects. If you already have three existing projects in your cloud account, you will need to delete one or more before you can create new projects for the exercises in this book.

 You can delete projects by selecting the OPEN action in the left sidebar of the Dashboard and then choosing DELETE from the pop-up menu on the right side of a listed project.

Importing Audio for the Project

In this section of the exercise, you will configure the Edit window and import audio to the project. The process you'll use will automatically create tracks for the imported audio files.

Configure the Edit window:

1. Choose **WINDOW > EDIT**, if needed, to bring the Edit window to the forefront and make it active.

2. Resize or maximize the Edit window for a full-screen view (or choose **WINDOW > ARRANGE > CASCADE** to arrange your open windows in a cascading fashion).

Import the project audio:

1. Choose **FILE > IMPORT** to display the **OPEN** dialog box for your system.

2. In the dialog box, navigate to your Documents folder (or other location where you saved the APB Media Files folder in Exercise 1).

3. Open the 02. Project Files folder within the APB Media Files folder.

4. Select the 01-Overboard.cgrp file and click **OPEN**.

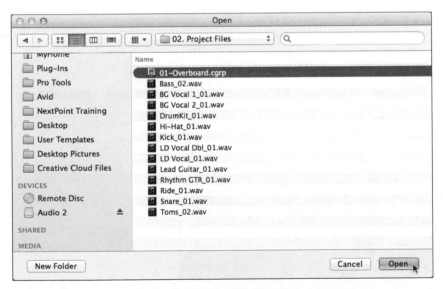

Figure 2.24 File selected in the Open dialog box (Mac OS shown)

5. When the **CLIP GROUP OPTIONS** dialog box displays, select the **NEW TRACKS** radio button and enable the checkbox for the **IMPORT TEMPO MAP FROM GROUP FILE** option. (See Figure 2.25.)

Figure 2.25 Settings configured in the Clip Group Import Options dialog box

6. Click **OK** to complete the import. Thirteen tracks will be added to your project, and the imported audio will be placed on the tracks. (The audio is included inside of the 01-Overboard clip group.)

> (i) If the Missing Files dialog box appears during the import, select Automatically Find and Relink and click OK to proceed.

Playing the Project

In this part of the exercise, you will ungroup the audio, configure the Playback Engine settings, and play back the project.

Ungroup the audio clips:

1. With the clip group still selected, choose **CLIP > UNGROUP** to ungroup the audio across all the tracks.

2. Press **RETURN** (Mac) or **ENTER** (Windows) to deselect the imported audio and place the Edit cursor at the start of the project.

Figure 2.26 Edit window with imported audio after ungrouping

Play back the project:

1.   Choose **SETUP > PLAYBACK ENGINE** to display the Playback Engine dialog box.

2.   Verify that your connected audio interface is displayed in the Playback Engine pop-up menu (if applicable). If needed, click on the pop-up menu to select the interface.

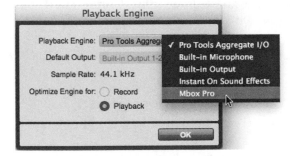

Figure 2.27 Selecting the Mbox Pro audio interface as the Playback Engine

> (i) Changing the selected audio interface will cause the project to save and close. This is normal behavior. Click OK to proceed through the displayed prompts, leaving the Playback Engine dialog box open.

3.   At the bottom of the Playback Engine dialog box, select the **PLAYBACK** radio button, if not already active.

4.   Click **OK** to accept the changes you've made and close the Playback Engine dialog box.

5.   If necessary, reopen your OverboardTRX session by selecting it under **FILE > OPEN RECENT**.

> (i) Changing your audio interface will generally reassign input and output paths for your project. This is normal behavior and will not affect the project. If you are prompted to save a report, choose No to dismiss the dialog box and proceed.

6.   Press the **SPACEBAR** to begin playback. The playback cursor will scroll across the screen and you will hear playback (if you have speakers or headphones connected to your system).

7.   While playing back the project, scroll the Edit window vertically using the scroll bar on the right side of the window (or another method of your choice) to view the audio waveforms on each track.

8.   When finished, press the **SPACEBAR** a second time to stop playback.

Finishing Up

To complete this exercise, you will need to save your work and close the project. You will be reusing this project in Exercise 5, so it's important to save and retain the work you've done.

Finish your work:

1. Choose **FILE > SAVE** to save the project.

2. Choose **FILE > CLOSE PROJECT** to close the project and return to the Dashboard.

> ⓘ **You cannot close a project by closing the Mix and Edit windows. Although it may appear closed, the project will remain open with no active windows.**

3. If desired, you can click **CANCEL** in the Dashboard to dismiss it and then exit Pro Tools | First by doing one of the following:

    • On a Mac-based system, choose **PRO TOOLS FIRST > QUIT PRO TOOLS | FIRST**.

    • On a Windows-based system, choose **FILE > EXIT**.

    You may have to wait while the audio uploads to the cloud. The synchronization dialog box will display while the audio uploads.

Figure 2.28 The synchronization dialog box

Pro Tools | First will automatically close when the upload is complete.

That completes this exercise.

Chapter 3

Audio Recording Concepts

...*What You Need to Record Audio*...

This chapter introduces you to the fundamentals of audio recording. We begin with a discussion on the basics of sound, including the principles of frequency and amplitude. We then discuss various types of microphones and their uses, before diving into a discussion on multi-track recording. We follow this by examining the process of converting audio signals between the analog and digital domains and exploring the role of the audio interface in this exchange. The characteristics of analog and digital audio discussed in this chapter are important considerations when it comes to optimizing your results with any DAW.

⊕ ## Learning Targets for This Chapter

- Understand the audio characteristics of frequency and amplitude

- Understand characteristics of traditional microphones and USB microphones

- Understand the purpose of multi-track recording

- Understand the basic principles of analog-to-digital conversion

- Recognize the role of the audio interface in modern digital recording

The process of recording audio has been commonplace for over 60 years, ever since magnetic tape-based recording processes began replacing earlier processes of inscribing a signal to a physical surface. In just the past 20 years or so, tape-based recording has itself largely given way to digital recording technology.

Regardless of the technology used to capture an audio recording, certain fundamental characteristics remain unchanged, including how an audio event moves through an acoustic environment and how that event is translated into an electrical signal that can be recorded. Recording in digital simply adds a dimension of collecting discrete measurements of the signal and storing those measurements as binary information.

The Basics of Audio

To understand the process of recording audio, it helps to first understand the basics of audio and sound waves. Sound waves are created when a physical object vibrates, causing a variation in the surrounding air pressure. By way of example, consider what happens when a guitar string is plucked.

The vibration of the guitar string, as it moves back and forth in a repeating cycle, causes a displacement of air particles. This results in a cyclical variation in air pressure, known as compression and rarefaction. The air pressure increases (compression) and decreases (rarefaction) in a way that corresponds directly to the pattern and frequency of the string's vibration. This cycling pattern of air pressure is referred to as a sound wave.

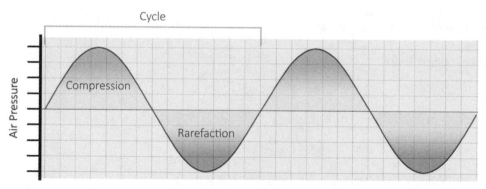

Figure 3.1 Cycles of compression (increasing air pressure) and rarefaction (decreasing air pressure) represented in a sound wave

Frequency

The frequency of the cycle of sound pressure variations determines our perception of the pitch of the sound. If the guitar string vibrates quickly, the air pressure variations will likewise cycle quickly between compression and rarefaction, creating a high-pitched sound. If the guitar string vibrates slowly, the air pressure will cycle slowly, creating a low-pitched sound.

We measure the frequency of these changes in *cycles per second* (CPS), also commonly denoted as *Hertz* (Hz). These two terms are synonymous—15,000 CPS is the same as 15,000 Hz. Multiples of 1,000 Hz are often denoted as kilohertz (kHz). Therefore, 15,000 Hz is also written as 15 kHz.

 The open "A" string on a guitar vibrates at a frequency of 110 Hz in standard tuning. Playing the A note on the 12th fret produces vibrations at 220 Hz (one octave higher).

The range of human hearing is generally accepted to be between 20 and 20,000 cycles per second. This is also commonly denoted as 20 Hz to 20 kHz. Therefore, to capture a full-spectrum recording, we must be able to represent all frequencies within this range.

Amplitude

The intensity of a sound, or the amount of change in air pressure it produces, creates our perception of the loudness of the sound. A sound's intensity is represented by the amplitude (height) of the sound wave. We measure amplitude in *decibels* (dB).

The decibel scale is defined by the dynamic range of human hearing, from 0 dB at the threshold of hearing to approximately 120 dB at the threshold of pain. The decibel is a logarithmic unit that is used to describe a ratio of sound pressure. As such, the decibel does not have a linear relation to our perception of loudness. An increase of approximately 10 dB is required to produce a perceived doubling of loudness.

By way of example, the amplitude of ordinary conversation is around 60 dB. Increasing the amplitude to around 70 dB would essentially double the loudness, similar to what you might face trying to hold a conversation in a room with the TV or radio on. Increasing the amplitude to 80 dB would double the loudness again, such as you might experience trying to hold a conversation in a crowded room.

Microphones

The most common technique used to capture an acoustic audio event for recording is to place a microphone somewhere near the sound source. Microphones come in many shapes, sizes, and price points, so it can help to know a little bit about how they work before selecting the microphone or microphones you plan to use.

Traditional Microphones

All microphones are transducers, meaning they change energy from one form to another. A traditional analog microphone simply converts the variations in air pressure into variations in an electrical current. Three basic types of microphones are commonly available to make this conversion: dynamic mikes, ribbon mikes, and condenser mikes.

Dynamic Microphones

A dynamic microphone consists of a diaphragm attached to a coil of wire encircling a magnet. When sound waves hit the diaphragm, it vibrates back and forth, thereby moving the coil of wire back and forth over the magnet. This movement induces a current in the coil, with compression creating a positive voltage and rarefaction creating a negative voltage.

The advantages of dynamic microphones are that they are rugged and durable. They can also handle high input signals without distortion. Dynamic microphones are commonly used in both studio and live performance environments.

Ribbon Microphones

A ribbon microphone consists of a thin metal foil or other conductive ribbon material suspended between the positive and negative poles of a magnet. As sound waves hit the ribbon, they cause it to vibrate; the ribbon's movement within the magnetic field induces a current within the ribbon itself.

The advantages of ribbon microphones include a warm, smooth tone and an ability to capture high-frequency detail. Some ribbon microphones can be delicate and expensive. Ribbon mikes tend to be better suited for use in a studio environment rather than live performance.

Condenser Microphones

Condenser microphones consist of a thin conductive diaphragm (front plate) affixed a small distance in front of a metal back plate. The two plates are typically energized with a fixed charge. When sound waves hit the front plate, the diaphragm vibrates, varying the distance between the two plates. This varies the capacitance of the circuit and creates an opposite change in electrical voltage.

 The capacitance is the ratio of the electric charge on the plates to the voltage difference between them. The capacitance increases as the plates move closer together and decreases as the plates move further apart.

Condenser microphones require power to operate, either from a battery or a phantom power source. Phantom power is typically 48 volts DC applied through a microphone cable to the condenser mike.

 Mixers, microphone preamps, and audio interfaces commonly provide the option to enable phantom power, often denoted as +48V on the device.

The advantages of condenser microphones include a wide, smooth frequency response and sharp, detailed transient response. Condenser mikes are particularly well suited for acoustic instruments and cymbals. Although condenser mikes are very popular for in-studio recording, they are also commonly used in live sound production as well, particularly as drum overhead mikes.

USB Microphones

Another option to consider for home or studio use with your DAW is the USB microphone. USB mikes function the same as their traditional microphone counterparts, in that they convert acoustical energy into electrical energy. However, a USB mike goes a step further using two additional circuits: a built-in preamp and an analog–to–digital converter. This additional circuitry allows the microphone to be plugged directly into your computer for use with your DAW without requiring a separate audio interface.

 For information on the analog-to-digital conversion process, see "Moving Audio from Analog to Digital" later in this chapter.

Most USB microphones are condenser mikes, although a few dynamic USB mikes are also available.

Popular choices among USB microphones include:

- **Blue Microphones**

  - **Snowflake USB Microphone**—Designed for mobile desktop recording at an affordable price ($)

  - **Snowball USB Microphone**—Designed for podcasting and other desktop recording ($$)

  - **Yeti USB Microphone**—Designed for studio vocals, musical instruments, voiceovers, field recordings, podcasting, and desktop recording ($$$)

  - **Spark Digital Lightning Microphone**—Designed for studio and desktop recording for voiceovers, vocals, and instruments at a premium price ($$$$)

- **CAD U37 USB Studio Condenser Recording Microphone**—Designed for desktop recording and voiceovers, vocals, and instrumental recording on a budget ($)

- **Audio-Technica ATR2100-USB Cardioid Dynamic USB/XLR Microphone**—Designed for stage and studio use at a reasonable price ($$)

- **Rode NT-USB USB Condenser Microphone**—Designed for studio-quality recording of vocals, instruments, and voiceovers with built-in monitoring control ($$$)

- **Apogee Mic 96k Professional Quality Microphone**—Designed for high-resolution studio-quality recording at a premium price ($$$$)

- **Rode Podcaster USB Dynamic Microphone**—Designed for studio-quality podcasting and other desktop recording at a premium price ($$$$)

Other Considerations

Aside from the characteristics of different types of microphones described above, a few other considerations should come into play when selecting the right mike for your needs.

Polar Pattern

A microphone's polar pattern describes how the microphone responds to sound coming from different directions. Typical choices include omnidirectional mikes, bidirectional mikes, and unidirectional mikes.

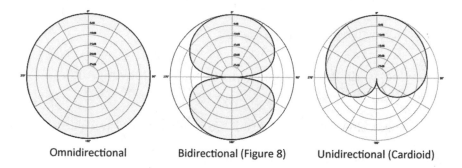

Figure 3.2 Common polar patterns: omnidirectional, bidirectional, and unidirectional

Omnidirectional. An omnidirectional mike will pick up sound equally from all directions. While this may be desirable for a microphone placed in the middle of a large conference table, it is usually not the best choice for studio recording where the goal is to isolate a sound source.

Bidirectional. Bidirectional mikes pick up sound primarily from the front and rear of the microphone, rejecting sound coming from the sides. This kind of mike may be desirable for across-the-desk interviews, two-part vocal recordings, or similar recordings of two opposite-facing sound sources. By rejecting sound from the sides, this type of mike will limit the amount of room acoustics and unwanted ambient noise in the recording.

Unidirectional (cardioid) . Unidirectional mikes are the most popular choice for recording isolated sound sources. These are also commonly referred to as cardioid microphones. Unidirectional, or cardioid, polar patterns are designed to pick up sound from the front of the microphone, while rejecting (or attenuating) sound coming from the sides or rear of the microphone.

Proximity Effect

Most unidirectional and bidirectional microphones exhibit a noticeable bass boost when used within a few inches of a target sound source. This phenomenon is known as the proximity effect and often results in an unwanted boomy sound. You can hear the effect by speaking into a microphone as you move up close to the front of the grill.

If you are aware of a mike's proximity effect, you can adjust the mike placement or roll off the bass frequencies with an equalizer to compensate.

Basic Miking Techniques

Microphone placement and position have a large impact on how well a microphone will perform at capturing the desired signal. The overall goal when setting up a microphone is to target the sounds you want to record while rejecting the sounds you don't. Several accessories are available to help with this process.

Microphone Accessories

The microphone accessories discussed below can assist you with mike placement, noise reduction, and sound isolation.

- **Mike Stand**—USB microphones designed for desktop use often come with a small stand or clip. For miking in a studio or open environment, however, you will need to invest in a full-sized mike stand. You might also consider a stand with a boom extension or gooseneck add-on for better reach and flexibility. You'll find a variety of stands and extensions readily available from your local music store or online retailer.

- **Windscreens and Pop Filters**—Windscreens and pop filters are designed to reduce unwanted noise resulting from wind or bursts of air hitting the microphone. These problems are especially prevalent for on-location field recordings and close-miked recordings of vocal or dialog performances.

> (i) In vocal performances, bursts of air are commonly produced from words that begin with "p" or "b" sounds. These bursts, or plosives, can ruin a recording if they hit a microphone's diaphragm directly.

- **Shock Mounts**—Shock mounts are designed to suspend a microphone, isolating it from any mechanical vibrations that may affect the mike stand. Such vibrations are commonly caused by loud music, noise carried through a floor or stage, or nearby thumps and bumps.

- **Acoustic Shields and Vocal Booths**—To improve sound isolation, especially for vocal and dialog recordings, you can consider using an acoustic shield. These products are designed to reduce the influence of ambient noise, room acoustics, and reflected sound on a recording. Acoustic shields are most effective at attenuating mid– and high–frequency audio.

  A more extreme approach is to build or install a fully–enclosed vocal booth or isolation room. These will be more effective at reducing unwanted noise than a shield, but they can also be expensive and complex to design.

  Note, also, that both shields and booths may colorize the audio, boosting or cutting certain frequencies of the performance. You may be able to correct for the colorization using an equalizer; however, you will need to determine whether the isolation gains are worth the trade-off.

Where to Shop for Audio Gear

While locally-owned music stores are becoming scarce, audio gear has never been easier to shop for. In addition to ubiquitous Guitar Center storefronts (718 locations in 44 states), numerous online retail outlets are available. Online options include guitarcenter.com, sweetwater.com, musiciansfriend.com, and vintageking.com, among others. Almost any audio equipment can be found with a quick Internet search!

Basic Setup and Connections

Setting up your microphone or microphones is a simple matter of finding the right mike position and establishing a connection to your computer.

- **Microphone Position**—The location of your microphone during a recording can have a dramatic influence on the recorded signal. Generally speaking, the closer the mike is to the target sound source, the "cleaner" the recording will be. That is to say, the recording will include more of the desired sound and less ambient noise.

  However, as noted above, certain mikes exhibit a proximity effect when placed close to their sound source. This can colorize the sound in ways that may be unwanted, depending on the situation.

- **Microphone Connection**—The way that your microphone connects to your computer will vary, depending on the type of mike you are using. Most analog microphones use a cable with XLR connectors (3-pin) to attach to your audio interface. The audio interface will in turn connect to your computer using a USB cable or other common digital computer connection.

Figure 3.3 Microphone XLR connection to an Mbox Pro audio interface

A digital USB microphone will connect directly to your computer, with no audio interface required.

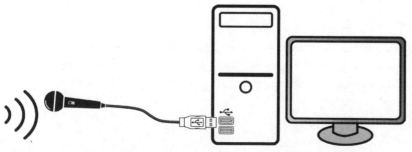

Figure 3.4 USB microphone connection to a desktop computer

Multi-Tracking and Signal Flow

The benefits of recording to a DAW are many. For starters, it allows you to record multiple takes and keep the best parts of each take. Additionally, it gives you the ability to edit and process a recording to improve the final results. But one of the greatest advantages is the freedom to record numerous isolated parts, each on its own track (known as multi-track recording).

What Is Multi-Track Recording?

The concept of multi-track recording has been around for many decades and is a fundamental aspect of audio production. Using this production method, each audio source is isolated as an individual recording on its own track. Each of these recorded tracks can then be edited and processed discretely. By playing back all of the individual tracks simultaneously, you can create a mix of the multiple sound sources as a final output.

By way of example, a music recording might include individual tracks for vocals, guitar, bass guitar, keyboards, and drums. By isolating each part on its own track, the volume levels, pan settings, EQ settings, and other processing can be set independently for each component.

Another advantage of multi-track recording is that individual parts can be recorded at different times. This is key if the performers cannot all be present in the same location at the same time. It also allows individual contributors to record multiple parts. For example, a musician can record both guitar and piano parts for a song. Or a voice actor can record dialog lines for multiple characters in a script for an animated short.

Figure 3.5 Multi-track music production session in Pro Tools|First

Not all recordings require multiple tracks. In some cases, you may want to record a mix of multiple sources to a single track. Some examples might include recording a live ensemble performance with a pair of microphones routed to a single stereo track or using an external mixer to sum multiple drum microphones to a stereo track. One reason for doing this is to simplify the recording and the number of tracks in your session. You might also use this approach if you do not have enough inputs on your system to record from many microphones at the same time.

Recording Signal Flow

Recording onto a computer involves routing a signal through various processing stages. This routing path is commonly referred to as the signal flow. Here, we will focus on a typical recording signal flow, from the sound source to the storage device (HDD, SSD, or cloud storage).

The sound originates at a source, such as a guitar, and travels through an environment by way of variations in air pressure, as discussed above. The air pressure changes are picked up by a microphone, converting the sound into an electrical signal. The electrical signal next travels down the microphone cable to an audio interface.

Within the audio interface, the signal is boosted, using a pre-amplifier (or *pre-amp*). The pre-amp is used to create a healthy signal level for recording. Next, the signal is sampled, using periodic measurements of the electrical voltage. The measured values are represented as strings of binary numbers and are passed along to the computer. At the computer, the binary numbers are stored on a hard disk drive or solid-state drive or cached and uploaded to cloud storage.

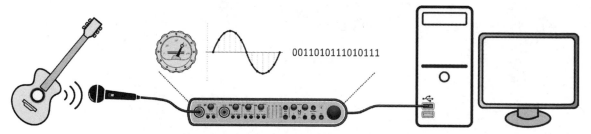

Figure 3.6 Recording signal flow from a guitar to a computer's hard drive

Moving Audio from Analog to Digital

As mentioned above, the practice of recording audio to a computer involves converting an electrical signal into individual, discrete binary measurements. This is the process known as analog-to-digital conversion.

Analog Versus Digital Audio

The variations in electrical voltage produced by a microphone represent a continuously changing analog audio waveform. In order to represent that information on a computer, the waveform must be converted into binary numbers that the computer can understand.

What Is Binary Data?

Binary data is comprised of binary digits, or bits. Each binary digit can represent only two possible values: *zero* or *one*. (At the most basic level, computers store and work with values using "switches" that are either off or on. A bit value of *zero* can be stored by toggling the associated switch off, while a bit value of *one* can be stored by toggling the switch on.)

In order to store values larger than one, computers use strings of multiple binary digits. For example, using a string of four binary digits, a computer can store values from zero (0000) to fifteen (1111). Using a string of eight binary digits, a computer can store values from zero up to 255. Using a 16-bit string, the computer can store values up to 65,535.

Once an audio signal has been converted to digital, the waveform can be stored, read, and manipulated by the computer. The digital audio file is comprised of individual measured values (samples) stored as strings of binary digits.

The Analog-to-Digital Conversion Process

Converting an analog signal to digital involves two critical parameters: the sample rate and the bit depth.

Sample Rate. The sample rate refers to the frequency at which the incoming electrical signal is measured by the audio interface. The sample rate must be high enough to accurately represent the original analog signal.

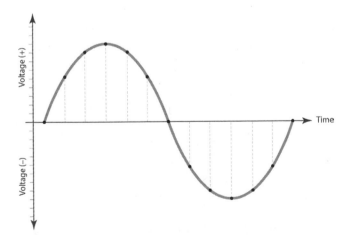

Figure 3.7 Sample intervals used to measure the changing voltage of an incoming audio signal

The sample rate required to accurately record a given signal is driven by a fundamental law of analog-to-digital conversion, known as the *Nyquist Theorem*. The Nyquist Theorem states that, in order to represent a given audio frequency, each cycle of the waveform must be sampled at least two times. Or, stated another way, the sample rate must be at least two times the frequency of the audio you wish to record.

Because we generally want to record full-spectrum audio – from 20 Hz to 20,000 Hz – the Nyquist Theorem tells us we need to use a sample rate of at least 40,000 Hz (or 40kHz): twice the upper end of this range. Most modern digital audio systems use a minimum sample rate of 44.1kHz.

Bit Depth.   The bit depth (or word length) refers to the number of binary digits included in each measurement string. The more binary digits used, the more accurate the measurements will be. Low bit-depth recordings exhibit a loss of audio detail—the result of a reduced dynamic range.

What Is Dynamic Range?

Dynamic range is the difference between the quietest signal that a system can represent and the loudest signal that the system can represent. Dynamic range is measured in decibels (dB). This is a relative measurement, not an absolute loudness value. The maximum absolute loudness of a system depends on the amount of amplification applied at the output; however, the dynamic range remains constant at all loudness levels, since it measures the relative *difference* between two levels.

You can estimate the dynamic range of a system by multiplying the bit depth by six. Said another way, each binary digit that is added to the word length provides approximately 6 dB of dynamic range.

The useful range of loudness values for speech and music is generally considered to be from 40 dB on the quiet end to 105 dB on the loud end: a 65-dB dynamic range. In order to produce that dynamic range, a digital audio system must provide a minimum 11-bit word length (65 dB divided by 6 dB per bit). Additional dynamic range is required to allow for headroom before clipping and to accommodate any inherent noise floor in the system. Most modern digital audio systems use a minimum bit depth of 16 bits.

The Audio Interface

As mentioned previously, an audio interface is a device used to provide analog-to-digital conversion for the audio coming into a system. It also provides digital-to-analog conversion for the audio playing out of the system. The audio interface is what allows you to get sound into and out of your computer.

Most audio interfaces also provide one or more microphone pre-amps. Pre-amps generally include a gain control that allows you to adjust the incoming signal and optimize record levels.

Audio Interface Considerations

A multitude of audio interfaces are available today, providing an enormous array of options. To narrow down your choices, it helps to decide on the characteristics that are important for your recording needs.

Some factors to consider include:

- What kind of input and output (I/O) connectivity do you need?

- What level of sound quality are you looking for?

- What sort of budget are you working with?

I/O Connectivity

If you plan to work exclusively in Pro Tools|First, you can consider an audio interface with up to 4 inputs, which is the maximum that Pro Tools|First currently supports. For the greatest flexibility, look for an audio interface with microphone (XLR) inputs.

If you are operating on a limited budget, you can consider an audio interface that includes just 1 or 2 microphone inputs. These may be supplemented with additional line- or instrument-level inputs. Line/instrument inputs can be useful for recording from an electric guitar or keyboard connected directly to the audio interface along with your miked source(s).

Most audio interfaces will include balanced stereo outputs, via a pair of ¼-inch jacks, for connecting to studio monitors. Many also include a stereo headphone jack with volume control. A headphone output is useful for monitoring playback from your DAW while recording: monitoring through headphones instead of your studio speakers helps prevent the playback from bleeding into a live microphone.

Sound Quality

Generally speaking, the "quality" of a digital audio file is a factor of the sample rate and bit depth used for the recording. But the recorded results are also influenced by the quality of the microphone pre-amps and the analog-to-digital (or A/D) converters in the audio interface.

Other factors also have a significant impact, including the recording environment and the quality and type of microphone(s) being used to capture the audio.

All of that is to say that you should not consider the specifications of sample rate and bit depth in isolation when seeking to optimize the quality of your recordings.

When to Use High-Resolution Audio

For a simple recording project, you may find yourself using a utilitarian microphone to record audio that has a limited dynamic range (such as when recording dialog for a podcast or webinar). You may also be recording in an untreated room or office environment. In such cases, recording with a high sample rate and bit depth will not have a beneficial impact: recording at 44.1kHz and 16-bit will certainly be sufficient.

Other times, you may be recording something with a wider dynamic range, such as a musical performance. This type of recording is often done using higher-quality microphones in a home-studio environment with at least some degree of acoustic treatment. In this case, you might want to consider using higher-resolution audio for better results and more editing flexibility. Recording at 24-bits is recommended in this situation to preserve the quality and dynamic range of the audio being captured.

In cases where you find yourself working in a professional studio environment—with top-of-line microphones, boutique pre-amps, and other high-end gear—you will almost certainly want to record at a sample rate of 96kHz or above (and 24-bit) to capture all the subtle nuances of the performance and the character of the associated equipment.

 Recording at 32-bit floating point is typically only necessary when you plan to do extensive additional processing to the audio files after recording. You will hear no audible difference in the quality of the captured audio over recording at 24-bits.

Nearly all of the audio interfaces on the market today support sample rates up to 96kHz, with many supporting up to 192kHz. Likewise, 24-bit A/D conversion is a near universal standard for bit depth. This means that your search for an audio interface for Pro Tools|First will not need to be based on the supported sample rate and bit depth of the device, as just about any device will fit the bill.

 Pro Tools|First supports audio with sample rates up to 96kHz.

Instead, look for an audio interface with a construction quality and price point that complements your recording goals and budget. For higher-quality audio, look for devices from "brand name" companies that have a reputation for high-end gear...but expect to pay a premium for them.

Budget

The ultimate deciding factor often comes down to budget. But you can weigh the options, such as I/O connectivity and brand reputation, against your budget to find the right compromise.

For example, if you need only a single mike input, you may opt for a high-end audio interface to maximize the sound quality. On the other hand, if having 4 mike inputs is an absolute requirement, but sound quality is less of a concern, you might select a more utilitarian audio interface instead to stay within budget.

In the end, be sure to consider the budget for your entire recording setup as a whole. You will want to balance the cost of your audio interface against the other considerations covered in this chapter to ensure that you are not spending too much in one area and neglecting others.

Working Without an Audio Interface

In some cases, you may decide to work without an audio interface. You could do this as an interim measure until you can save up for the audio interface you want. You could also do this as way to run your DAW when you are away from your audio interface, such as when on the road with a laptop.

In either case, Pro Tools | First allows you to utilize the built-in audio on your computer (if available) in lieu of a dedicated audio interface.

On Mac-based systems, no special hardware or software setup is required to work without an audio interface. Launching Pro Tools | First without an interface connected will cause the software to use the Pro Tools Aggregate I/O as the audio engine, automatically connecting the available inputs and outputs on your computer to the software.

On some Windows-based systems, Pro Tools | First will be able to utilize the computer's input and output options right out of the box. Other systems may need a driver installed to allow Pro Tools | First to access the computer's sound card options. The go-to resource for this is ASIO4ALL, a universal ASIO driver for Windows Driver Model (WDM) audio. ASIO4ALL is an independently developed freeware utility.

 ASIO stands for Audio Stream Input/Output, a computer soundcard driver protocol developed by Steinberg Media Technologies.

In most cases, you simply need to download and install the ASIO4ALL software. Once installed, ASIO4ALL will allow you to run Pro Tools | First on a Windows machine with no audio interface connected and play back through the computer's built-in speakers or headphone jack.

 To download ASIO4ALL, go to www.asio4all.com **and download the latest version in the language of your choice.**

Review/Discussion Questions

1. When a sound event occurs, what are the changes in air pressure called (i.e., the areas where air pressure increases and decreases)? (See "The Basics of Audio" beginning on page 64.)

2. What is meant by the frequency of an audio waveform? How does the frequency of a sound wave affect our perception of the sound? (See "Frequency" beginning on page 64).

3. What characteristic affects our perception of the loudness of a sound? How is loudness measured? (See "Amplitude" beginning on page 65.)

4. What is the purpose of a traditional microphone? What three basic types of microphones are commonly available? (See "Traditional Microphones" beginning on page 65.)

5. How are USB microphones different from traditional microphones? What is the advantage of using a USB microphone over a traditional microphone? (See "USB Microphones" beginning on page 67.)

6. What are the differences between omnidirectional microphones, bidirectional microphones, and unidirectional microphones? Which is the most common type of mike for recording isolated sound sources? (See "Polar Pattern" beginning on page 68.)

7. What are some accessories available to help you with mike placement, noise reduction, and sound isolation when recording? (See "Microphone Accessories" beginning on page 69.)

8. How is multi-track recording different from recording to a single audio file? What are some advantages of multi-track recording? (See "What Is Multi-Track Recording?" beginning on page 71.)

9. What two parameters are critical for the analog-to-digital conversion process? What minimum specifications are used for these parameters in modern digital audio systems? (See "The Analog-to-Digital Conversion Process" beginning on page 73.)

10. What is the purpose of an audio interface? (See "The Audio Interface" beginning on page 74.)

11. What are some factors to consider when selecting an audio interface for use with your DAW? (See "Audio Interface Considerations" beginning on page 75.)

12. How is working without an audio interface useful? What additional hardware or software options might you need in order to run Pro Tools|First without an interface? (See "Working Without an Audio Interface" beginning on page 77.)

Selecting Your Audio Production Gear

🎧 Activity

In this exercise, you will define your audio production needs and select components for a home studio based around Pro Tools|First software. By balancing your wants and needs against a defined budget, you will be able to determine which hardware and software options make sense for you.

🕐 Duration

This exercise should take approximately 10 minutes to complete.

◎ Goals/Targets

- Identify a budget for your home studio
- Explore microphone options
- Explore audio interface options
- Explore speakers/monitoring options
- Consider other expenses
- Identify appropriate components to complete your system

Getting Started

To get started, you will create a list of needs and define an overall budget for your home studio setup. This budget should be sufficient to cover all aspects of your initial needs for basic audio production work. At the same time, you'll want to be careful to keep your budget realistic so that you can afford the upfront investment. Keep in mind that you can add to your basic setup over time to increase your capabilities.

Use the table below to outline your basic requirements and to serve as a guide when you begin shopping for options. Place an **X** in the appropriate column for your expected needs in each row.

Do not include MIDI gear in this table, as we will address that separately.

 This exercise assumes that you own a compatible computer with built-in speakers for playback. Do not include a host computer in this table.

Function or Component	Not Required	Minimum Configuration	Maximum Configuration for Pro Tools | First
Audio Interface: Output Channels (Playback)	–	1-2 Inputs	4 Inputs
Audio Interface: Input Channels (Recording)	–	2 Outputs (for stereo playback)	4 Outputs (for stereo playback and output to external gear)
Output Device(s)	Built-in Computer Speakers	Headphones	Stereo Monitor Speakers
Input Device(s) (Microphones)	–	USB Microphone	XLR Microphone(s) (specify type and number)
Accessories and Other (List or Describe) (Stands, Soundproofing, Software Add-Ons, etc.)			

Available Budget for the Above: _____

Identifying Prices

Your next step is to begin identifying prices for equipment that will meet your needs. Using the requirements you identified above as a guide, do some Internet research at an online music retailer of your choice to identify appropriate options for each of the items listed in the table below. You may also want to browse some manufacturers' websites for more information.

Component	Manufacturer and Model	Unit Cost
Audio Interface		
Microphones		
Headphones		
Monitor Speakers		
Accessories/Other		
TOTAL		

Finishing Up

To finalize your purchase decisions, compare the total in the table above to the budget you allocated. If you find that your budget is not sufficient to cover the total cost, you will need to determine which purchase items you can postpone or consider bundle options. On the other hand, if you have money left over in your budget, you can consider upgrade options.

Bundle Options

One way to save some money is to look for gear bundles. These options can be much more affordable than buying the same components separately. Following are some good examples of bundles from Focusrite:

- Scarlett Solo Studio

- Scarlett 2i2 Studio

- iTrack Solo Studio

Each of the above bundles includes a Focusrite audio interface, a large–diaphragm condenser microphone, and a pair of closed-back studio headphones. As an added bonus, each bundle also includes the Pro Tools|First – Focusrite Creative Pack, a collection of 12 additional plug-ins for Pro Tools|First.

For more information, check out the details on the Focusrite website:

- Scarlett interfaces: https://us.focusrite.com/scarlett-range

- iTrack Solo interface: https://itrack.focusrite.com/products/itrack-solo-studio

- Pro Tools|First – Focusrite Creative Pack: https://us.focusrite.com/scarlett-pro-tools-first

Upgrade Options

If you are looking to expand your project count beyond the basic options provided with Pro Tools|First, you can consider an Avid Cloud Collaboration Premium Plan. The three premium plan options provide increased cloud storage and local save options for Pro Tools|First, enabling unlimited project counts. You can find details on Avid's website here:

- http://www.avid.com/avid-cloud-collaboration-for-pro-tools/how-to-get-it#Get-more-projects

If you need more audio processing options for Pro Tools|First, you can consider the First Air Effects bundle and/or other plug-in bundles available from Avid. More information on these options can be found here:

- First plug-In bundles: http://www.avid.com/pro-tools-first/first-plug-in-bundles

Chapter 4

MIDI Recording Concepts

...What You Need to Record MIDI...

Understanding MIDI is essential to producing music using a DAW. In this chapter, we'll take a look at some basic MIDI concepts that will get you started creating tracks. We'll begin by taking a quick look at the history of MIDI and how the MIDI protocol works. Next we'll check out some of the types of MIDI controllers that are currently available. Then we'll look at how to set up the controller to communicate with your DAW. This will lead us into a discussion on the fundamental differences between MIDI and audio data. Finally, we'll take a quick look how to begin working with virtual instruments.

◈ Learning Targets for this Chapter

- Understand the basic history of MIDI

- Learn about the MIDI protocol

- Recognize types of MIDI controllers

- Learn how to set up your controller and DAW

- Recognize the differences between MIDI and audio

- Begin tracking with virtual instruments

The term MIDI stands for Musical Instrument Digital Interface. MIDI is a protocol for connecting electronic musical instruments, computers, and other devices, allowing them to communicate with one another.

The MIDI standard was developed in the 1980s to allow musical performance information to be shared among and between devices. The standard provides specifications for describing musical events, such as note values and durations, allowing musical performances to be represented numerically.

A Brief History of MIDI

Before MIDI, there was really no standardized way to have synthesizers and other electronic musical instruments communicate with each other. Early voltage-controlled analog synthesizers by Bob Moog and Don Buchla (et al.) could send *voltage* information to each other. But they couldn't communicate more complex musical ideas, such as a discrete note with all of its pertinent information (pitch, amplitude, duration, etc.).

Image courtesy of Perfect Circuit Audio

Figure 4.1 A Buchla 200e analog modular synthesizer

Digital Control

Another major drawback to analog synthesizers was that individual sounds could not be saved; favorite sounds had to be rebuilt by hand to be reused. Practitioners would actually make little drawings that showed where cables were patched and the position of each knob. (See Figure 4.2.) Some would even take Polaroid pictures so they'd have a photograph of the patch. (Interestingly, this way of working is making a huge comeback with the current Eurorack synthesizer craze!)

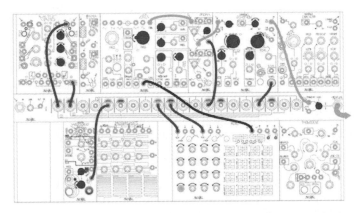

Figure 4.2 A patch "sheet" from a modern Eurorack analog synth

By the early 1980s, despite still using analog circuitry to generate sounds, most synthesizers had made the move to digital control for things like patch storage and recall (saving sounds and recalling them later). This created the possibility of having a common digital communication standard that would allow an electronic music instrumental to speak to any other instrument, regardless of the manufacturer.

The Birth of MIDI

In 1981, a proposal for a "Universal Synthesizer Interface" (USI) was presented at a meeting of the Audio Engineering Society (AES). This lead to the original MIDI 1.0 Specification. The specification was finalized in 1983 by a group that would become the MIDI Manufacturers' Association. The term *MIDI* was coined, as an acronym for Musical Instrument Digital Interface.

Image courtesy of Perfect Circuit Audio

Figure 4.3 Sequential Circuits Prophet 600 (1982)

At the 1983 National Association of Music Merchants (NAMM) trade show, the first public unveiling of MIDI occurred. A MIDI connection was demonstrated between a Sequential Circuits Prophet 600 (shown in Figure 4.3) and a Roland Jupiter 6. Soon, every major manufacturer had added MIDI connectivity to their synthesizers, drum machines, sequencers, and other devices.

The MIDI standard also helped pave the way for computer-based music. In 1984, Passport Designs released their MIDI/4 sequencer that ran on a personal computer.

The MIDI Protocol

The complete MIDI protocol is quite complicated, but it can be informative to take a look at the basics. MIDI messages can be divided into three basic categories: MIDI notes, program changes, and controller messages.

MIDI Notes

MIDI notes are probably the most important part of the protocol. Note data is the building block for almost all the work you'll do with MIDI.

One thing to understand about MIDI messages is that almost all parameters have a range of values spanning from 0 to 127. So, for instance, the pitch of a MIDI note is represented using a range of 0 to 127. A value of 0 represents the "C" note two octaves below the bottom of a piano. We refer to this note as C-2.

Middle C is typically assigned a note value of 60 and referred to as C3 (although some manufacturers use C4 instead). Figure 4.4 provides a diagram of note values.

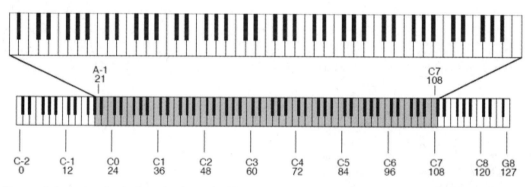

Figure 4.4 A standard piano keyboard with note names and MIDI note numbers

The other important bit of note information is the velocity, or how hard a note is played. Velocity is also represented using a range of 0-127, with the value of 64 falling right in the middle (sort of a *mezzo forte* in musical terms). Playing a note lighter will result in a lower velocity value, whereas playing harder will result in a higher value.

So, a MIDI note is a combination of a note number (pitch) and a velocity number. We refer to this combination as a **NOTE ON** command, because it activates the note in a technical sense. The Note On is eventually followed by a **NOTE OFF** command, which tells the device to stop playing the note. The Note Off command is the same note number, paired with a velocity of zero. The Note On and Note Off events are really all we need to send a note between two MIDI devices.

Pro Tools provides an "Event List" that shows the note information for a track. From left to right, this list displays the bar and beat location where each note starts, the associated note number (pitch), the attack velocity, the release velocity (rarely used), and the note length.

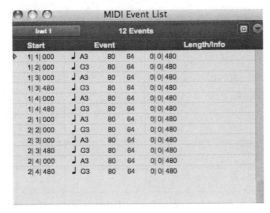

Figure 4.5 The MIDI Event List in Pro Tools

Program Changes

As mentioned above, patch storage and recall was an early advantage of digital control for synthesizers. The MIDI protocol improved upon this, enabling patch change commands (also known as program changes) to be sent to and from devices.

Like other MIDI messages, patch change commands use a range of values from 0 to 127. Thus, most banks of sounds on a MIDI keyboard will have 128 sounds. Table 4.1 shows an example bank of 128 sounds that many synthesizers support. This is part of the *General MIDI* standard.

Table 4.1 General MIDI Instrument Families

Program Change #	Family Name	Program Change #	Family Name
1 – 8	Piano	65 – 72	Reed
9 – 16	Chromatic Percussion	73 – 80	Pipe
17 – 24	Organ	81 – 88	Synth Lead
25 – 32	Guitar	89 – 96	Synth Pad
33 – 40	Bass	97 – 104	Synth Effects
41 – 48	Strings	105 – 112	Ethnic
49 – 56	Ensemble	113 – 120	Percussive
57 – 64	Brass	121 – 128	Sound Effects

Controller Messages

The final category of MIDI messages we'll consider is the category of controller messages—also known as MIDI continuous control (CC) messages. These are messages that can be used for purposes such as capturing the expressiveness of a MIDI performance (pitch bend or mod wheel movements) or performing studio mixing tasks (volume or pan changes). MIDI CC data represents an essential part of how keyboardists actually *play* their instrument.

Table 4.2 provides a list of standard MIDI continuous control defaults. Notice that certain controller numbers are "undefined," leaving room to make custom assignments.

Table 4.2 MIDI Controller Numbers (Excerpt)

Controller Number	Hex	Controller Name
0	00h	Bank Select
1	01h	Mod Wheel
2	02h	Breath Controller
3	03h	Undefined
4	04h	Foot Controller
5	05h	Portamento Time
6	06h	Data Entry MSB
7	07h	Main Volume
8	08h	Balance
9	09h	Undefined
10	0Ah	Pan

MIDI Controllers

To get started working with MIDI, it helps to have a MIDI controller. A MIDI controller is a device that generates MIDI performance data and transmits it to another device, such as a DAW, for processing. You can use a MIDI controller for recording MIDI notes and performance data into your DAW or for triggering a sound module or virtual instrument.

A variety of different MIDI controllers are available today. The most common designs continue to be based on the piano. With origins in the 18th century, the familiar black and white piano keyboard is a staple in the MIDI controller market. However, the last decade or so has seen an explosion in MIDI controller innovation. Newer concepts include drumpad controllers (inspired by the drum machine designs of the 1980s), grid controllers (originally introduced to augment the grid-based interface of Ableton Live), and mixer controllers (borrowing their faders and knobs from established analog and digital mixer designs).

Digital Pianos and Synthesizers

Many keyboard-based devices on the market can be classified as *tone-generating keyboards*. These are keyboards capable of generating their own sounds. Although generally designed for stand-alone performance, most tone-generating keyboards also provide MIDI connectivity. This allows you to use the keyboard to generate MIDI performance data and record it on your DAW. It also allows the keyboard to receive MIDI data from elsewhere and use it to trigger the device's onboard sounds.

Tone-generating keyboards generally fall into two categories: digital pianos and synthesizers:

- **Digital Pianos**—Digital pianos are exactly what the name implies: they look like a scaled-down version of a real piano. Digital pianos typically feature a full 88-key keyboard (often with simulated piano action known as *hammer action*). This type of keyboard is designed to compete head-to-head with real acoustic pianos; thus they are very simple to operate.

  Digital pianos generally offer a limited range of sounds (such as piano and organ). However, more expensive models may include additional sounds and auto-accompaniment features that can generate bass lines and drum patterns. Perhaps the most distinguishing feature of a digital piano is the presence of built-in speakers, which synthesizers rarely offer. (See below.)

Figure 4.6 Yamaha Arius Digital Piano

- **Synthesizers**—The term "synthesizer" encompasses a wide range of vintage and modern instruments. The term was originally used to describe analog devices that employed a combination of oscillators and filters to create sounds. These devices generated approximations of acoustic instruments (such as flute or violin) as well as otherworldly sounds that didn't bear resemblance to traditional instruments.

  But synthesizers quickly evolved to encompass both analog and digital technologies, with newer incarnations capable of using older analog-style synthesis as well as modern digital techniques such as sampling, physical modeling, and frequency modulation (FM) synthesis.

Modern synthesizers come in a variety of sizes, ranging from small, highly-portable two-octave (25-key) models to full 88-key piano–sized models.

Figure 4.7 Moog's classic MiniMoog synthesizer (1970)

If you already own a digital piano or synthesizer, look for a MIDI 5-pin connector or USB port for connecting it to your DAW. If you don't already own such a device, you can consider using a keyboard controller instead.

Keyboard Controllers

Keyboard controllers are essentially piano-style controllers that provide MIDI output, which you can use to create or record a MIDI performance. However, they do not include any onboard sound or tone-generating capabilities. This means that you cannot use a MIDI controller as a stand-alone instrument. Instead, the keyboard is designed to control other hardware synthesizers, sound modules, or virtual instruments.

The keyboard controller serves as a kind of universal MIDI input device. Using a piano keyboard as the performance interface, keyboard controllers enable any user with basic piano skills to create just about any kind of MIDI performance with little to no added learning curve.

Keyboard controllers come in a variety of sizes and price points. Users on a limited budget can consider a basic 25- to 37-key controller for under a hundred dollars. More sophisticated models with up to 88 keys can be found in the hundred-fifty to five hundred dollar range. These commonly include knobs, faders, and drumpads that can be mapped to control almost any function of the target instrument.

Figure 4.8 M-Audio Oxygen 49 keyboard controller

Drumpad Controllers

Most modern drumpad controllers are descended from Roger Linn's ingenious designs from the 1980s. The most iconic of Linn's designs was the Akai Professional MPC60, introduced in 1988. The 4×4 layout of pads that Linn pioneered has since become a standard pad arrangement for dozens of products.

The pads themselves are carefully designed to have a great feel that helps the player to perform dynamic drum and percussion grooves.

Figure 4.9 Akai Professional MPD218 drumpad controller

Grid Controllers

Today, the grid controller is probably the most popular controller type after the piano-style keyboard. Grid controllers have become popular for studio work, but they have also been embraced by live performers in a variety of genres, including EDM and hip-hop.

The grid controller design was inspired by Ableton Live's session view, with each pad used to trigger clips, play drum sounds, and adjust controls such as volume. Some grid controllers, such as Novation's Launchpad Pro and Ableton's Push 1 & 2, can be used to enter notes as well. These include options for restricting notes to a musical scale so that no wrong notes can be played! And, while grid controllers are generally optimized to work with Ableton Live, they can be used with an increasing number of DAWs.

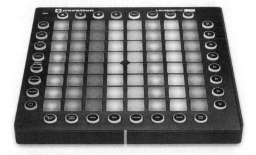

Figure 4.10 Novation Launchpad Pro grid controller

Alternate Controllers

You can also find some very innovative new controller styles on the market these days, offering alternatives to the standard keyboard, pad controller, or grid controller.

A primary focus of such alternative controllers currently is Multidimensional Polyphonic Expression (MPE). MPE is a new industry-wide standard that uses a separate MIDI channel for each touch. This channel-per-note configuration permits the controller to transmit discrete vibrato, glissando (pitch slides), note pressure, and other expressive information for each note that is played.

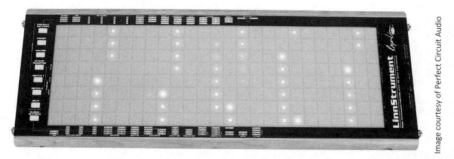

Image courtesy of Perfect Circuit Audio

Figure 4.11 Roger Linn's Linnstrument is one example of an alternate controller

What to Look for in a MIDI Controller

Deciding which controller or controllers to purchase can be an overwhelming task! The most important thing is to determine which activities you will be performing frequently, which you'll be doing only occasionally, and which you won't be doing at all. Here are some suggestions based on the strength of various controller types for typical music production tasks:

- Entering Notes:
  - Keyboard (best choice)
  - Grid (good alternative)
- Playing Beats:
  - Drumpad (best choice)
  - Grid (good alternative)
  - Keyboard (also good)
- Arranging:
  - Grid

Purchasing a Keyboard Controller

If you decide to purchase a keyboard controller, you'll need to decide on a few other attributes. The most important is probably the number of keys (note range). Your needs here will generally be determined by your proficiency as a keyboard player.

If you are an accomplished keyboardist who plays with two hands simultaneously, you will probably feel most comfortable with a keyboard featuring 61 keys or more. A full-sized, 88-key controller will offer the widest note range and the best feel. On the other hand, if you play using just one hand at a time, you may be satisfied with a smaller 25-key model.

Aside from note range, you'll also want to consider a device's support for velocity sensitivity, aftertouch, pitch and mod wheel controls, and other mappable controls like knobs and sliders.

Velocity Sensitivity

As mentioned previously, representing how hard each note is played is often a key ingredient to the expressiveness of a performance. Most moderately sophisticated keyboard controllers will be velocity sensitive, meaning they measure how hard each key is struck. However, some budget models may not include this capability, representing a significant limitation for many types of MIDI recording.

Aftertouch

When available, aftertouch lets a performer add expressive inflections to a sustained note or chord. Aftertouch can be used to add vibrato, pitch bends, and swells by varying the pressure on the held keys. When using a virtual instrument that supports it, aftertouch can be essential to making the instrument sound realistic. (Think of guitar solos and horn parts, for example: how often are sustained notes completely static?) Here again, budget keyboard controllers often do not include support for this parameter. Be prepared to do some comparison-shopping when trying to get the most bang for your buck.

Pitch and Mod Wheel Controls

These are additional options for adding expressiveness to a performance. Pitch bend and mod wheel controls are common on synthesizers but may not be included on some MIDI controllers. A traditional pitch wheel adds pitch bend (portamento) control, allowing the player to bend a note (or chord) up or down in a continuously variable manner. Pitch bend controls are sometimes included in non-wheel format, such as in a joystick, knob, or ribbon format.

Modulation wheels (or mod wheels for short) are typically used to set a vibrato amount. However, the mod wheel can also be mapped to other parameters, such as volume swells, tremolo, and filter sweeps.

Other Mappable Controls

Additional buttons, knobs, and sliders may be included on mid-sized and full-sized keyboard controllers. These controls can be mapped to plug-in parameters and other MIDI controls. In some cases, they can even operate functions in your DAW, such as transport controls and volume faders.

Setup and Signal Flow

Once you've selected a MIDI controller, you'll need to establish communication between the controller and your computer. Almost all modern MIDI controllers use USB rather than an actual MIDI cable to communicate. Configuring such a device can be as simple as plug-and-play, if the device is USB class-compliant. However, some devices require that you install specific drivers built for your computer and operating system.

Plug-and-Play Setup

For "class-compliant" USB devices, no drivers are required to communicate with your computer. You can verify that a device is class-compliant by checking the specifications on the manufacturer's website. Alternatively, you can connect the device to your computer and launch the appropriate software utility to verify communication.

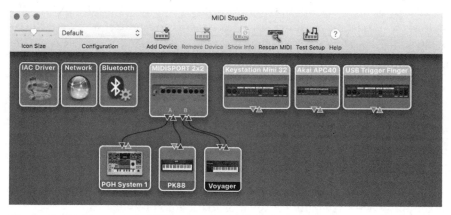

Figure 4.12 An example MIDI setup in Apple's Audio MIDI Setup utility; class-compliant devices will appear here automatically

MIDI Cables and Jacks

If you are using a device that has regular MIDI connections (not USB), you will have to deal with MIDI cables and jacks. A MIDI cable is technically called a 5-pin DIN cable and has connectors as shown in Figure 4.13.

Figure 4.13 A pair of MIDI cables

MIDI data is actually transmitted using only two pins on the 5-pin connector.

An important aspect of a MIDI cable is that it can carry *16 channels* of information. That means you could have up to 16 patches playing on one synthesizer, and they could all be addressed individually using a single MIDI cable.

The jacks that MIDI cables plug into are typically called *ports*. These can include an input, an output, and sometimes a "thru" connection.

Figure 4.14 A typical configuration of MIDI ports on a device

The MIDI In port receives incoming MIDI data from an outside source; this is commonly used to play back a MIDI performance coming from a DAW or other source using the onboard sounds of the device. The MIDI Out port sends MIDI data out from the device, for recording to a DAW or for triggering a different sound module. The MIDI Thru port passes the signal from the In port directly out to another device, without modifying it by any performance being done on the device. This can be very handy if you have a small MIDI interface with only a couple of ports, or if you have a complex live performance setup and don't want to lug an interface around.

Using a MIDI interface

Although most modern controllers use USB, you may encounter a hardware device (such as an older synthesizer) that uses traditional 5-pin MIDI cables to communicate. If so, you'll need a way to connect the MIDI cables to your computer, because the computer will not have the appropriate jacks for MIDI. You can accommodate these connections using an audio interface with MIDI jacks (quite common on all but the smallest interfaces).

Figure 4.15 MIDI jacks on the back of a Focusrite 2i4 audio interface

As an alternative to an audio interface, you can use a dedicated MIDI interface to route MIDI data to your computer. MIDI interfaces come in a variety of shapes and sizes and can have as many as eight jacks for MIDI input and output.

Figure 4.16 M-Audio Uno MIDI interface

Considerations for Using Multiple MIDI Devices

Even the smallest studio will often have more than one MIDI device. This could entail any combination of keyboard, drumpad, grid, and mixer controllers. Aside from the ergonomic issues of placing multiple controllers in the physical space, you'll also need to consider whether you want the devices to control specific instruments or to all control the currently selected instrument.

In most DAWs, the ideal solution is to leave inputs on your MIDI tracks assigned to "ALL" so that the currently selected instrument will respond to any controller that you touch. This makes it very easy to play keyboard for a piano part, then switch over to the drumpads to perform a beat, all without having to stop and change the MIDI routing.

MIDI Versus Audio

One of the more difficult concepts to grasp when you begin working with a DAW is the difference between MIDI and audio. While most novice audio producers have a decent understanding of how audio data is recorded and represented in a DAW, many do not have a similar understanding with regard to MIDI data.

What Is MIDI?

As discussed earlier in this lesson, MIDI is a protocol that facilitates communication between a huge range of hardware and software devices. MIDI data is not audio, but rather a series of messages that can communicate information such as notes (pitch), duration, velocity (how hard a key or pad is pressed), dynamics (volume), and more. A tone-generating hardware or software instrument can receive MIDI messages and convert them into audio data.

In other words, the MIDI data has the potential to become music that we can hear, but there's no way to listen to the MIDI data by itself.

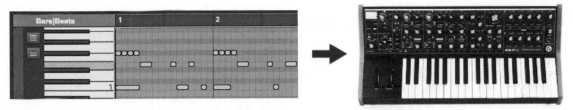

Figure 4.17 MIDI data (in piano roll format) must be sent to a tone-generating device to become music that we can hear

MIDI messages share some features with traditional music notation. Both contain the information necessary to play a piece of music, but neither are capable of actually becoming music on their own. Like MIDI, the notes of a musical score aren't audio, but instead represent the potential for audio once they are played using an instrument.

MIDI and notation contain information that can convey essential musical elements such as pitch, duration, velocity, and dynamics. Almost every DAW allows MIDI data to be viewed and edited as music notation (in addition to piano roll, event list, and other more modern formats).

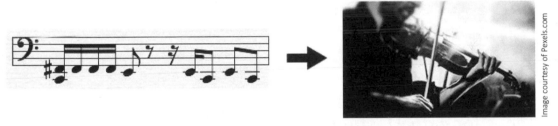

Figure 4.18 Music notation must be read by a musician to become music we can hear.

Monitoring with Onboard Sound Versus Virtual Instruments

If you are using a tone-generating keyboard such as a digital piano or synthesizer, you will need to decide whether you want to monitor from the onboard sound of the device or, alternatively, silence the onboard sounds and instead listen to a virtual instrument inside of your DAW.

It is rare that you will want to hear the sound of the controller while recording MIDI data into your DAW. (In fact, this can result in an annoying doubling of the controller audio with the DAW audio.) In the majority of situations, you'll want to monitor from the associated virtual instrument's output alone. This can be accomplished by turning off "Local Control" on the keyboard device. This setting will disable the internal sounds of the device while still sending MIDI data out to the DAW.

You may need to refer to the user guide or manufacturer's website to find the local control setting on your particular device.

Tracking with Virtual Instruments

Most modern music production studios incorporate software instruments, or virtual instruments, into their toolkit. In fact, a number of software manufacturers are known primarily for their virtual instrument offerings, including Native Instruments, Arturia, and Spectrasonics. Virtual instruments encompass a huge range of musical devices, including digital synthesizers, analog-modeling synthesizers, samplers, drum machines, and much more. They have become so ubiquitous in the DAW world that every major manufacturer offers a range of free or paid virtual instruments.

Figure 4.19 Native Instruments Kontakt sampler

Creating Tracks for Virtual Instruments

Working with virtual instruments in your DAW can seem a bit confusing at first. It's not quite as simple as just creating a track and pressing record! The first step to working with virtual instruments is to create the appropriate track type, which is usually referred to as an "Instrument" or "MIDI" track depending on the DAW. These tracks are capable of recording and editing MIDI data, routing the MIDI data to a virtual instrument, and then mixing the virtual instrument's resulting audio output.

Let's take a look at a couple of example configurations.

Virtual Instruments in Pro Tools|First

Routing MIDI to a virtual instrument in Pro Tools|First is quite similar to the process in many other DAWs, including standard Pro Tools, Cubase, and Logic.

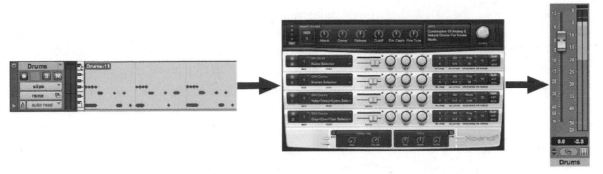

Figure 4.20 When MIDI is routed to the Xpand!2 plug-in, the plug-in's audio output is processed in the track's Fader section.

In Figure 4.20, the Drums track sends its MIDI data to the Xpand!2 virtual instrument plug-in, which is inserted on the same track. Then, Xpand!2 converts the MIDI data to audio, with the sound being determined by the patch/preset that is currently selected. Next, the audio output from Xpand!2 is routed through the audio section of the Drums track, where its volume, pan, and other audio attributes can be adjusted as desired. Finally, the audio output of the track is routed to the audio interface, so that it can be monitored through speakers or headphones.

Virtual Instruments in GarageBand

GarageBand provides another example of this concept, although the approach used in the software is somewhat different. (See Figure 4.21.) Note that GarageBand doesn't offer a mixer view, so the track is only visible in a horizontal layout that is similar to the Edit window in Pro Tools.

In GarageBand, the sound module is assigned by selecting the desired source from the Sound Library, rather than by placing a virtual instrument plug-in on the track.

Figure 4.21 Using a drum instrument in GarageBand

In Figure 4.21, we can see the MIDI data in the familiar piano roll format on the track. That MIDI data is being routed to the East Bay drum kit (whose controls are displayed at the bottom). The kit converts the MIDI data to audio. The audio output actually appears on the horizontal controls just to the left of the MIDI data, where the volume and pan attributes can be modified. From there, the audio goes to the interface output.

Summary

As you can see, the function of a virtual instrument is quite similar regardless of the DAW you choose. Professional-level DAWs offer sophisticated routing and additional views for working with MIDI data (as well as audio). By contrast, entry-level DAW options (such as GarageBand) aim to keep things as simple as possible. Regardless of where you begin, once you have gained basic familiarity with your chosen DAW, you'll find it relatively easy to apply that knowledge to any other DAW you should encounter.

Review/Discussion Questions

1. What were some of the drawbacks of historical analog synthesizers? (See "A Brief History of MIDI" starting on page 86.)

2. How did digital control of synthesizers pave the way for the development of MIDI? (See "A Brief History of MIDI" starting on page 86.)

3. What are the three basic categories of MIDI messages? (See "The MIDI Protocol" starting on page 88.)

4. What is the standard range of values for all MIDI messages? (See "The MIDI Protocol" starting on page 88.)

5. What MIDI note number is typically used to represent middle C on a piano? Is this number the same with every device? (See "The MIDI Protocol" starting on page 88.)

6. What are the two components of a MIDI Note On command? (See "The MIDI Protocol" starting on page 88.)

7. What is the name for a patch change command when using MIDI? (See "The MIDI Protocol" starting on page 88.)

8. What type of MIDI data can be used to increase the expressiveness of a MIDI performance? (See "The MIDI Protocol" starting on page 88.)

9. What are two categories of tone-generating keyboards? (See "MIDI Controllers" starting on page 90.)

10. Aside from keyboards, what are some other types of MIDI controllers? (See "MIDI Controllers" starting on page 90.)

11. What does it mean when a USB device is labeled "class-compliant?" (See "Setup and Signal Flow" starting on page 96.)

12. How can MIDI notes be converted to an audio signal that we can hear? (See "MIDI Versus Audio" starting on page 98.)

13. How can a virtual instrument plug-in be assigned in Pro Tools|First? (See "Tracking with Virtual Instruments" starting on page 100.)

Selecting Your MIDI Production Gear

🎧 Activity

In this exercise, you will define your MIDI production needs and select components to complement the Pro Tools|First system you configured in Exercise 3. By identifying the type of MIDI production work you will be doing, you will be able to select an appropriate MIDI control or controllers to meet your needs.

🕐 Duration

This exercise should take approximately 10 minutes to complete.

✤ Goals/Targets

- Identify a budget for your MIDI hardware

- Explore controller options

- Consider other expenses

- Identify appropriate components to complete your system

Getting Started

To get started, you will create a list of requirements for your MIDI controller and define an overall budget for your MIDI setup. Once again, make sure your budget is sufficient to cover all your immediate needs, while remaining realistic about what you can afford. You can always add to your basic MIDI setup over time with more devices and virtual instruments.

Use the table below to identify your basic MIDI requirements and to serve as a guide when you begin shopping for a controller. Place an **X** in the appropriate column(s) for each row.

Criteria	Rating			
Piano Keyboard Skills	Novice / Hunt and Peck	Competent Beginner	Intermediate	Advanced
Intended Uses	Drum Programming, Effects, Short Musical Parts, Loops, EDM	Background Music Production, Simple Keyboard Parts and Other Instruments	Lead Instrument Parts, 2-Handed Performances, Complex Arrangements	Orchestral Scores and Arrangements
Feature Requirements	Basic MIDI Input	Velocity Sensitivity	Pitch Bend and Mod Wheel	Aftertouch
Accessories and Other (List or Describe) (Keyboard Stands, Foot Pedals, etc.)				

If your **X**'s fall predominantly in the left half of this table, you may want to consider a drum pad or grid controller, or look for a budget-model keyboard controller. If your **X**'s fall predominantly in the right half, you should probably target a full-sized and fully featured keyboard controller. If your MIDI needs are extensive, you may want to consider selecting more than one type of controller to purchase.

Available Budget for MIDI Gear: _____

Identifying Prices

Your next step is to begin identifying prices for the type of controller and accessories that will meet your needs. Using the requirements you identified above as a guide, conduct some research online to identify available options. List potential matches in the table below, along with short descriptions (including number of keys, if applicable) and prices.

Type of Controller	Manufacturer and Model/Description	Price
Accessories/Other		

Finishing Up

To finalize your purchase decisions, total the cost of each option plus your required accessories and compare them to the budget you allocated. If you find that your budget is not sufficient to cover your preferred choice, consider a different option with the plan to upgrade in the future.

If you are able to purchase your first choice items and have money left over in your budget, you can look at software add-ons to supplement your collection of virtual instruments. For example, you might consider the First Air Instruments bundle available from Avid. These are the same virtual instruments available in commercial versions of Pro Tools.

More information on the virtual instruments included in the First AIR Instruments bundle can be found here: http://www.avid.com/pro-tools-first/first-plug-in-bundles.

Chapter 5

Pro Tools Concepts, Part 1

...What You Need to Know to Get Started with Pro Tools|First...

This chapter introduces you to some basic operations and functions you need to be familiar with to get started working in Pro Tools|First. We cover how to create a new project, how to access and use the main windows, and how to create tracks. We also cover basic navigation and selection techniques, including transport controls, zooming and scrolling operations, and uses for Timeline selections and Edit selections. These foundational concepts will help you get up and running and remain productive as you work.

◈ Learning Targets for This Chapter

- Learn how to create a new Pro Tools|First project

- Recognize uses for the Edit window, Mix window, and Transport window

- Become familiar with the basic controls in each main window

- Learn how to create tracks and understand the supported track types in Pro Tools|First

- Understand the difference between mono tracks and stereo tracks and recognize when to use each

- Learn how to navigate in the Edit window by scrolling and zooming

- Learn playback and selection techniques

If you need professional-level audio production capabilities on a limited budget, Pro Tools|First is an excellent place to start. The techniques and workflows you use in Pro Tools|First will transfer seamlessly to standard Pro Tools software (and Pro Tools|HD), should you decide to upgrade in the future. And Pro Tools|First allows you to work on projects shared by other Pro Tools users, making collaboration easy. Yet despite its robust capabilities, Pro Tools|First has a simplified feature set and streamlined user interface, allowing you to get up and running quickly with a minimal learning curve.

Creating a Session or Project

When you launch a Pro Tools product (Pro Tools|First, standard Pro Tools, or Pro Tools|HD), the first thing you see after the startup completes is the Dashboard. The Dashboard is your springboard for creating a new Pro Tools production or opening an existing Pro Tools file.

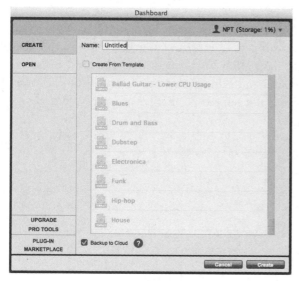

Figure 5.1 The Dashboard in Pro Tools|First

A Pro Tools production can be created as either a *session* or a *project*. The difference between these formats is where the document file and associated media files are stored. A Pro Tools session document is stored on a local drive (either the computer's internal drive or an external, connected drive). A Pro Tools project document is stored using the cloud-based storage provided by your Avid Master Account.

Pro Tools|First is limited to project documents only, meaning all of your Pro Tools|First productions will be stored using your Avid cloud allocation. If needed, you can upgrade to an Avid Cloud Collaboration Premium Plan, which gives you access to additional cloud storage as well as the ability to save projects offline, for unlimited project creation.

Pro Tools software and Pro Tools|HD systems can create either local session documents or cloud-enabled projects.

To create a new, blank project in Pro Tools|First, do the following:

1. Display the Dashboard, if not currently showing, by choosing **FILE > CREATE NEW**.

2. Verify that the **CREATE** action is selected in the left sidebar.

3. Type a name for the project in the **NAME** field at the top of the Dashboard.

4. Verify that the **CREATE FROM TEMPLATE** option is deselected (unchecked).

5. Click the **CREATE** button at the bottom of the Dashboard.

   A new project will be created using the cloud storage associated with your Avid Master Account.

 In standard Pro Tools and Pro Tools|HD, the Dashboard is also used to specify parameters for your project or session, such as the sample rate and bit depth.

Main Windows

The main windows in Pro Tools include the Edit window, the Mix window, and the Transport window. Each of these windows can be accessed under the **WINDOW** menu at the top of the screen. Some differences exist in these windows in Pro Tools|First, as compared to standard Pro Tools and Pro Tools|HD, but the differences are minor.

In this section, we cover the features of these main windows in Pro Tools|First. Where appropriate, we point out some of the differences in standard Pro Tools.

Edit Window

The Edit window is where you will do most of your work recording, arranging, and editing audio and MIDI data. This window provides a timeline display of the audio waveforms and MIDI performances on tracks in your session or project.

To access the Edit window when it is not displayed, choose **WINDOW > EDIT WINDOW**.

By default, the audio and MIDI data on your tracks will be displayed as *clips* in the Edit window. Clips are representations of audio or MIDI files or file sections in a Pro Tools session or project.

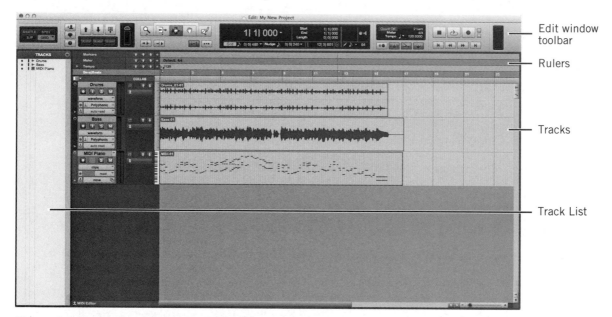

Figure 5.2 Edit window in Pro Tools | First

Edit Window Toolbar

The toolbar area at the top of the Edit window provides a variety of functions, including the Edit Mode buttons, the Track Collaboration tools, the Edit tools, the Main Counter, the MIDI controls, and the Transport controls.

Edit Mode Buttons

The buttons on the left side of the toolbar activate each of Pro Tools' four Edit modes.

Figure 5.3 Edit mode buttons (Slip mode active)

The Edit modes (Shuffle, Slip, Spot, and Grid) affect the movement and placement of audio and MIDI data.

- **Shuffle Mode**—In this mode, clip movement is constrained by other clips, and edits affect the placement of all subsequent clips on the track. When you move a clip, it will snap to the previous or next clip on the track. Removing part of a clip will cause all clips to the right to slide over by the amount of time removed. Clips cannot be overlapped in this mode.

- **Slip Mode**—In this mode, clip movement and placement is unconstrained. Removing a portion of a clip will leave blank space (silence) in the affected area of the track, and edits will not affect the placement of other clips on the track. It is also possible to move a clip so that it overlaps or covers another clip on the track.

- **Spot Mode**—This mode is similar to Slip mode, with the exception that you can move or place clips at precise locations by specifying the location numerically in a dialog box. The dialog box allows you to specify the start or end location for the selected clip.

- **Grid Mode**—In this mode, clip movement is constrained by the current Grid value setting. Selections are similarly constrained, snapping to the nearest Grid increment. As in Slip mode, removing part of a clip will leave blank space on the track without affecting other clips, and clips can be overlapped when moved.

Track Collaboration Tools

The track collaboration tools are used when you collaborate on a project with another Pro Tools user. These tools consist of two components: the Global Track Collaboration tools and the Track Collaboration controls.

The Global Track Collaboration tools are displayed in the Edit window toolbar. These tools let you post and receive all shared track data.

Figure 5.4 Global Track Collaboration tools in the Edit window

The Track Collaboration controls are displayed at the head of each track in the Edit window. These controls are used to share a track with a collaborator, take or release ownership of a track, upload changes on a track, or download changes to a track.

Figure 5.5 Track Collaboration controls at the head of a track

Edit Tools

The Edit tools are used to work with audio and MIDI data on tracks.

Figure 5.6 Edit tools in Pro Tools|First

The Edit tools in Pro Tools|First include the Zoomer tool, the Trim tool, the Selector tool, the Grabber tool, and the Pencil tool.

- **Zoomer tool**—This tool can be used to zoom in and out on a particular area of a track. Zooming in lets you examine a clip or waveform up close. Zooming out lets you get an overview of the clips on your tracks.

- **Trim tool**—This tool can be used to trim excess audio or MIDI material from the beginning or ending of a clip. Trimming modifies clips nondestructively, leaving the underlying source material unchanged.

- **Selector tool**—This tool can be used to position the playback point or to select an area of a track for playback or editing. Selected areas appear highlighted by a dark overlay in the Edit window.

- **Grabber tool**—This tool can be used to select an entire clip with a single mouse click. The Grabber is also used to move clips within a track or between tracks.

- **Pencil tool**—This tool is commonly used for creating and editing MIDI notes. It can also be used for editing automation and for editing waveform data at the sample level.

> **(i)** Standard Pro Tools and Pro Tools|HD also include a Scrubber tool in the Edit tool cluster (between the Grabber and Pencil tools).

Counters Display

The Counters display area in the Edit window includes the Main Counter as well as the Timeline Selection Fields. In Pro Tools|First, this area also includes selectors for setting the Grid and Nudge values.

Figure 5.7 Counters display area in Pro Tools|First

The unit of measurement in the Counters display area is based on the project Time Scale.

 The project Time Scale defaults to Bars|Beats in Pro Tools|First. The project Time Scale can be changed to Min:Secs by clicking on the selector (down arrow) next to the Main Counter display.

- **Main Counter**—The Main Counter is a numeric display showing the location of the Edit cursor (or the selection start, if a selection is active).

- **Timeline Selection Fields**——These fields include the Start, End, and Length displays to the right of the Main Counter. The Start value will always be equivalent to the Main Counter display in Pro Tools|First. The End and Length fields show the selection end location and selection length, respectively, whenever a selection is active.

- **Grid and Nudge Selectors**——These selectors are displayed underneath the Main Counter in Pro Tools|First and are used to set the Grid value and Nudge increment, respectively.

 Details on using the Grid and Nudge functions are provided in Chapter 6.

Rulers

Rulers are horizontal displays that appear at the top of the Edit window, below the Edit window toolbar and above the tracks display area. The Rulers in Pro Tools|First include Conductor Rulers (Markers, Meter, and Tempo) along with a Main Timebase Ruler.

 Standard Pro Tools and Pro Tools|HD provide additional Conductor Rulers, including Key and Chord rulers, as well as a variety of Timebase Rulers, including Samples, Timecode, and Feet+Frames rulers.

The Main Timebase Ruler provides measurement indicators for identifying specific locations on a project's timeline. The Main Timebase Ruler can be toggled between Bars|Beats and Min:Sec, by changing the project Time Scale from the Main Counter.

 See "Monitoring Your Timeline Location" later in this chapter for details on changing the project Time Scale.

Track List

The Edit window in Pro Tools|First includes a Track List on the left side of the window. The Track List can be used for selecting, arranging, and showing/hiding the tracks in your project. You can adjust the side column width as needed to view longer track names.

Standard Pro Tools and Pro Tools|HD also provide a right side column, displaying the Clip List. Both side columns can optionally be hidden in these versions of the software.

Mix Window

The Mix window provides a mixer-like environment for recording and mixing audio. In this window, tracks appear as mixer strips. Each strip includes controls for inserts, sends, input and output assignments, panning, and volume.

Figure 5.8 Mix window in Pro Tools|First

To access the Mix window when it is not displayed, choose **WINDOW > MIX**.

 You can also toggle from the Edit window to the Mix window (and vice versa) by pressing **COMMAND+=** on the Mac or **CTRL+=** on windows.

Track List. Like the Edit window, the Mix window includes a Track List on the left side for selecting, arranging, and showing/hiding the tracks in your project.

Signal Routing Controls. The top portion of each track's mixer strip provides controls for routing signals for the track. These include Insert selectors for applying plug-in processors, Send selectors for routing to an output or bus, an Input selector for routing audio into the track for recording or processing, and an Output selector for routing audio out of the track for playback.

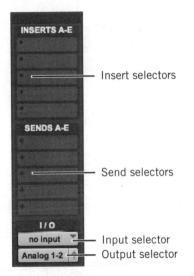

Insert selectors

Send selectors

Input selector
Output selector

Figure 5.9 Signal routing controls

Record and Playback Controls. The bottom portion of the mixer strip provides controls for setting record and playback options. These include Pan controls for positioning the signal within the stereo field; buttons to enable Input monitoring, Record, Solo, and Mute functions; and a Volume Fader for setting the output level.

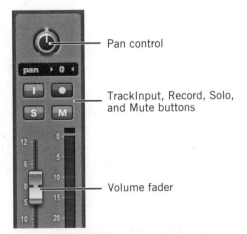

Pan control

TrackInput, Record, Solo, and Mute buttons

Volume fader

Figure 5.10 Record and playback controls

Transport Window

The Transport window provides buttons for various transport functions, such as play, stop, fast-forward, and rewind. This window also displays Global Track Collaboration tools, a Counters display, and a MIDI Controls section.

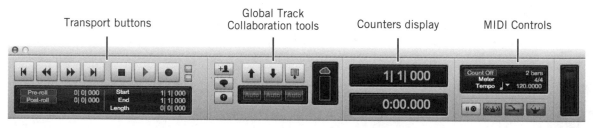

Figure 5.11 Transport window in Pro Tools | First

Global Track Collaboration Tools. The Global Track Collaboration area of the Transport window is identical to this section in the Edit window toolbar, providing tools for uploading and downloading project data using your Avid cloud storage. These tools are used primarily for work with remote collaborators.

Counters Display. The Counters display area shows the location of the cursor or selection in Bars|Beats (Main Counter) and in Min:Secs (Sub Counter). These displays are reversed when the Main Time Scale is set to Min:Secs.

MIDI Controls. The MIDI Controls section lets you configure playback and recording options. Controls in this area include the Count Off, Meter, and Tempo displays; the Wait for Note button for MIDI recording; the Metronome button for enabling the click; the MIDI Merge button, which is used for certain MIDI record workflows; and the Tempo Ruler Enable button for activating and deactivating the tempo map.

Working with Tracks

Once you've created a project in Pro Tools | First, you will need to create tracks for your project and give them meaningful names. Tracks are where your audio and MIDI performances are recorded and edited. Audio and MIDI data can be copied and duplicated in different locations to create repeating patterns, to arrange song sections, or to assemble material from multiple takes.

Adding Tracks

To add tracks to your project, you can use the New Tracks dialog box. This dialog box lets you configure the number and type of tracks needed. In Pro Tools | First, you can add up to 16 tracks of each main type, plus up to 4 Master Fader tracks. Tracks can be configured as either mono or stereo.

Figure 5.12 The New Tracks dialog box

To access the New Tracks dialog box, choose **TRACK > NEW**, or press **COMMAND+SHIFT+N** on Mac (**CTRL+SHIFT+N** on Windows). Use the selectors in the dialog box to configure the type of track to add.

Pro Tools|First supports the following five track types:

- **Audio**—This track type lets you record or import audio clips and work with them in a waveform-based display format.

- **MIDI**—This track type lets you record, create, import, and edit MIDI clips. MIDI tracks cannot route audio signals; therefore, this track type does not have a channel format (mono or stereo).

- **Instrument**—This track type combines the functions of MIDI tracks and Aux Input tracks, making it ideal for composing with virtual instrument plug-ins.

- **Aux Input**—This track type is used to route live audio signals through the Pro Tools mixer. Aux Input tracks are often used as effects channels and submix destinations.

- **Master Fader**—This track type is used to control output levels for signals routed to an audio interface or a computer's on-board outputs. A Master Fader track is typically used to monitor, process, and control the mix signal going to the main stereo outputs.

You can add multiple tracks of different types simultaneously by adding rows to the New Tracks dialog box. To add a new row, click on the plus button (**+**) at the end of an existing row.

Figure 5.13 Multiple tracks and track types configured in the New Tracks dialog box

Mono Versus Stereo Tracks

Tracks that route or process audio signals offer a choice between mono and stereo channel formats. Either format will allow you to pan the track's playback in order to position the audio output within the stereo field. The distinction between them is the channel format of the track's *input* signal. In other words, the channel format you choose should be based on whether the incoming audio is mono or stereo.

For example, you will typically use mono audio tracks to record vocal and dialog performances, since the source signal will usually be a solo voice recorded with a single microphone. The same holds true for recording many types of close-miked acoustic instruments, as well as electric instruments that are connected directly to an audio interface. Common exceptions would include stereo-miked instruments, such as pianos, and electronic instruments that provide stereo outputs, such as drum machines and synthesizers.

MIDI Versus Instrument Tracks

To record a MIDI performance, you can use either a MIDI track or an Instrument track. Both track types allow you to record incoming MIDI data from a connected controller. You can also edit MIDI notes, adjust note velocities, and record and edit MIDI CC data on either track type.

Configuring MIDI Tracks for Playback

During playback, a MIDI track makes no sound on its own. In order for the notes on a MIDI track to trigger audio, the MIDI output from the track must be routed to a sound module or virtual instrument. For example, the MIDI playback can be routed out of Pro Tools to an external synthesizer to generate sound. The synthesizer sounds could then be monitored externally, by using an amplifier, or internally, by routing the synthesizer's audio through an Aux Input track in Pro Tools.

Alternatively, the MIDI output can be routed directly to a virtual instrument plug-in on an Aux Input track within Pro Tools. In this scenario, the virtual instrument acts as the sound module, generating an audio signal that plays through the Aux Input channel.

Configuring Instrument Tracks for Playback

In most cases, you'll find it easier to work with MIDI on an Instrument track. Using an Instrument track lets you place a virtual instrument directly on the track, using an Insert selector. The MIDI on the track then triggers the virtual instrument during playback.

Because an Instrument track combines the functions of a MIDI track with those of an Aux Input track, it allows you to route both MIDI and audio signals simultaneously.

Click Tracks

When using Pro Tools|First to record music, it can be helpful to use a click track. A click track provides a metronome-based click that performers can use as a reference tempo while recording. Once you've created a click track, the click sound can be toggled on/off using Metronome button in the Transport window.

To add a click track to your project, choose **TRACK > CREATE CLICK TRACK**. Pro Tools|First will automatically add an Aux Input track with the Click II plug-in on Insert A.

Clips Versus Files

Each recording you complete on a track in Pro Tools or Pro Tools|First is stored as a separate audio file on disk (or in your cloud storage account). In your project, these audio files are represented as *whole file clips* on the associated tracks. Whole file clips include all of the original, unedited audio from the parent file on disk.

When you edit a whole file clip, such as by trimming off the start or end of the recording, you create a *subset clip*. A subset clip is a pointer that references a portion of the audio within the parent audio file.

By working with clips rather than the original files, Pro Tools can perform non-destructive audio editing. This means the original audio files are unaltered by the edits you perform. As a result, you can easily recover or reference "missing" audio after an edit using trimming, healing, and other techniques.

Basic Navigation

As a project grows, both in overall length and in track number, it becomes increasingly important to be able to navigate through the project quickly. In this section, we cover basic navigation techniques for use with playback, recording, and editing in a project.

Using the Transport Controls

The Transport window provides buttons for controlling playback and cursor position. The transport buttons are also displayed in the Edit window toolbar.

Figure 5.14 Transport buttons in the Transport window (left) and in the Edit window toolbar (right)

The transport buttons provide the following functions:

- **Play**—The Play button initiates playback from the current cursor location. The play function can also be initiated by pressing the **SPACEBAR** when the transport is stopped.

- **Stop**—The Stop button stops a playback or record pass. The stop function can also be initiated by pressing the **SPACEBAR** when the transport is in motion.

- **Record**—The Record button places the project in Record Ready mode, in preparation for a record pass on any record-enabled track(s).

- **Return to Zero**—The Return to Zero button returns the cursor to the start of the timeline. This function can also be initiated by pressing the **RETURN** key on Mac (or the **ENTER** key on Windows).

- **Rewind**—The Rewind button moves the cursor backwards while held. This function is available both when the transport is stopped and while it is in motion.

- **Fast Forward**—The Fast Forward button moves the cursor forward while held. This function is available both when the transport is stopped and while it is in motion.

- **Go to End**—The Go to End button moves the cursor to the end of the project. The end location is determined by the longest track in the project. This function can also be initiated by pressing **OPTION+RETURN** on Mac (or **ALT+ENTER** on Windows).

Zooming and Scrolling in the Edit Window

As mentioned earlier in this chapter, you can use the Zoomer tool to zoom in on an area of a track. Clicking on a track with the Zoomer tool will zoom in horizontally for the entire Edit window, accordingly. To reverse this behavior and zoom out, hold the **OPTION** modifier on Mac (or **ALT** on Windows) while clicking with the Zoomer tool.

 The Option/Alt modifier in Pro Tools and Pro Tools|First commonly provides a *reverse* operation for tools and actions.

You can also zoom in and out horizontally using the Plus and Minus buttons and the zoom slider located along the bottom in the right corner of the Edit window.

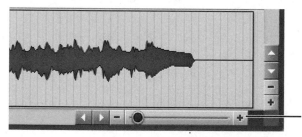
—— Horizontal zoom controls

Figure 5.15 Zoom in/out buttons (Plus and Minus) and zoom slider in the Edit window

Alternate Zoom Functions

Pro Tools|First provides additional zoom functions that can speed up your workflow when you need to quickly zoom in and out. Available options include the following:

- **Zoom In**—To zoom in from the keyboard, press the **T** key. Each key press zooms in one level.

- **Zoom Out**—To zoom out from the keyboard, press the **R** key. Each key press zooms out one level.

Standard Pro Tools and Pro Tools|HD require Commands Keyboard Focus mode to be active in order to use the R and T keys for zooming.

- **Zoom to All**—To fit the entire contents of the project timeline within the Edit window, press **OPTION+A** on Mac (or **ALT+A** on Windows). This will zoom horizontally to accommodate the longest displayed track in the project.

 You can also activate the Zoom to All feature by double-clicking on the Zoomer tool icon in the Edit window toolbar.

Horizontal Scrolling

When zoomed in on your project, you will commonly need to scroll the Edit window left or right to access a desired location on screen. The following options can be used to scroll the Edit window horizontally:

- Drag left and right using the scroll bar at the bottom of the window.

- Press **RETURN** on Mac (**ENTER** on Windows) to jump to the start of the project.

- Press **OPTION+RETURN** on Mac (**ALT+ENTER** on Windows) to jump to the end of the project.

- Press the **LEFT ARROW** or **RIGHT ARROW** key to center the cursor location on screen (with no selection active).

- With a selection active, press the **LEFT ARROW** key to center the start of the selection and the **RIGHT ARROW** key to center the end of the selection.

- On Mac, press **OPTION+PAGE UP** to scroll the display one screen earlier and **OPTION+PAGE DOWN** to scroll the display one page later. (On Windows, press **ALT+PAGE UP** and **ALT+PAGE DOWN**, respectively.)

You can also swipe left/right with a Magic Mouse, trackpad, or similar device to scroll the Edit window earlier or later.

Vertical Scrolling

When working on a project with many tracks (or with tracks set to large display sizes), you will commonly need to scroll the Edit window up or down to access a desired track on screen. The following options can be used to scroll the Edit window vertically:

- Drag up or down using the scroll bar on the right side of the window.

- Press the **HOME** key to scroll to the top of the window.

- Press the **END** key to scroll to the bottom of the window.

- Press the **PAGE UP** key to scroll up by one screen.

- Press the **PAGE DOWN** key to scroll down by one screen.

Controlling Playback Behavior

You can position the cursor for playback using Transport controls, such as fast-forward and rewind. However, you can also manually position the cursor anywhere within your project to set a playback location. You can also set the scrolling behavior that the Edit window uses during playback.

Setting a Playback Location

To set the playback location, do one of the following:

- Click anywhere on a ruler or a track with the **SELECTOR** tool. A blinking cursor will appear on the ruler or track, indicating the current timeline location.

(i) **The blinking cursor displayed on a ruler is known as the Timeline location in Pro Tools; the blinking cursor on a track playlist is known as the Edit cursor.**

- Click in the Main Counter, enter a time location, and press **RETURN** or **ENTER**. The Edit cursor will move to that location.

- Click and drag with the Selector tool on a ruler or a track to make a selection. The selected area will appear highlighted with a dark overlay.

- Click on a clip on a track with the **GRABBER** tool to select it. The clip will appear highlighted with a dark overlay.

When you click the **PLAY** button in the Transport (or press the **SPACEBAR**), the project will begin playback from the current cursor location or the start of the selection. A solid, non-blinking line, called the *playback cursor*, will move across the screen during playback, indicating the current playback point.

Playback will continue until you press the **STOP** button (or press the **SPACEBAR** a second time) or until the playback cursor reaches the end of the selection.

Setting Scrolling Options

All varieties of Pro Tools software provide scrolling options that let you specify how the contents of the Edit window are displayed during playback and recording. The most commonly used scrolling options are No Scrolling and Page Scrolling (described below). Additional options are available for advanced workflows.

- **No Scrolling**—This option prevents the Edit window from scrolling during playback and recording. In this mode, the playback cursor moves off screen and the Edit window remains stationary during transport operations.

■ **Page Scrolling**—This option allows the Edit window to scroll one screen (or "page") at a time as the playback cursor moves across the timeline. In this mode, the playback cursor moves across the screen until it reaches the right edge of the Edit window. At this point, the entire contents of the window will scroll by one screen, and the playback cursor will continue from the left edge of the window.

To set the current scrolling option, choose **OPTIONS > EDIT WINDOW SCROLLING** and select the desired scrolling mode from the submenu.

Monitoring Your Timeline Location

When navigating a project to set locations for playback, recording, or editing, you'll find it useful to reference the location indicators that Pro Tools|First provides for you. These indicators include the Counter displays and the Main Timebase ruler, described earlier in this chapter.

Counter Displays

You can refer to the Main Counter to determine the current cursor location. You can also click on a field in the Main Counter and manually enter a location. Typing in a value in the Main Counter and pressing **RETURN** (Mac) or **ENTER** (Windows) will move the cursor to the specified location.

You can also refer to the Start, End, and Length displays to the right of the Main Counter for information on an existing selection. By keeping an eye on these displays as you click and drag with the Selector tool, you can gauge the location and duration of selections as you make them. Here again, you can click in one of these fields to type in a value, setting them to precise numeric locations.

Ruler Displays

In Pro Tools|First, the Main Timebase Ruler displays time increments in Bars|Beats by default. This can be useful for music production, allowing you to easily identify where Bar 8 ends and Bar 9 begins, for example.

For some projects, it can be helpful to set the Main Timebase to Min:Sec instead. Doing so will change the ruler increments and the Counter displays to show time in minutes and seconds, relative to the project start.

To toggle the Main Timebase to display in minutes and seconds, click on the Timescale Selector (down arrow next to the Main Counter) and select **MIN:SECS** from the pop-up menu.

Figure 5.16 Selecting the Min:Secs timescale from the Main Counter display

Selections

Making proper selections is an important part of any work you will do in a project. Here, we discuss some of the basics of making and working with selections.

Timeline Selections Versus Edit Selections

Pro Tools provides two basic types of selections: *Timeline selections* and *Edit selections*. Timeline selections are represented by a dark overlay on the Main Timebase Ruler indicating the selected time range. A Timeline selection sets the range for playback and record operations.

To create a Timeline selection, click and drag with the **SELECTOR** tool directly on the Main Timebase Ruler (Bars|Beats or Min:Secs) or on any Conductor Ruler (Markers, Meter, or Tempo). You can also adjust the Timeline selection by clicking and dragging on the **TIMELINE SELECTION IN** and **OUT POINTS** (blue arrows) in the Main Timebase Ruler.

Figure 5.17 Timeline selection on the Bars|Beats ruler from Bar 3 to Bar 5

By contrast, Edit selections are selections made on track playlists. An Edit selection encompasses a range of audio, MIDI, or blank space on one or more tracks. In Pro Tools|First, an Edit selection will always have a corresponding Timeline selection. Adjusting either selection will affect the other.

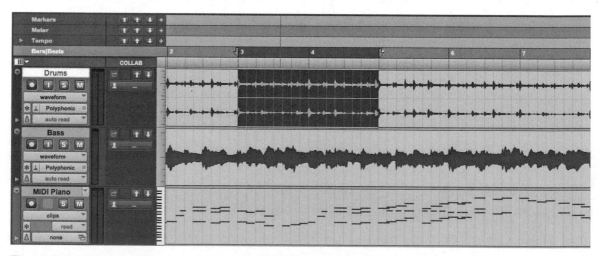

Figure 5.18 Edit selection on the Drums track from Bar 3 to Bar 5

Selection Scenarios

To help illustrate the different types of selections, consider the following scenarios:

- **Making a Selection for Playback**—To select a range of time for playback, you can use either a Timeline selection or an Edit selection. Technically, the Timeline selection determines the playback range, but since an Edit selection will always have a corresponding Timeline selection in Pro Tools|First, either selection type will work for playback purposes.

  When playing back a selected range, all tracks will be included, subject to any Solo or Mute setting you may have made.

- **Making a Selection for Editing**—To select a range for editing, you must make an Edit selection on the associated track or tracks. For example, to delete a portion of the audio on a track, you would select the target area on the track and press the **DELETE** key on Mac (or **BACKSPACE** on Windows).

  When editing a selected range, only the tracks that contain an Edit selection will be affected.

- **Making a Selection for Recording**—To select a range for recording, you can use either a Timeline selection or an Edit selection. As with playback ranges, record ranges are based on the Timeline selection, which can also be set by making an Edit selection on a track.

  Note that it does not matter which track or tracks contain the Edit selection; recording will be performed only on tracks that are record-enabled.

Review/Discussion Questions

1. What is the difference between a Pro Tools project and a Pro Tools session? Which option is available in Pro Tools|First? (See "Creating a Session or Project" starting on page 110.)

2. Which window displays the audio waveforms and MIDI performances in a timeline display on tracks in your Pro Tools|First project? (See "Edit Window" beginning on page 111.)

3. What are the four Edit modes available in Pro Tools and Pro Tools|First? (See "Edit Window Toolbar" beginning on page 112.)

4. Which Edit tool can be used to select an entire clip with a single mouse click? (See "Edit Window Toolbar" beginning on page 112.)

5. What is the Main Timebase Ruler used for? What measurement units are available for the Main Timebase Rule in Pro Tools|First? (See "Rulers" beginning on page 115.)

6. How are tracks displayed in the Mix window? What are some track controls available in this window? (See "Mix Window" beginning on page 116.)

7. What are some controls available in the Transport window? What kinds of options can you configure using the MIDI Controls section in this window? (See "Transport Window" beginning on page 118.)

8. What track types are supported in Pro Tools|First? What type of track lets you route live audio through the Pro Tools mixer and can be used as an effects return or submix destination? (See "Adding Tracks" beginning on page 118.)

9. What is the difference between a MIDI track and an Instrument track? Which type can be used to record MIDI information? Which type can be used to host a virtual instrument? (See "MIDI Versus Instrument Tracks" beginning on page 120.)

10. What are clips in Pro Tools? How is an audio clip different from an audio file? (See "Clips Versus Files" beginning on page 121.)

11. What are some ways to zoom in and out in Pro Tools|First? What are some ways to scroll the Edit window to the left or right? (See "Zooming and Scrolling in the Edit Window" beginning on page 122).

12. Which Edit tool can be used to set a playback location by clicking on a track? Which Edit tool can be used to make a selection for playback by clicking on a clip? (See "Setting a Playback Location" beginning on page 124.)

13. What location indicators does Pro Tools provide for you to help you monitor your timeline location or selection details? (See "Monitoring Your Timeline Location" beginning on page 125.)

14. What is the difference between a Timeline selection and an Edit selection in Pro Tools? In what scenarios would you use each? (See "Timeline Selections Versus Edit Selections" beginning on page 126.)

Configuring and Working on a Project

🎧 Activity

In this exercise, you will configure the display for the project you created in Exercise 2. You will also practice making selections and changing the Main Timescale to measure selections in different timebase units. By using Zoom functions and working in Grid mode, you will be able to make very accurate selections on track playlists and on the timeline.

⏱ Duration

This exercise should take approximately 10 minutes to complete.

⊕ Goals/Targets

- Adjust the width of the Track List

- Toggle the Main Timescale between Bars|Beats and Min:Secs

- Make selections with the Selector tool

- Use Grid mode and set the Grid value

Getting Started

To get started, you will open the multi-track project you created in Exercise 2. This will serve as the starting point for this exercise.

Open your existing OverboardTRX project:

1. Launch Pro Tools|First, if it isn't already running. Once startup completes, the Dashboard window should display.

2. If the Dashboard is not visible, select **FILE > OPEN PROJECT** to display it.

3. If necessary, click the **OPEN** action on the left side of the Dashboard.

4. Select your **OverboardTRX-xxx** project from the list of available projects.

5. Click **OPEN**. The project will open as it was when last saved.

Configuring the View

Before starting work on a project, it can be helpful to adjust the view in Pro Tools|First to optimize the window displays. In this section of the exercise, you will adjust the Track List in the Edit window and hide the Transport window for an unobstructed view.

Adjust the width of the Track List:

1. Position the mouse cursor along the right-edge boundary of the Track List, so that the double-headed cursor appears.

Figure 5.19 Double-headed cursor displayed at the border of the Track List

2. Click and drag on the border of the Track List to increase its width. Expand it enough to see each of the complete track names without using excessive space. It may take several attempts to get the width just the way you want it.

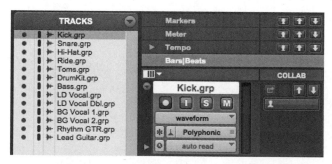

Figure 5.20 Track List adjusted to show completed track names

Hide the Transport window:

■ Choose **WINDOW > TRANSPORT** to deselect it and hide the Transport window.

Making Selections

The tracks in this session represent a segment of the song "Overboard" by The Pinder Brothers. To get familiar with the audio in this project, you will start by selecting audio segments and measuring their duration.

Select audio on the Kick.grp track:

1. Activate the **SELECTOR** tool in the Edit window toolbar.

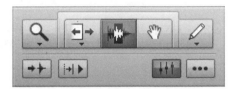

    Figure 5.21 Selector tool active in the Edit window toolbar

2. Click at the start of the Kick.grp track and drag across the active waveform area of the track. Do not include the "silent" part at the end of the audio clip.

    Figure 5.22 Selection on the Kick.grp track

3. Refer to the Counters area in the Edit window toolbar to determine the length of your selection, in bars and beats. In the example shown below, the selection starts at Bar 1, Beat 1 (1|1|000) and ends at Bar 36, Beat 1 (36|1|000), for a 35-bar selection length (35|0|000).

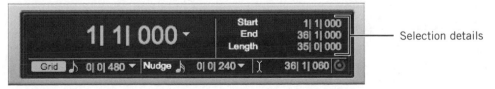

    Figure 5.23 Selection details in the Counters area of the Edit window toolbar

4. Change the project Time Scale to Min:Secs by clicking on the pop-up selector (down arrow) next to the Main Counter display. (See Figure 5.24.)

Figure 5.24 Changing the project Time Scale from the Main Counter

5. Refer to the **LENGTH** field in the Counters area to determine the length of your selection in minutes and seconds. The audio on this track is approximately one minute, twelve and a half seconds in duration (1:12.500).

6. Click on the pop-up selector next to the Main Counter display a second time and change the project timescale back to Bars|Beats.

Adjust the zoom for a better view:

1. Use one of the following methods to zoom in a few levels:

   - Activate the **ZOOMER** tool (magnifying glass icon) and click on the track playlist.

Figure 5.25 Zoomer tool positioned in the middle of the Kick.grp track playlist

   - Click on the Zoom In button (plus sign) in the bottom corner of the Edit window.

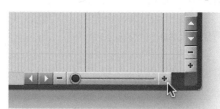

Figure 5.26 Zoom In button in the Edit window

   - Press the **T** key on the keyboard.

   Each action will zoom in horizontally by one level.

2. Zoom in sufficiently to see each bar number on the Bars|Beats ruler.

3. Press the **RIGHT ARROW** key on your keyboard to scroll the end of the selection to the center of the Edit window.

Figure 5.27 Close-up view of the end of the selection on the Kick.grp track

4. Double-click on the **ZOOMER** tool to zoom back out and see the full length of the track in the Edit window.

Select a timeline range for the guitar solo:

1. Click on the **GRID** button on the left side of the Edit window toolbar to activate Grid mode.

Figure 5.28 Activating Grid mode in the Edit window toolbar

2. Click on the **GRID VALUE SELECTOR** along the bottom of the Counters area.

Figure 5.29 Grid Value selector beneath the Main Counter display

3. From the Grid Value pop-up menu, select **1 bar** as the grid size.

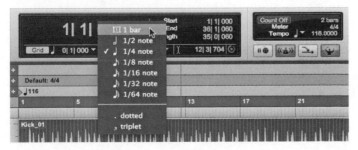

Figure 5.30 Selecting the Grid value

4.   Activate the **SELECTOR** tool.

Figure 5.31 Selector tool active in the Edit window toolbar

5.   Click in the Rulers area at **Bar 19** and drag to **Bar 27** to create an 8-bar timeline selection. Keep an eye on the **Start, End,** and **Length** fields in the Counters area to verify your selection.

Figure 5.32 Eight-bar timeline selection from Bar 19 to Bar 27

6.   Press the **SPACEBAR** to begin playback of the selected range. In normal playback mode, playback will stop automatically at the end of the selection.

Finishing Up

Feel free to experiment further with the project. Practice making selections based on the grid. Also try setting the grid to different values to make selections that start and end in between bars. When finished, return to the start of the project and save the work you've done.

Saving the project changes:

1.   Click the **RETURN TO ZERO** button in the Transport controls or press **RETURN** (Mac) or **ENTER** (Windows) to place the cursor at the start of the project.

2.   Choose **FILE > SAVE** to save the project.

3.   Choose **FILE > CLOSE PROJECT** to close the project and return to the Dashboard.

That completes this exercise.

Chapter 6

Pro Tools Concepts, Part 2

...What You Need to Know to Work with Pro Tools | First...

We begin this chapter with an overview of recording audio and MIDI performances using Pro Tools. Next, we explore options for importing existing audio and MIDI data into your session. And finally, we take a look at basic editing techniques that can be used to fine-tune audio and MIDI performances.

◈ Learning Targets for This Chapter

- Learn how to record audio

- Learn basic MIDI recording techniques

- Learn how to import audio and MIDI

- Understand how Edit modes affect selections and edit operations

- Learn basic techniques for working with clips and selections

When starting a new Pro Tools|First project, the first step is typically to either record or import some audio or MIDI data into your session. This can be accomplished in a number of ways, but generally you'll either record new clips directly onto an Audio or Instrument track in your project or import existing clips from various locations on your computer.

Setting Up for Recording

When beginning a music project, it can be beneficial to set the project tempo for Pro Tools|First prior to starting to record. This will allow you to use a click track as a tempo reference during recording, helping the musicians keep the performance consistently in time. Additionally, recording to a click will ensure that the music aligns to the Bars|Beats ruler. As a result, any selections and edits you make can easily be aligned to the music by working in Grid mode.

 The project tempo defaults to 120 beats per minute (BPM) in Pro Tools|First.

To set the project tempo, do the following:

1. Click in the Tempo field within the MIDI Controls section of either the Edit window toolbar or the Transport window. The default value of **120** will become highlighted.

Figure 6.1 Tempo field selected in the MIDI Controls

2. Do one of the following:

    *   Type in the tempo value that you'd like to use (in BPM).

    *   Tap the **T** key on your computer keyboard repeatedly at the tempo you'd like to use. Pro Tools|First will average the tempo as you tap.

3. Press **RETURN** or **ENTER** to accept the tempo value.

To use a click track with the project, do the following:

1. Choose **TRACK > CREATE CLICK TRACK**. A new click track will be added to the project.

2. Enable the **METRONOME** icon in the MIDI Controls, or choose **OPTIONS > CLICK**.

Recording Audio

Recording audio is one of the most fundamental aspects of working with any modern DAW. Working in Pro Tools|First gives you non-linear access to all of the audio in your project. This means you can jump directly to any location without needing to fast–forward or rewind like you would with a tape recorder.

Pro Tools|First provides a truly intuitive workflow for quickly getting your musical ideas recorded onto a track. And thanks to the huge hard drives included with most modern computers, you'll rarely have to worry about running out of recording space.

Making a Record Selection

Before you begin recording, you'll need to specify where you want the record pass to begin and end. Audio engineers call the beginning and end of the target area the "punch-in point" and "punch-out point," respectively. You can designate punch-in and punch-out points in a number of ways in Pro Tools|First. You can also choose to just specify the punch-in point and leave the punch-out point open-ended, letting Pro Tools|First continue recording until you manually stop the record take.

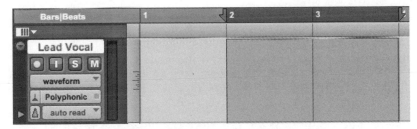

Figure 6.2 A record selection prepared on a lead vocal track

To set a record location without specifying a stopping point:

- Click with the **SELECTOR** tool on a track or a ruler to position the Edit cursor or Timeline location.

To set a record range, do one of the following:

- Click and drag with the **SELECTOR** tool on a track or ruler to create an Edit selection or Timeline selection.

- Click with the **SELECTOR** tool to specify the punch-in point. Then Shift-click at a later location to specify the punch-out point. This will create a selection between the two locations.

- Use the Grabber to select an existing clip that matches the desired record duration and location. (For example, you might use a previously recorded clip covering of the first verse of a song.)

Record-Enabling Audio Tracks

Once you've set a location for recording, you'll need to specify which tracks to record on. A common beginner mistake is to assume that Pro Tools will record on any track where you've made a selection or positioned the Edit cursor. In reality, the position of the cursor determines only the *timeline* location for recording; it has no bearing on the track or tracks where the recording will be completed.

To specify a destination track, you simply need to record–enable the target track in the Edit or Mix window.

Figure 6.3 A record-enabled track in the Edit window

To record–enable a track in Pro Tools | First:

1.   Locate the desired track in the Edit or Mix window.

2.   Do one of the following:

   • Click the **RECORD ENABLE** button on the track (button with a white circle icon).

   • Select the track and press **SHIFT+R** on your computer keyboard.

 In commercial versions of Pro Tools, click on the track playlist to position the Edit cursor prior to using the Shift+R shortcut.

Monitoring Record-Enabled Audio Tracks

Whenever you click **PLAY** (or press the **SPACEBAR**), you will hear any clips already in place on your tracks. Tracks that have no clips will remain silent. This is true even when a track is record-enabled and you begin playback: you will hear any existing clips on that track and *not* the live input from your audio interface.

This can be a little confusing, especially if you are trying to audition a part before starting to record. Fortunately, you can listen to (or *monitor*) the live input at any time by enabling the target track's TrackInput monitoring control.

Figure 6.4 A track with the TrackInput button enabled in the Edit window

To enable TrackInput on an Audio track in Pro Tools | First:

1. Locate the desired track in the Edit or Mix window.

2. Do one of the following:

   • Click the **TRACKINPUT** ("I") button on the track.

   • Select the track and press **SHIFT+I** on your computer keyboard.

Auto Input Monitoring

The alternative to using TrackInput monitoring mode is known as Auto Input monitoring, which is Pro Tools' default mode. While recording in Auto Input monitoring mode, Pro Tools automatically switches between monitoring the live input during record passes (ignoring existing clips on the track) and monitoring track material during playback passes (ignoring live input).

Using Auto Input monitoring mode lets you use pre-roll to start playback earlier than the desired punch-in point. This will allow you to hear playback from the track before the take begins, which is generally a more musician-friendly approach. It also allows you to listen back to the last recorded take without switching monitoring modes.

Initiating a Record Take

Once you have record–enabled one or more tracks, you can initiate a record take in Pro Tools | First. The most common technique for beginners is to press the **RECORD** button followed by the **PLAY** button in either the Transport window or the Edit window toolbar.

Figure 6.5 The Transport controls in the Edit window toolbar

Pro Tools also provides a number of keyboard shortcuts that can be used to initiate record. All of these shortcuts immediately initiate recording without requiring that you press **RECORD** and **PLAY** separately. If you record frequently, these are some of the first shortcuts that you'll want to learn!

To immediately begin recording, do one of the following:

■ Press **COMMAND+SPACEBAR** (Mac) or **CTRL+SPACEBAR** (Windows).

(i) Mac users may need to use System Preferences to disable Command+Spacebar as the keyboard shortcut for Spotlight in order to use this shortcut in Pro Tools.

■ Press function key **F12**.

(i) Mac users may need to enable standard function key behavior in System Preferences and disable F12 as the Mission Control shortcut for the "Show Dashboard" function to use this shortcut in Pro Tools.

■ Press the **[3]** key on the numeric keypad.

Stopping a Record Take

If you've created a selection for recording, Pro Tools | First will automatically stop the record take when it reaches the end of the selection (the punch-out point). However, if you are recording without a selection, the record take will continue until you manually stop the transport. Pro Tools | First provides several techniques for stopping a record take.

To immediately stop a record take, do one of the following:

■ Press the **STOP** button in the Transport controls.

■ Press the **SPACEBAR**.

■ Press the **[0]** key on the numeric keypad.

At times you may want to stop a take prematurely due to a problem in the record pass. Often a musician will make a mistake right at the beginning of the take and won't want to continue. Fortunately, Pro Tools provides a helpful shortcut that will both stop the take and delete the partially recorded clip. Obviously, you'll only want to use this option if you're absolutely certain that the take is not worth keeping.

To immediately stop a record take and delete the recorded clip:

■ Press **COMMAND+PERIOD** (Mac) or **CTRL+PERIOD** (Windows). Pro Tools will abort the pass and discard the recorded audio without saving it to disk.

Recording MIDI

Although the MIDI communication protocol is more than 30 years old, understanding how to record and edit MIDI data is more relevant today than ever. Advances in virtual instrument design and computer processing speed over the past decade have made virtual instruments an indispensible part of the modern music production workflow. The fundamental workflow for recording MIDI is similar to that for recording audio. However, some important differences apply in MIDI production. But don't worry; you don't need a PhD in synthesis to start making music with the MIDI feature set in Pro Tools!

Monitoring a MIDI Controller

The monitoring workflow is one area that differs significantly when recording MIDI versus recording audio. This is because an audio signal can be monitored directly, whereas MIDI data must be routed to an instrument to become an audible signal. The routing can seem a little complicated at first, but once you understand the basics you'll be able to take advantage of this powerful technology.

 For basic information on routing MIDI data to virtual instruments, see "Tracking with Virtual Instruments in Chapter 4.

Routing MIDI data to a virtual instrument is slightly different for MIDI tracks versus Instrument tracks. On a MIDI track, the I/O view is used to choose a destination for the MIDI data. On an Instrument track, the Instrument view is used to route the MIDI data to its destination.

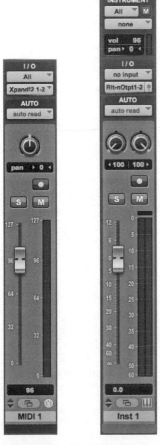

Figure 6.6 The I/O view on a MIDI track (left) and the Instrument view at the top of an Instrument track (right)

To add to the routing confusion, the Instrument view is actually hidden by default in Pro Tools | First.

To display the Instrument view, do one of the following:

- To display in the Mix window, choose VIEW > MIX WINDOW VIEWS > INSTRUMENTS.

- To display in the Edit window, choose VIEW > EDIT WINDOW VIEWS > INSTRUMENTS.

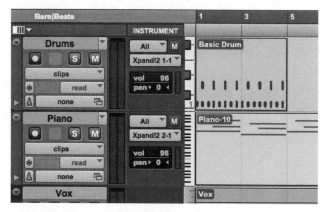

Figure 6.7 The Instrument view displayed at the head of the tracks in the Edit window

 Pro Tools|First automatically assigns the MIDI output to the first virtual instrument plug-in assigned on an Instrument track.

Record-Enabling MIDI and Instrument Tracks

Record-enabling MIDI and Instrument tracks is quite similar to recording-enabling Audio tracks.

To record-enable a MIDI or Instrument track in Pro Tools|First:

1. Locate the desired track in the Edit or Mix window.

2. Do one of the following:

    - Click the Record Enable button on the track.

    - Press SHIFT+R on your computer keyboard.

 In commercial versions of Pro Tools, click on the track playlist to position the Edit cursor prior to using the Shift+R shortcut.

Using Wait for Note

The Wait for Note option keeps Pro Tools|First in a record-ready state until it receives the first note or other bit of MIDI data from your controller. This can solve some common problems that you'll encounter when recording MIDI.

- **Problem #1**—Your MIDI controller is on the other side of your studio or home production space, and you have to get there quickly to play a part you're trying to record. This is not only annoying, but it makes playing the first few notes that much more of a challenge.

- **Solution**—With **WAIT FOR NOTE** enabled, you can take your time getting to your controller because the record pass won't begin until you play the first note.

- **Problem #2**—When beginning a MIDI recording take, you may play the first note just a tiny bit before the start of the record selection when using the count off feature. As a result, Pro Tools|First may not record the first note.

- **Solution**—With **WAIT FOR NOTE** enabled, the first note initiates the record pass, so it's not possible to play a note before recording has begun. Sweet!

To enable Wait for Note, do the following:

- Click on the **WAIT FOR NOTE** button in the MIDI Controls section of the Edit window toolbar or the Transport window.

 —— Wait for Note button

Figure 6.8 The Wait for Note button in the Edit window toolbar

Using MIDI Merge Mode

MIDI Merge mode is another powerful option for recording MIDI data. When disabled, each successive record pass results in a new MIDI Clip on the track. But with MIDI Merge mode enabled, successive passes add MIDI data, merging it into the existing clip. MIDI Merge mode is great for recording the left hand and right hand parts of a piano performance separately, for example, and combining them both in the same clip.

MIDI Merge mode is also an essential tool for recording drum parts. You can start by recording just one or two drum pieces in the first pass (such as kick and snare) and then merge in additional pieces on subsequent passes (see Figures 6.9 and 6.10 below).

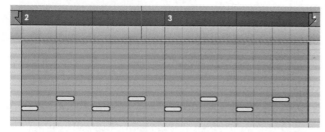

Figure 6.9 The first pass of a drum recording with just kick and snare

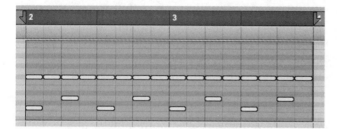

Figure 6.10 The second pass of a drum recording with hi-hat merged into the clip

To enable MIDI Merge mode, do one of the following:

- Click the **MIDI MERGE** button in the MIDI Controls section of the Edit window toolbar or the Transport window.

- Press the **[9]** key on the numeric keypad.

MIDI Merge button

Figure 6.11 The MIDI Merge button in the Edit window toolbar

Importing Audio and MIDI

If you're not ready to record in Pro Tools, or if you'd like to use existing media from your hard drive instead, you can import audio or MIDI files into your Pro Tools|First project to get started. There are a number of ways to import audio and MIDI files into Pro Tools|First.

Supported Audio Files

Before you attempt to import an audio file, you'll want to make sure that it is in a format that can be imported into Pro Tools|First.

The following file types can be imported:

- AAC Audio

- ACID files

- AIFF

- MP3

- QuickTime (Mac only)

- ReCycle (REX 1 and 2)

- Sound Resource (AIFL – Mac Only)

- WAV

 Pro Tools|First cannot import copy-protected AAC or MP4 files.

Importing from the Desktop

An easy way to get started importing is to use the drag–and–drop method. Like commercial versions of Pro Tools, Pro Tools|First fully supports drag–and–drop importing of audio and MIDI files from the Mac Finder or Windows Explorer. Simply select the desired files on your computer and drag them into your Pro Tools|First project. (We look at the different destinations available for dropped files below.)

Importing from Soundbase

Another way to import audio and MIDI files into Pro Tools|First is to use the built-in Soundbase browser. Soundbase is a browser window that functions similar to a Mac Finder or Windows Explorer window. You use Soundbase to browse and search any mounted volume on your computer. However, Soundbase offers features that are tailored to working with audio and MIDI files.

To open the Soundbase browser, do one of the following:

- Select **WINDOW > SOUNDBASE**.

- Press **OPTION+CONTROL+I** (Mac) or **ALT+START+I** (Windows).

- Click on the **QUICK BUTTONS** icon in the Edit window toolbar and then click **SOUNDBASE**.

The Soundbase browser window will open. (See Figure 6.12.)

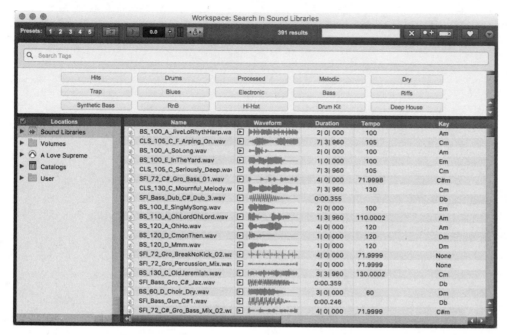

Figure 6.12 The Soundbase browser showing the Locations pane on the left and Soundbase tags at the top

Typically a browser window is used in one of three ways: manually browsing, searching for files, and using Soundbase to locate tagged files.

To manually browse for files after opening Soundbase:

■ Use the shortcuts in the Locations pane on the left to browse any of the following:

- Your installed sound libraries

- Your connected volumes

- The current project's media

- Any catalogs you've created

- Your user locations

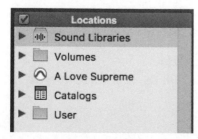

Figure 6.13 The Locations pane in the Soundbase browser

To search for files using standard browser functionality:

1. Select Volumes in the Locations pane on the left side of the browser window.

2. Press **COMMAND+F** (Mac) or **CTRL+F** (Windows).

3. Type a search term into the Browser Search Field.

To locate tagged files using Soundbase:

1. Select Sound Libraries in the Locations pane on the left side of the browser window.

2. Select one or more Tags in the Soundbase pane to locate audio files with compatible metadata.

Figure 6.14 The Soundbase pane in the Workspace browser

 Pro Tools | First comes with a 500 MB loop library from Loopmasters. The included files are fully tagged and are searchable under Sound Libraries.

File Drag and Drop Locations

Once you've located a file on your desktop or using Soundbase, you'll want to consider your options for dragging and dropping the file into Pro Tools | First. Imported files can be dragged to the Track List, to a blank area in the Edit window, or onto an existing track.

 When importing MIDI to a new track, the MIDI Import Options dialog box will display so you can choose between a MIDI track and an Instrument track.

To import a file to the Track List:

1. Select an audio or MIDI file in Soundbase, the Mac Finder, or Windows Explorer.

2. Drag and drop the file into the Track List. A new track will be added to the project containing the imported audio or MIDI data.

To import a file to the Edit window:

1. Select an audio or MIDI file in Soundbase, the Mac Finder, or Windows Explorer.

2. Do one of the following:

   - Hold the **SHIFT** key while dragging and dropping the file anywhere in the Edit window.

   - Drag and drop the file onto the empty space at the bottom of the Edit window.

   A new track will be added to the project containing the imported audio or MIDI data.

To import a file to an existing track:

1. Select an audio or MIDI file in Soundbase, the Mac Finder, or Windows Explorer.

2. Drag and drop the file to the desired location on an existing track.

Using the Import Command

Audio and MIDI files can also be imported into Pro Tools|First using the **FILE > IMPORT** command. This option uses a basic file dialog box to let you locate files anywhere on your computer's hard drive. Imported files will be placed at the start of new tracks in Pro Tools|First.

Due to the familiar interface, new Pro Tools users may find this option to be the easiest.

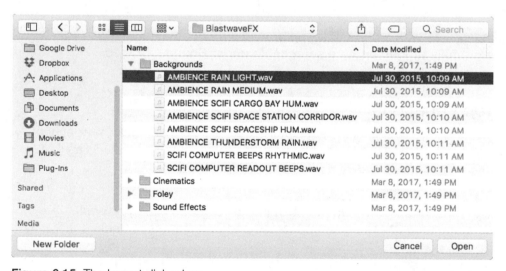

Figure 6.15 The Import dialog box

Edit Modes and the Grid

Before you start editing clips, it helps to have a good understanding of the Edit modes that are available in Pro Tools|First. The active mode will impact the movement and placement of clips and the function of various Edit tools. You should also know how to modify the grid value so that clips will align properly when working in Grid mode.

The Edit Modes

Four basic Edit modes are available in Pro Tools|First: Shuffle, Spot, Slip, and Grid. As discussed in Chapter 5, you can select a mode by clicking on the associated button in the Edit window toolbar.

Figure 6.16 The Edit modes buttons in the Edit window toolbar (Slip mode active)

Shuffle Mode

Shuffle mode places serious constraints on how clips are moved and edited. With Shuffle mode active, clip movements are constrained by other clips: you can only position a clip at the beginning of the session or immediately before or after another existing clip. You cannot place or move clips such that they overlap each other, and a number of edit commands are unavailable.

Furthermore, adding a clip to a track will move all of the subsequent clips on the track later in time by the new clip's length. Cutting or deleting a clip or selection will move all of the existing clips on the track earlier in time by the amount removed. Suffice it to say, Shuffle Mode is not a mode that novice users will use very often when working with Pro Tools|First.

Spot Mode

Spot mode is another mode that novice uses may not use much. However, its functionality is quite simple. With Spot mode active, dropping a clip onto a track or clicking on an existing clip with the Grabber tool will open the Spot dialog box. This dialog box can be used to enter an exact time location for the clip. The Spot dialog box can be set to use either Bars|Beats or Min:Secs as its time scale.

Spot mode is rarely used for music production, although it can be useful if you know the exact Bar|Beat location where you want to move a clip.

Figure 6.17 The Spot dialog box

Slip Mode

Slip mode is generally considered the simplest Edit mode in Pro Tools. This mode places no constraints on how clips can be moved and edited. With Slip mode active, clips can be moved to any location on a track, even on top of another clip. (The topmost clip will be the audible one).

Adding new clips to a track in Slip mode has no impact on the position of other clips on that track. Deleting a clip or selection will result in silent space on the track.

Grid Mode

Grid mode is essentially a variation on Slip mode. It offers much of the same freedom to move and edit clips on tracks. However, with Grid mode active, clips will snap to the nearest grid interval when moved, as specified by the Grid Value. Selections that you create will also align to the grid automatically. Grid mode makes it very easy to edit a music project, because all of your edits can occur on a bar or beat.

Setting the Grid Value

When working in Grid mode, you'll want to set the Grid value to an appropriate size. You can set the Grid value in a number of ways, but the easiest way is to use the Grid Value pop-up selector in the Counters display area of the Edit window toolbar.

 Commercial versions of Pro Tools place the Grid Value pop-up selector in its own area on the Edit window toolbar, to the right of the Counters display.

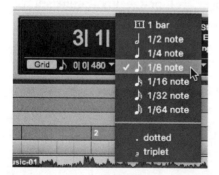

Figure 6.18 The Grid Value pop-up selector in the Counters display area of the Edit window

In Pro Tools|First, the available grid values are always linked to the currently active Main Time Scale. If the Main Time Scale is set to Bars|Beats, the available grid values will range from 1 bar to 1/64 note. If the Main Time Scale is set to Min:Secs, the available grid values will range from 1 second to 1 millisecond.

To set the Grid value:

■ Click the Grid Value pop-up selector and select the desired grid size.

To use a dotted or triplet value when the Main Time Scale is Bars|Beats:

■ After selecting a grid size in Bars|Beats, click the Grid Value pop-up selector a second time and select DOTTED or TRIPLET.

To show or hide the grid lines in the Edit window:

■ Select or deselect the GRID button next to the Grid Value display. (The Grid button will have a green highlight when grid lines are enabled.)

Working with Clips and Selections

Once you've recorded or imported some audio or MIDI material, it's time to start editing! Pro Tools|First shares many of the same powerful editing features as the full versions of Pro Tools.

Selecting an Edit Tool

To get started editing, you'll need to select the proper Edit tool in Pro Tools|First. You can select tools in several ways. One of the most obvious methods is to click directly on the desired tool in the toolbar. However, it can often be faster to use keyboard shortcuts.

Figure 6.19 The available Edit tools in the Pro Tools|First toolbar

The keyboard shortcuts for Edit tools, which are some of the first you should learn, are pretty easy to remember. They simply use Function keys **F5** through **F8**, from left to right, for the first four tools, and **F10** for the last tool.

■ To enable the Zoomer tool (magnifying glass), press **F5** on your computer keyboard.

■ To enable the Trim tool, press **F6**.

■ To enable the Selector tool, press **F7**.

■ To enable the Grabber tool, press **F8**.

■ To enable the Pencil tool, press **F10**.

Commercial versions of Pro Tools include a Scrubber tool between the Grabber and Pencil tools; this tool is enabled by pressing **F9**. (Scrubber functionality is not available in Pro Tools|First.)

Basic Editing Techniques

DAWs provide a variety of ways that you can slice and dice audio and MIDI clips. You'll become familiar with a multitude of editing techniques in Pro Tools | First as you work, but for now we'll cover the basics techniques you'll need to get started.

A basic list of editing techniques:

- Selecting clips
- Moving clips
- Cutting, Copying, and Pasting clips

These are the basic building blocks that you'll want to learn. Let's go through each in some detail.

Making Selections

Selecting material is one of the most basic and frequently used techniques in the DAW world. It serves as a building block for further editing. Many other commands require a clip (or portion of a clip) to be selected first before they can be executed. In Pro Tools | First, you can make selections in a number of ways.

To select an entire clip, do one of the following:

- Using the Grabber tool, click on the target clip.
- Using the Selector tool, double-click on the target clip.

To select a portion of a clip:

- Using the Selector tool, click and drag within the target clip.

(i) **Selections can include multiple clips, partial clips, and blank areas between clips. Edit operations will utilize the entire selection and preserve blank areas, as appropriate.**

Moving Clips

At times you may want to move a clip to a new location on a track or onto a completely different track. While you can use Cut/Copy/Paste for this purpose, it's usually faster to simply drag the clip to the desired location using the Grabber tool.

To move a clip to a new location on the same track:

- Using the Grabber tool, click and drag the clip horizontally.

To move a clip to a different track:

- Using the Grabber tool, click and drag the clip vertically.

 When dragging a clip to a different track, you can hold Control (Mac) or Start (Windows) to constrain the clip and prevent it from moving left or right.

Cutting, Copying and Pasting Clips

For edits involving partial clips or long selections, you'll often want to use Cut/Copy/Paste commands. These commands can be accessed at the top of the Edit menu in Pro Tools|First, but you'll definitely want to use the keyboard shortcuts to save time. Pro Tools|First uses standard keyboard shortcuts for each of these operations:

- Cut operation—**COMMAND+X** (Mac) or **CTRL+X** (Windows)

- Copy operation—**COMMAND+C** (Mac) or **CTRL+C** (Windows)

- Paste operation—**COMMAND+V** (Mac) or **CTRL+V** (Windows)

Advanced Editing Techniques

Beyond selecting and moving your audio or MIDI data, you'll often need to use slightly more advanced editing techniques. Some useful options include trimming the start/end of a clip, splitting a clip into two or more separate clips, and adding fades to clips. All of these operations use non-destructive editing in Pro Tools|First.

Non-Destructive Audio Editing

Non-destructive editing is an import concept to understand when editing audio data in a DAW. Essentially, non-destructive editing means that any changes you make to an audio clip in Pro Tools will not affect the original audio file stored on disk. This gives you the freedom to try any number of different edits without fear of permanently modifying the original file.

 A few rare operations perform destructive editing in Pro Tools|First. For example, If you zoom in to the sample level and draw over an audio clip's waveform with the Pencil tool, you will actually be editing the original audio file on disk.

Editing MIDI Clips

While editing audio data is almost always non-destructive, the same is not true for MIDI data. This is because MIDI clips in Pro Tools are stored within the project file, and not in a separate file on disk. As a result, some MIDI editing commands *will* modify the original clip. Although it is possible to use the undo command to revert a clip back to the original, this option is typically useful only immediately after making an unwanted change.

Trimming the Start and End of Clips

Trim operations are used constantly when editing audio in Pro Tools | First. A trim will essentially add or subtract audio from the beginning (head) or end (tail) of a clip.

Trimming allows you to make a whole-file clip shorter (turning it into a subset clip) by removing audio from the start or end of the clip. You can also make a subset clip longer again at *any time* in the future by trimming it back out. In other words, subset clips still have access to *all* of the original audio data from the parent file (or whole-file clip). This lets you recover any missing audio that you later decide to keep.

 You will only be able to trim the clip start or end up to the boundary of the underlying audio data in the parent file. Once you reach the file boundary, you won't be able to trim the audio any further.

To trim off the start of clip:

1. Using the Trim tool, click and hold inside the clip near the clip start.

2. While continuing to hold the mouse, drag to the right to remove audio and move the clip start later.

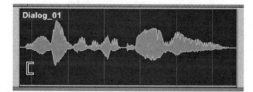 

Figure 6.20 Dialog clip before trimming (left) and after trimming (right)

To trim off the end of clip:

1. Using the Trim tool, click and hold inside the clip near the clip end.

2. While continuing to hold the mouse, drag to the left to remove audio and move the clip end earlier.

Splitting a Clip into Two or More Clips

Another very common editing technique is to split a clip into two or more smaller clips. In Pro Tools | First, you can use a simple edit command to perform this function: **EDIT > SEPARATE CLIP > AT SELECTION**.

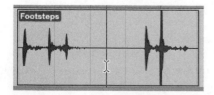 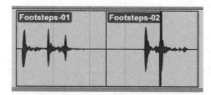

Figure 6.21 A single clip before separating (left) and the result of separating at the cursor location (right)

To split a clip into two clips:

1.   Using the Selector tool, click at the desired location inside a clip to position the edit cursor.

2.   Do one of the following:

   •   Select **EDIT > SEPARATE CLIP > AT SELECTION**.

   •   Press **COMMAND+E** (Mac) or **CTRL+E** (Windows).

Fading Clips

Last but certainly not least, you can apply fades to your audio clips. Fades are not only used to gradually fade audio in and out, but they can also be used to prevent undesirable pops and clicks at the beginning and end of clips. Here, we'll focus on the basics of creating and editing fades in Pro Tools | First.

To create a fade in or fade out:

1.   Make a selection with the Selector tool that spans across the start or end of a clip.

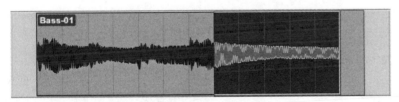

Figure 6.22 Selection across the end of a Bass clip

2.   Open the Fades dialog box by doing one of the following:

   •   Select **EDIT > FADES > CREATE**.

   •   Press **COMMAND+F** (Mac) or **CTRL+F** (Windows).

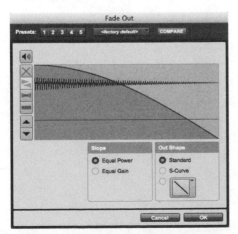

Figure 6.23 The Fade Out dialog box

3.   Adjust the fades settings as desired (or use the defaults); then click **OK** to apply the fade.

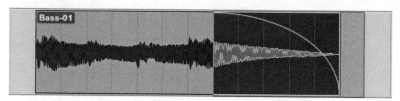

Figure 6.24 Fade out curve applied to the end of the clip

In addition to fade–ins and fade–outs, the Fades operation can be used to create crossfades. Crossfades are useful to smooth out an edit location, by fading out the audio from before the edit point while simultaneously fading in the audio from after the edit point.

To create a crossfade:

1.   Make a selection with the Selector tool across the junction between two adjacent clips.

2.   Select **EDIT > FADES > CREATE**, or press **COMMAND+F** (Mac) or **CTRL+F** (Windows) to open the Crossfade dialog box.

3.   Adjust the fades settings as desired (or use the defaults); then press **OK** to create the crossfade.

If you decide to modify the fades later, you can return to the Fades dialog box by double-clicking on the fade curve on the track with the Grabber tool. You can also move fade curves using the Grabber tool and resize fades using the Trim tool, just like editing clips.

Review/Discussion Questions

1. Which Edit tool can be used to specify a starting point ("punch in") for recording without specifying a stopping point ("punch out"). (See "Making a Record Selection" beginning on page 139.)

2. What are some ways that you can specify both a starting and stopping point for a record take? (See "Making a Record Selection" beginning on page 139.)

3. What are three ways that you can immediately begin a record take in Pro Tools|First? (See "Initiating a Record Take" beginning on page 141.)

4. What are two ways that you can immediately stop a record take? How can you immediately stop a record take and delete the recorded clip? (See "Stopping a Record Take" beginning on page 142.)

5. What are two ways that you can display the Instrument view? (See "Monitoring a MIDI Controller" beginning on page 143.)

6. In what two windows can you enable Wait for Note? What is the purpose of this option? (See "Using Wait for Note" beginning on page 145.)

7. How is MIDI Merge useful when recording drum parts? (See "Using MIDI Merge Mode" beginning on page 145.)

8. What types of audio files can be imported into Pro Tools|First? What are some examples of files that cannot be imported? (See "Supported Audio Files" beginning on page 146.)

9. What three locations are available as destinations for files you import using the drag–and–drop method? (See "File Drag and Drop Locations" beginning on page 149.)

10. What are the available Edit modes in Pro Tools|First? (See "The Edit Modes" beginning on page 151.)

11. Which function keys on the computer keyboard can be used to select the Edit tools? (See "Selecting an Edit Tool" beginning on page 153.)

12. Which Edit tool must be used to select a portion of a clip? (See "Making Selections" beginning on page 154.)

13. Which Edit tool must be used to drag and drop a clip to a new location in the session? (See "Moving Clips" beginning on page 154.)

14. When is audio editing a destructive process? What about MIDI editing? (See "Advanced Editing Techniques" beginning on page 155.)

15. What Pro Tools|First command is used to split a clip into two separate clips? (See "Splitting a Clip into Two or More Clips" beginning on page 156.)

Importing and Editing Clips

🎧 Activity

In this exercise, you will learn how to perform basic editing techniques in Pro Tools|First. You'll begin by creating a new project. Then you'll import a clip group and a MIDI file into the project and configure the tracks. Finally, you'll do some basic audio editing to remove unnecessary content from an audio clip.

🕐 Duration

This exercise should take approximately 15 minutes to complete.

⊕ Goals/Targets

- Create a new blank project document

- Import audio and MIDI into the project

- Assign the Xpand!2 virtual instrument for the MIDI parts

- Remove audio at the beginning of two drum tracks for a 4-bar intro

- Save your work for use in Exercise 7

Getting Started

To get started, you will create a new project to use for the exercise.

Create the project:

1. Create a new project by selecting **FILE > CREATE NEW** or pressing **COMMAND+N** (Mac) or **CTRL+N** (Windows). The Dashboard will open.

2. Click the **CREATE** action on the left side of the Dashboard, if not already active.

3. Make sure that the **CREATE FROM TEMPLATE** checkbox is not selected (unchecked).

4. Name the project **Lights** and add your initials to the end of the filename.

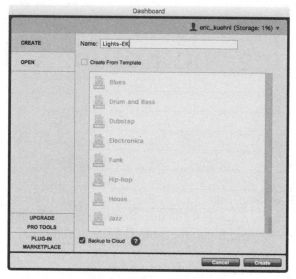

Figure 6.25 The Dashboard with the correct settings to create the project

5. Click the **CREATE** button at the bottom of the Dashboard to create the project. A new project will be created and will display on screen.

6. Choose **WINDOW > EDIT**, if needed, to bring the Edit window to the forefront and make it active.

7. Maximize or resize the window as needed for a full-screen view.

Importing Audio

In Exercise 2, you used a clip group to import the audio files into your first project. Here, you'll use a similar technique to start a second project. You'll be using this new project for the remainder of the exercises in this book.

Import the clip group into your project:

1. Choose **FILE > IMPORT** to display the **OPEN** dialog box for your system.

2. In the dialog box, navigate to your **Documents** folder (or other location where you saved the **APB Media Files** folder in Exercise 1).

3. Open the **06. Lights** folder within the **APB Media Files** folder.

4. Select the **01-Lights.cgrp** file and click **OPEN**.

5.   When the **CLIP GROUP OPTIONS** dialog box displays, select the **NEW TRACKS** radio button. Do not enable the checkbox for the **IMPORT TEMPO MAP FROM GROUP FILE** option.

6.   Click **OK** to complete the import. Ten tracks will be added to your project, and the imported audio will be placed on the tracks.

> **ⓘ**   If the Missing Files dialog box appears during the import, select Automatically Find and Relink and click OK to proceed.

Next you will ungroup the imported files and rename the tracks.

Ungroup the audio:

1.   With the imported audio still selected, choose **CLIP > UNGROUP** to ungroup the audio.

2.   Press **RETURN** (Mac) or **ENTER** (Windows) to move the Edit cursor to the beginning of the project.

Rename the tracks:

1.   Rename each of the tracks to remove their extensions as follows:

• Double-click on the nameplate of the Kick.grp track. The Track Name dialog box will display.

• Modify the displayed name to remove the .grp extension.

• Click the **NEXT** button at the bottom of the dialog box to move to the next track.

Figure 6.26 Clicking the Next button in the Track Name dialog box

• Repeat the process for each track in the project.

When finished, your project should look similar to Figure 6.27 below.

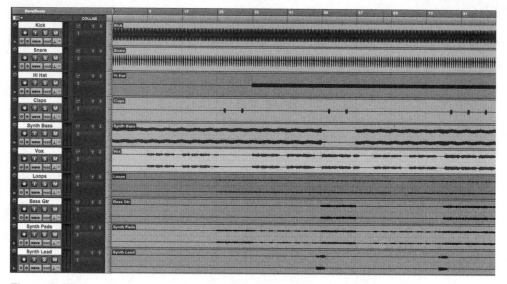

Figure 6.27 An overview of the ungrouped project audio with the tracks renamed

Importing MIDI

In this part of the exercise, you will import two MIDI clips using a Standard MIDI file.

Import the MIDI data:

1.   Choose FILE > IMPORT to display the OPEN dialog box for your system.

2.   In the dialog box, locate and select the Exercise-06.mid file inside the 06. Lights folder.

3.   Click OPEN to import the file. The MIDI Import Options dialog box will display.

Figure 6.28 The MIDI Import Options dialog box

4. In the MIDI Import Options dialog box, set the destination to **NEW TRACK(S) > INSTRUMENT TRACK**.

5. Click **OK**. The two MIDI clips will automatically be placed on Instrument tracks at the correct locations in the project.

Assigning Virtual Instruments

With the MIDI clips imported to Instrument tracks, you'll next need to assign virtual instruments on those tracks. You'll use the Xpand!2 virtual instrument plug-in on both tracks and then select appropriate presets.

Insert Xpand!2 on the Instrument tracks:

1. Choose **WINDOW > MIX** to activate the Mix window and bring it to the forefront.

2. Resize or maximize the Mix window as needed to get a full-screen view.

3. Locate the Inserts panel for the Piano track.

4. Click on the first insert on the Piano track and choose **MULTI-CHANNEL PLUG-IN > INSTRUMENT > XPAND!2 (STEREO)** from the pop-up menu.

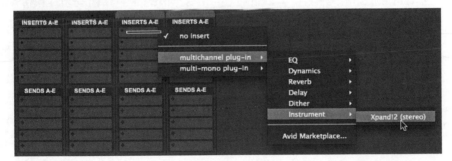

Figure 6.29 Selecting Xpand!2 from Insert Selector A on the Piano track

The Xpand!2 plug-in window will display.

5. Click on the Librarian menu (displaying <factory default>) and choose the **14 E PIANOS+CLAV > +01 MARK 2** preset. (See Figure 6.30.)

6. Close the plug-in window when done.

Figure 6.30 Choosing a preset using the Librarian menu

7. Repeat the above process on the **Strings** track, assigning the **16 STRINGS > +01 BIGGER LEGATO STRINGS** preset for this second copy of Xpand!2.

8. Close the plug-in window when finished.

Preview the project:

1. Choose **WINDOW > EDIT** or press **COMMAND+=** (Mac) or **CTRL+=** (Windows) to toggle back to the Edit window.

2. Press the **SPACEBAR** to begin playback and listen to the project in its current state.

3. Pay particular attention to the number and type of instruments that you hear. Feel free to solo and mute tracks to isolate certain elements and get familiar with the different parts.

Removing Unwanted Audio

In this part of the exercise, you will remove some drum parts at the beginning of the song. This will create a more dramatic intro featuring the Synth Bass part.

Remove the unwanted audio:

1. Using the **ZOOMER** tool, click on the **Kick** track to zoom in two or three levels for a better view.

2. Set the project to **GRID** mode. (Click on the Grid button on the left side of the Edit window toolbar.)

3.   Set the Grid value to **1 BAR** using the Grid Value selector beneath the Main Counter.

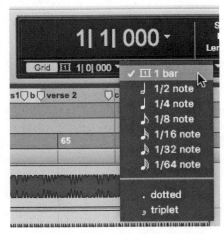

Figure 6.31 Setting the Grid value to 1 bar

4.   Using the **SELECTOR** tool, click and drag to select the first four bars on the **Kick** track (1|1|000 to 5|1|000). You can verify the selection using the Selection Indicators in the Edit window toolbar.

5.   Press **DELETE** to delete the selection.

6.   Repeat Steps 3 and 4 for the **Snare** track.

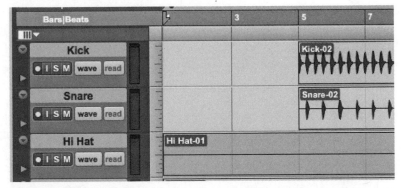

Figure 6.32 The first four bars removed from the Kick and Snare tracks

Finishing Up

To complete this exercise, you will need to save your work and close the project. You will be reusing this project in Exercise 7, so it's important to save and retain the work you've done.

Before you wrap up, you should also listen to the project to hear the changes you've made.

Finish your work:

1. Choose **FILE > SAVE** to save the project. The changes you've made will be saved in your local project cache and your Avid Cloud Account.

2. Press **RETURN** (Mac) or **ENTER** (Windows) to position the Edit cursor at the beginning of the project.

3. Press the **SPACEBAR** to begin playback. Only the synth bass should be audible for the first four bars, creating a nice intro.

4. When finished, press the **SPACEBAR** a second time to stop playback.

5. Choose **FILE > CLOSE PROJECT** to close the project and return to the Dashboard. If you are notified that tracks with changes have not been uploaded to the cloud, simply click **CLOSE** or **SAVE** to proceed. (You do not need to upload track changes unless you are using Cloud Collaboration features.)

> (i) To ensure that all audio files are saved in your Avid Cloud Account, be sure to let in-progress file uploads complete prior to quitting Pro Tools|First.

That completes this exercise.

Chapter 7

Mixing Concepts

...What You Need to Know to Mix a Project...

This chapter introduces you to mixing concepts, from setting levels and panning to the role of EQ and dynamics processing on the tracks in a mix. We discuss how to keep a mix from clipping, the difference between gain-based processing and time-based processing, and the differences between insert processing and send-and-return processing. The chapter ends with a discussion of mixing in the box and some suggestions for maximizing your results when mixing in Pro Tools | First.

✛ Learning Targets for This Chapter

- Set effective levels for your tracks

- Recognize the role of EQ and dynamics processing in creating a balanced mix

- Use panning to create a sense of space and positioning in your mix

- Understand how inserts and sends can be used to add processing to tracks

- Recognize the advantages of in-the-box mixing

After you have recorded, imported, or otherwise created the media that you want to use in your project, you can set about the task of mixing the audio. Mixing is the process of setting the basic levels, positioning, and sonic characteristics of your tracks. Essentially, this is where you determine how the various parts of the project will blend together to create a cohesive result during playback.

Basic Mixing

Although mixes can get very complex on large sessions, the basic process is fairly simple. The primary goal when creating a stereo mix is to set the levels for each of the tracks using the tracks' volume faders and to position each of the tracks within the stereo field using the tracks' pan controls. Other options include using inserts and sends to process each track and add effects.

Setting Levels

Setting the levels for your tracks is typically done in the Mix window. Here you'll find volume faders for each track, which you can use to adjust each track's overall output level.

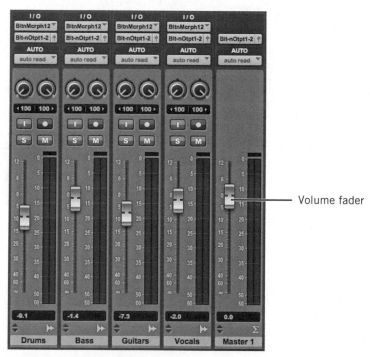

Volume fader

Figure 7.1 Volume faders in the Pro Tools | First Mix window

Level Considerations

The purpose of adjusting the output level of a track is to make the track audible without obscuring other tracks or causing the track to become overly prominent in the mix. During the recording process, audio is often recorded louder than it needs to be in the final mix. Additionally, as you begin summing multiple tracks together, the overall output level for the project will increase. For these reasons, it helps to pull all of the faders down quite a bit when you begin mixing and then gradually adjust the levels of each track as needed.

Allowing one track to be heard above all the others is not only a matter of raising its volume fader, however. A common mixing dilemma is that making one track louder will cause another, equally important track to become overshadowed and indistinct.

Getting a Good Music Mix Is More Than Setting Levels

Raising the fader on a guitar track enough to get it to cut through the mix can make the vocal track hard to hear. Raising the fader on the vocal track may then begin to obscure the impact of the drums. And raising the faders on the drum tracks can affect the bass guitar, which may now be barely audible. By the time you bring up the level on the bass guitar to compensate, you may be right back where you started, with the guitar track no longer cutting through the mix. Only now, everything is louder!

In the quest for the ultimate mix, where "everything is louder than everything else," often you simply end up with a very loud mix and still cannot distinguish individual parts.

As you start setting the initial levels for your mix, try to achieve a good overall balance. Don't get overly concerned if you find that certain tracks start to compete with one another. These issues can be addressed later using panning, EQ and dynamics processing, and other techniques that help give each track its own unique space in the mix.

Beware of Clipping

Among the problems caused by loud tracks, the output levels of your mix may get too "hot," leading the signal to clip at the digital–to–analog converters. This will cause the mix to become distorted on playback during the loudest moments.

Digital distortion is always detrimental to sound quality and should be avoided at all costs. Therefore, it is better to mix too quiet than it is to mix too loud. You can always increase the overall output levels of a mixed stereo file at a later stage if needed. But you cannot remove clipping from the stereo file after the fact.

Metering on Source Tracks

To help you keep an eye on your audio levels, each track includes a standard meter display to the right of the track fader. At the top of each meter is a clip indicator for the track. The clip indicator will light whenever the signal from the track exceeds full-scale audio.

Meters in the Pro Tools mixer measure loudness in decibels relative to full-scale audio (dBFS), with full scale represented by 0 at the top of the meter. Digital clipping occurs whenever a signal exceeds 0 dBFS at an input or output.

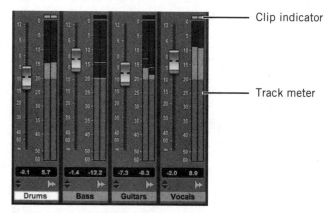

Clip indicator

Track meter

Figure 7.2 Meters on tracks in Pro Tools | First

Audio tracks show *pre-fader* metering by default. This means that the meter reflects the level from the source audio on the track (disk file) rather than the output level of the track. A lit clip indicator on an Audio track does not necessarily mean the output levels are too hot—the volume fader could be pulled way down, reducing the playback amplitude. Similarly, not having a lit clip indicator does not mean a track will play back cleanly: if the volume fader is set high, the output levels could be pushed into clipping, which won't be shown on the track meter.

 Track metering does reflect plug-in processing done on the track, including changes made by EQ or dynamics processors. Any boost or cut to the signal caused by plug-ins will be represented on the meter.

Metering on Master Fader Tracks

In order to ensure that the output levels of your mix are not too hot, it's a good idea to add a stereo Master Fader track to your project. As discussed in Chapter 5, a Master Fader track can be used to monitor and control the output levels for your project.

The level meter on a Master Fader track reflects the overall output of the entire mix. This is a summed total of the signals from each contributing track.

Clip indicators on Master Fader tracks light red when the summed signal level exceeds the capabilities of the digital-to-analog converters. In this case, you can reduce the levels on each of the contributing tracks in your mix, or reduce the overall output level using the Master Fader itself.

While working on your mix, keep an eye on the meters on the Master Fader track. If the Master Fader begins clipping, reduce the output levels before continuing.

Clips Versus Overs

The clip indicators in Pro Tools|First light in yellow on Audio tracks, Instrument tracks, and Aux Input tracks to indicate an overage on the track (a signal exceeding 0 dBFS en route to an internal destination). This is distinguished from the red clip indicators on Master Fader tracks, which indicate a true clip (a signal that will distort an output or disk file, if not attenuated).

The Role of EQ and Dynamics Processing

As mentioned above, setting the fader levels is not the only consideration when it comes to allowing each track to be heard in a mix. Other important considerations include the track's frequency spectrum and the track's dynamic response.

The frequency spectrum of a track, or the amount of energy the track has at different audio frequencies, can be shaped using equalization (or EQ for short). You can use EQ processing to help reduce low-end rumble, high-end hiss, and other unwanted noise in a signal. You can also use EQ to shape a signal and create a unique tone for each track. This allows certain target frequencies or frequency ranges to be more prominent than others. By selectively boosting and cutting frequencies on each track, you can balance the audio spectrum in the mix, and give each track its own sonic footprint.

 In the interest of keeping track levels in check, it is generally better to focus on cutting the frequencies you don't want rather than boosting the frequencies you wish to emphasize.

The dynamic response of a track refers to the range of amplitude values on the track. Said another way, the track's dynamics relate to the differences in loudness from one part of the track to another. The momentary loudness peaks (or *transients*) on a track are often much louder than the track's average levels. These loudness peaks can begin to obscure other tracks (or cause clipping) long before the source track's overall amplitude is where you want it in your mix.

A solution to this problem is to use compression on the track. Compression helps reduce the loudness in peak areas without affecting the average loudness. Using compression in combination with an appropriate amount of make-up gain can help you increase the level on a track without obliterating the other tracks in your mix.

For details on using EQ and dynamics processing, see the associated discussions in Chapter 8 of this book.

How to Set Levels

When it comes to setting the relative levels of your tracks, it helps to get familiar with the audio characteristics of each track first. Then consider how those characteristics contribute to the overall mix. Use the following steps as a guide to get started:

- **Listen to the track in isolation**—Use the Solo function to isolate each track in turn and familiarize yourself with its sonic characteristics. When working on a music mix, consider how the track supports the rhythm, groove, harmony, and melody of the piece. When working with non-musical material, consider how the track contributes to the tone and emotion of the mix, and listen for the clarity of the track.

- **Listen to the track in context**—Unsolo the track to determine the appropriate level for the track relative to the other tracks in the mix. Can you still hear the important sonic elements that you heard when the track was soloed? Or is the track completely lost among competing sounds?

- **Listen to the mix without the track**—Mute the track to gauge its contribution to the mix and how necessary it is. Does the mix sound lacking without the track? Or is the mix suddenly clearer without the track competing for sonic space?

- **Check the track throughout the piece**—Toggle the mute and solo state of the track on/off to hear the track isolated, in context, and removed from the mix in multiple locations throughout the composition. Are there some parts of the mix where the track is more important than others? Should the levels change for different sections of the mix?

- **Make adjustments in iterations**—Return to the track and adjust the levels as you make other changes to the mix. Setting levels is an iterative process that will require fine-tuning as your mix begins to take shape. Be sure to consider how each track's contribution changes as you begin setting levels on other tracks, adjusting pan positions, and adding processing to the mix.

Work your way though each track in the project, listening and adjusting levels as you go to create a good overall balance. Don't worry if there are aspects of the mix you aren't completely happy with at this point; you will be refining the result as you progress through later stages of the mixing process.

Panning

The pan controls on each track allow you to position the track within the stereo field. In a stereo mix, you will have two track formats to consider: mono tracks and stereo tracks.

Pan Controls on Mono Tracks

Mono tracks will have a single pan control that allows you to position the track's output as desired in the stereo spectrum. Panning a track hard left will cause it to play out of the left speaker only; panning to center will cause the track to play at equal volume out of both speakers; and panning hard right will cause the track to play out of the right speaker only.

Pan control

Figure 7.3 Mono tracks panned hard left, center, and hard right (from left to right)

Pan Controls on Stereo Tracks

Stereo tracks will have two pan controls: one for each channel in the audio signal. Panning both channels to the same position will create a mono signal, allowing you to position the signal at a specific point within the stereo field, just as with a mono track.

On stereo tracks, you will typically leave the pan controls set hard left (for the left channel) and hard right (for the right channel) to preserve the stereo separation between the channels in the source audio. Panning each control partially towards the center will collapse the stereo spread, reducing the panoramic width of the track.

You can also pan each channel to its opposite extreme, effectively flipping the stereo image and reversing the signal's placement in the mix.

Figure 7.4 Stereo tracks with default panning (FX 1), mono panning (FX 2), and inverted panning (FX 3)

Panning Examples

As you refine your mix, you'll want to consider the panoramic position of each track, along with the overall distribution of the tracks. Positioning individual tracks at distinct locations will give each track its own space in the mix and will help you give your mix width and realism.

- **Center–panned tracks**—Certain tracks tend to work best in the center of a mix. These typically include the tracks that provide the main focus or lead part for the piece, such as a narration or voiceover track or a lead vocal track. In music production it is also common to place the main rhythmic elements at or near the center of the mix, such as the kick drum, snare drum, and bass guitar.

- **Hard–panned tracks**—Tracks that provide flavor, color, or character to a mix are often effective when panned hard left or right. These are typically supplemental tracks such as a shaker or harmonica in a music mix or ambient accents such as a distant siren or muffled argument from an adjacent room in a fiction narrative.

(i) Hard panning can also be effective on main tracks, especially in a sparse mix.

One potential problem with using hard-panned tracks is that they can become inaudible to a listener who is on the opposite side of the listening space from the sound source, such as when the stereo speakers are placed wide apart in a living room. Also, if the stereo playback should drop a channel, everything hard-panned to the dropped side would be lost.

These problems can be mitigated by not panning fully left/right, by including some reverb from a hard-panned track in the opposite channel, and by using psycho-acoustic processing to place an image in a stereo field by means of timing offsets while keeping the signal in both channels.

 For an example of hard panning, check out the electric guitar on early albums by Van Halen. Hard panning is prominent in songs such as "Little Dreamer," "Beautiful Girls," "Hang 'Em High," and numerous others.

- **Tracks panned off–center**—Often tracks are placed off center to create realism and a sense of space in the mix. This technique is commonly used to position characters around a room in a dialog mix. In music mixing, it is common to pan individual drum tracks to emulate the layout of the drum kit (placing hi-hat and splash cymbal on the left, rack toms across the middle, and floor tom and ride cymbal on the right, for example). Another common technique is to pan backing vocal tracks, placing high harmonies on the left, mid-range parts near the center, and low harmonies on the right, for example.

- **Other ideas**— It can be very effective to offset parts that have similar impact in a mix. For example, panning a doubled vocal part to left and right extremes can create a sense of width in the mix. Similarly, panning a rhythm guitar part opposite a Rhodes piano part can help each part contribute equally without competing with one another.

 For examples of effective panning for multiple vocal parts, take a listen to "Ziggy Stardust," "Changes," and other classics by David Bowie. Bowie often used opposite-panned vocal doubles and harmonies during key sections for emphasis.

Processing Options and Techniques

When it comes to adding processing to your tracks, you have two broad categories to consider: gain-based processing and time-based processing. You also need to consider when and how any processing should be added to your mix. Here we'll cover some options available in Pro Tools | First. All of these options apply equally to commercial versions of Pro Tools software.

Gain-Based Processing

Gain-based processors include any processors that affect the amplitude of the audio signal in some way. Examples include EQs, compressors, noise gates, expanders, and similar dynamics processors.

When adding gain-based processing to a signal, you will typically assign the processor as an insert to an individual track. This type of processing is usually applied to the entire signal (100% wet), rather than being mixed together with a dry signal. The processing is also commonly track-specific.

For example, when using an EQ plug-in to eliminate low-frequency rumble, you will want 100% of the source signal to be affected. And you will adjust the EQ parameters to address the specific frequency characteristics of the source signal on the track.

Time-Based Processing and Effects

The other type of processing can broadly be classified as time-based processing and effects. This includes processors that affect the signal in the time-domain, such as reverbs and delays, and modulation effects, such as choruses, flangers, and phasers. These processors typically get applied to only a portion of the signal and mixed back in with the dry signal.

Time-based processors are commonly used as shared effects, across multiple tracks in a mix. This helps provide consistency in the mix and makes more efficient use of your processing resources.

Inserts Versus Sends

Pro Tools|First allows you to add signal processing to a track using inserts and sends. An insert is an audio patch point that places a signal processor directly into the signal path of the track. When using an insert, all of the audio on the track must pass through the insert on its way to the track's output.

Pro Tools|First provides 10 insert positions on each track, allowing you to process the track's signal through multiple successive plug-ins, as needed.

 See Chapter 8 in this book for details on using inserts for plug-in processing.

By contrast, a send provides a signal path that can be used to route audio from one or more source tracks to a parallel destination for processing. In Pro Tools|First, signals from sends are typically returned to the mix by way of an Aux Input track. Processing is commonly added to the signal using a plug-in insert on the Aux Input track.

 In this send-and-return configuration, the Aux Input track is commonly referred to as the *return* track.

When creating a send for internal plug-in processing, you will use a bus to route signals from the source track(s) to the destination Aux Input track.

Processing with External Gear

In Pro Tools|First, you can also choose to route the signal from a send through external hardware, provided you have sufficient I/O on your audio interface. In this case, the send will route out of your audio interface, through an external processor, and back into your audio interface before the signal is returned to the mix. (See Figure 7.5.) As above, the signal is returned to the mix using an Aux Input return track.

Figure 7.5 External reverb connected to an audio interface for use with Pro Tools|First

Mixing in the Box

Although it is possible to use external gear for send-and-return processing in Pro Tools|First, mixing completely "in the box" offers numerous advantages. Mixing in the box simply means that all signal processing is provided by internal software plug-ins, so the mix does not rely on any external gear.

Advantages of In-the-Box Mixing

The advantages of working completely in the box include the following considerations:

- **Portability**—Creating your Pro Tools|First mix entirely in the box means that you can open the project from any Pro Tools workstation anywhere in the world, as long as you have an Internet connection. Barring any missing plug-ins, the mix will sound the same from any system.

  If you were to use external gear, you will need to take the gear with you to work on the mix from a different location.

- **Recallability**—Saving the project will save all plug-in settings and levels, allowing them to recall exactly as they were the next time the session is used. This is not the case when using external gear, as you will need to reconfigure all settings on the external hardware to match your last used settings for the project.

- **Time savings**—Reconfiguring hardware is not only inconvenient, it can be quite time-consuming. It also requires keeping detailed notes of settings and configurations, and updating those notes every time you change a setting.

- **Dynamic automation**—Plug-in settings can be automated, enabling you to incorporate dynamic changes in your mix. All automation settings are saved and recalled with the project, ensuring that it plays back consistently every time.

Getting the Most Out of an In-the-Box Mix

To get the most out of an in-the-box mix, you will want to consider how much control you need to have over the sonic characteristics of your mix. Ideally, this is something you would begin thinking about at the project inception, prior to starting to record.

For example, you'll need to decide early on if you want to be able to control the dynamics of each track entirely from within the project, or if it is OK to apply some compression to individual signals prior to the recording input stage. Likewise, you'll need to decide whether to record sources such as guitar tracks from an amp, with the guitarist's effects processing chain already in place, or to record a direct signal from the guitar and add amp simulators and stomp-box effects as plug-ins inside of Pro Tools|First.

Aside from considerations about when to apply processing, you will also need to take steps to maximize the results of any processing you apply from within Pro Tools|First. Use the following simple suggestions as a starting point:

- **Learn how to set plug-in parameters**—To effectively use the plug-ins that are provided with Pro Tools|First, you will need to know how to set the parameters properly and recognize what each parameter is used for. Take time to experiment and practice using each plug-in on material you are familiar with.

- **Avoid using copies of the same plug-in on many different tracks**—Learn how to use send-and-return processing to apply the same effects to multiple tracks, rather than placing individual copies of the same plug-in on each track. Not only does using multiple copies of a plug-in require more processing power than using a single copy, but you'll find that keeping the settings in sync across multiple tracks can become tedious and time-consuming.

- **Invest in good quality plug-ins**—The plug-in collection that comes with Pro Tools|First is sufficient to get you started. As you expand beyond that basic set, invest in quality processors that enhance your sonic palette. Don't be afraid to spend some money to get what you want, but keep in mind that many high-quality plug-ins are available at very reasonable prices. Spend some time reading or viewing product reviews, and check out trial versions, if available. Once you know what you want, keep an eye out for discounts and sale prices.

(i) **Plug-in manufacturers commonly offer discounts and promotional pricing during national holidays, trade shows, and similar events.**

Review/Discussion Questions

1. What are some reasons for lowering the faders across your entire project as you begin to set levels for your mix? (See "Level Considerations" beginning on page 170.)

2. Why is it important to avoid clipping in your mix? How can you tell if the project is clipping at the outputs? (See "Beware of Clipping" beginning on page 171.)

3. How can equalization be used to help a track cut through a mix? (See "The Role of EQ and Dynamics Processing" beginning on page 173.)

4. What is meant by the dynamic response of a track? What can be done to "tame" excessively loud peaks on a track? (See "The Role of EQ and Dynamics Processing" beginning on page 173.)

5. How are the pan controls different between mono tracks and stereo tracks? What accounts for this difference? (See "Panning" beginning on page 174.)

6. Describe some examples of panning techniques that can be useful or effective in a mix. (See "Panning Examples" beginning on page 176.)

7. How does gain-based processing affect an audio signal? Give some examples of gain-based processors. (See "Gain-Based Processing" beginning on page 177.)

8. What are some available time-based processors? How are time-based processors typically applied to tracks? How is this different from the way gain-based processors are used? (See "Time-Based Processing and Effects" beginning on page 178.)

9. How are inserts different from sends, in the way they process audio? What is the role of an Aux Input track in a send-and-return configuration? (See "Inserts Versus Sends" beginning on page 178.)

10. What is meant by "in-the-box" mixing? What are some advantages of mixing in the box? (See "Mixing in the Box" beginning on page 179.)

11. Why is it important to begin thinking about in-the-box mixing from the project inception? (See "Getting the Most Out of an In-the-Box Mix" beginning on page 180.)

12. How can you maximize the results of any processing you apply from within Pro Tools|First? (See "Getting the Most Out of an In-the-Box Mix" beginning on page 180.)

Creating a Basic Mix

🎧 Activity

In this exercise, you will perform basic mixing tasks in Pro Tools | First. You'll start off by adjusting levels to get a good basic mix. Then you'll explore some strategies to prevent clipping on loud tracks. Finally, you'll adjust pan settings to enhance the mix and create space for the different instruments.

🕐 Duration

This exercise should take approximately 20 minutes to complete.

⊕ Goals/Targets

- Configure a Master Fader for the project

- Set levels for different tracks in the project

- Set panning for different tracks in the project

- Save your work for use in Exercise 8

Getting Started

To get started, you will open your completed project from Exercise 6. This will serve as the starting point for this exercise.

Open your existing Lights project:

1. Select **FILE > OPEN PROJECT** or press **COMMAND+O** (Mac) or **CTRL+O** (Windows). The Dashboard will open.

2. If necessary, click the **OPEN** action on the left side of the Dashboard.

3. Select your **Lights-xxx** project from the list of available projects.

4. Click **OPEN**. The project will open as it was when last saved.

5. If needed, choose **WINDOW > MIX** or press **COMMAND+=** (Mac) or **CTRL+=** (Windows) to display the Mix window and make it active.

Creating a Rough Mix

At this point, you're ready to start mixing. As you adjust the volume faders on the tracks in your project, you will want to keep an eye on your output levels. However, you won't be able to use the meters on the source tracks for this since Pro Tools|First uses pre-fader metering by default.

 Pre-fader metering is designed for recording: it shows you the incoming signal level being written to disk, regardless of the fader position on the track.

In order to monitor your output levels, you'll need to add a Master Fader track to your session.

Add a Master Fader track:

1. Choose **TRACK > NEW** or press **COMMAND+SHIFT+N** (Mac) or **CTRL+SHIFT+N** (Windows). The New Tracks dialog box will appear.

2. Configure the settings for one new stereo Master Fader track.

Figure 7.6 The New Tracks dialog box configured for a stereo Master Fader track

3. Click **CREATE**. A new Master Fader track will appear.

4. If needed, move the track to the far right in the Mix window. To do this, simply click on the track nameplate and drag the track to the new position.

5. Double-click on the nameplate for the Master Fader track and rename it to **Stereo Mix**.

6. Press the **SPACEBAR** to begin playback.

7. Listen to the levels of each track. Begin evaluating what changes you'll need to make to even out the different parts so that each part can be heard clearly without "jumping out" of the mix and sounding too prominent.

8. See the suggestions below to help you evaluate the tracks and begin making changes.

General Mixing Suggestions

Here are some general tips for setting the rough levels for tracks:

- Solo a track and listen closely to the content. What are the most important details of that instrument? When you unsolo the track can you still hear those details clearly in the overall mix? If not, you may need to increase the level of the track.

- Mute a track and listen to the mix. Does the mix sound empty without that track? Do you even notice that it is missing? You may decide to leave the track muted or reduce the level of the track.

- While listening through the whole song, consider whether a track is only necessary in a particular section of the song. Most songs build in complexity as they progress. You might want to consider muting or reducing the volume of a track at the beginning of the song or during verses. Then you can unmute or increase the volume of the track later in the song or during choruses.

- Keep revisiting the various sections of the song. As you make changes in one section, it may change how you feel about other sections.

Suggestions for This Project

Here are some suggestions to help you create a rough mix of your project.

- Display the Memory Locations window to help you navigate the project while working in the Mix window. Choose **WINDOW > MEMORY LOCATIONS.** Click on the listed locations in this window as you work to jump to different song sections.

> (i) **The Memory Locations window displays markers that have been set up for a Pro Tools project or session. The markers for this project were imported with the MIDI file that you added in Exercise 6.**

- Listen to the mix going into Chorus 1. The Synth Lead and Piano tracks are a bit too loud in these sections. Try reducing the level of each track by about -5 dB.

- Listen to the mix in Chorus 2. The Strings track is much too loud. Try reducing the level on this track by around –8 dB.

- Throughout the song, the vocal track (Vox) gets a little bit lost in the mix. Try increasing the level on this track by around +1.5 dB.

- The Bass Gtr track gets a little too loud during both choruses. Try reducing the volume on this track by about -2 dB.

Adjusting Levels to Prevent Clipping

When mixing a project, it is fairly common to have some tracks that show clipping (or "overs") on individual track meters or on the Master Fader. This can be tricky to deal with when you're first developing your mixing skills. Fortunately, you have a number of ways to address clipping in Pro Tools|First.

General Level Suggestions

Here are some tips for dealing with clipping:

- If an individual track is causing clipping at the outputs (as displayed on the Master Fader), the first thing to do is reduce that track's level. If you can prevent clipping while the resulting level still sounds good in the mix, you're all set. If the resulting level is too quiet, you'll need to try another approach.

- Another option is to reduce the levels of all of the tracks. To do this, first reduce the level of the track that is causing the clipping until the clip goes away. Take note of how much you reduced the track from its prior level in the mix (such as –6 dB). Then reduce the level of each track in the session by the same amount. Afterwards, you may need to bring up the level of the Master Fader to get back to a reasonably loud mix.

- A third option to prevent clipping is to simply lower the fader on the Master Fader track to correct the clip at the output stage. While clipping on an individual track may not be detrimental to the final mix, you never want to have clipping on the Master Fader track.

Suggestions for This Project

The individual tracks in this mix are well below clipping, so you should not need to reduce them further. But the overall mix is clipping. You'll use the Master Fader to solve that problem.

Correct clipping at the output stage:

1. Play through the song.

2. Keep an eye on the **Stereo Mix** Master Fader track, watching the level on the meters, the clip indicator at the top of the meters, and the peak level indicator at the bottom right. (See Figure 7.7.)

3. Take note of the loudest areas of the project. After playing the song all the way through, you should have an idea of where the signal is peaking.

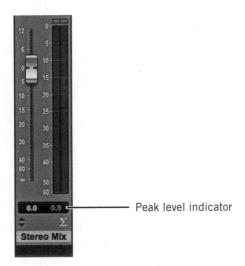

Peak level indicator

Figure 7.7 The peak level indicator on the Master Fader can be seen at the bottom right in red.

4. Reduce the level of the **Stereo Mix** track by at least the amount shown in red in the peak level indicator. (Alternatively, if the peak is below zero, you could raise the level until the peak is just below clipping.)

> (i) **Hold Command (Mac) or Ctrl (Windows) when moving a track's volume fader to have fine control over the level.**

5. Do one of the following to reset the peak level indicator:

    *   Click on the peak level indicator itself.

    *   Choose **TRACK > CLEAR ALL CLIP INDICATORS.**

6. Play through the song again to verify that the peak levels now remain below clipping. If clipping still occurs, reduce the Master Fader level further and test again.

Adjusting Panning

In this part of the exercise, you'll adjust the panning for your tracks. The project includes both mono and stereo tracks. Mono tracks can be easily positioned to any location in the stereo field. Stereo tracks are often adjusted to have a narrower or broader width. Both of these techniques can be used to add interest to the mix, and can also create space where each track can be heard and appreciated.

General Panning Suggestions

Here are some general tips for panning tracks:

- For each mono track, solo the track and adjust the panning. Listen for a particular pan position that just "feels right" for the track or instrument. Unsolo the track to check how its position works in the overall mix.

- For each stereo track, try adjusting the panning so that the width is narrower. You can often create more space in the mix by narrowing some stereo tracks. See if any tracks sound better left at the default (widest) pan setting instead.

- Try panning some tracks in unusual ways. Mono tracks can be panned all the way left or right to create a novel sound. Stereo tracks can be shifted so that they are not symmetrical in the left and right channels. Just be careful because extreme panning can also distract from the listening experience.

Suggestions for This Project

Here are a few thoughts for altering the panning of your project:

- Try setting the Hi Hat track slightly to the left (<15) and the Claps track slightly to the right (15>). This can help to create a more interesting mix of the percussion elements. (You can hear the effect of these changes in each of the choruses, where both tracks are contributing to the mix.)

- Create some space for the vocal by narrowing the panning on the Vox track a bit. Try setting the left pan to <50 and the right pan to 50>.

- Narrow the stereo image of the bass guitar to help it stand out. Try setting the left pan on the Bass Gtr track to <20 and the right pan to 20>. (You can hear the contribution of this track during each of the choruses.)

- Move the part on the Strings track to the left a bit by setting the right pan control to center (0). (You can hear the contribution of this track in chorus 2.)

Finishing Up

To complete this exercise, you will need to save your work and close the project. You will be reusing this project in Exercise 8, so it's important to save and retain the work you've done.

Before you wrap up, you can also listen to the project to hear the mixing changes you've made.

Finish your work:

1.   Choose FILE > SAVE to save the project.

(i)   **The changes you've made will be saved in your local project cache and your Avid Cloud Account.**

2.   Press **RETURN** (Mac) or **ENTER** (Windows) to position the Edit cursor at the beginning of the project.

3.   (Optional) Press the **SPACEBAR** to begin playback and listen through the project. Press the **SPACEBAR** a second time when finished to stop playback.

4.   Choose **FILE > CLOSE PROJECT** to close the project and return to the Dashboard. If you are notified that tracks with changes have not been uploaded to the cloud, simply click **CLOSE** or **SAVE** to proceed.

(i)   **You do not need to upload track changes unless you are using the Cloud Collaboration features in Pro Tools|First.**

That completes this exercise.

Chapter 8

Signal Processing

...What You Can Do to Optimize Your Audio...

This chapter begins with an overview of using plug-ins in Pro Tools|First. We take a look at some general categories of plug-ins—including EQ, Dynamics, and Time-Based effects—and provide some suggestions for using various plug-in processors and parameters. We also look at the process of creating send-and-return configurations and discuss how this setup can be useful.

✥ Learning Targets for This Chapter

- Understand basic plug-in functionality in Pro Tools|First

- Become familiar with the major plug-in categories

- Learn how to use basic plug-in parameters

- Explore send-and-return configurations

Plug-ins are the key to one of the most important aspects of working with a DAW: processing audio and adding effects. Innovations in plug-in design were a key factor in the rise of the DAW as the dominant platform for producing music and creating audio for film, TV, and video·games. Without great–sounding plug-ins for equalization, dynamics processing, and time-based effects such as reverb and delay, the DAW revolution might never have occurred.

In this chapter, we take a look at how to use plug-ins in Pro Tools|First and review the most common types of plug-ins that are used in today's production workflow.

Plug-In Basics

The sheer variety of plug-ins that are available today can seem completely overwhelming when you're just getting started. In order to ease the learning curve, Avid has selected a core set of plug-ins and included them in Pro Tools|First. While the selection is somewhat limited, this limitation may actually be a blessing in disguise! Learning just a few plug-ins well is a realistic goal for those who are new to the DAW world. And, because there are only a few major categories of plug-ins, the knowledge that you gain now can easily be applied to other plug-ins down the road as you expand your processing palette.

Viewing Inserts on Tracks

Before you can place a plug-in on a track, you'll need to know how to display the desired inserts view in both the Mix and Edit windows.

 In Version 12.8, Pro Tools|First provides up to ten inserts on each track, in two groups of five: Inserts A-E and Inserts F-J.

To show (or hide) an inserts view in the Edit window, do one of the following:

■   Select **VIEW > EDIT WINDOW VIEWS** and select either **INSERTS A-E** or **INSERTS F-J** from the submenu.

Figure 8.1 Showing inserts using the main View menu

- Click on the **EDIT WINDOW VIEW SELECTOR** and select either **INSERTS A-E** or **INSERTS F-J**.

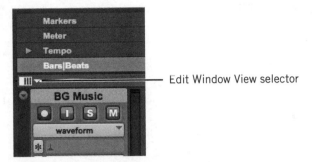
Edit Window View selector

Figure 8.2 The Edit Window View selector, above the tracks display in the Edit window

- **RIGHT-CLICK** on the name of a visible view (such as Instrument or I/O) and select **INSERTS A-E** or **INSERTS F-J** from the pop-up menu.

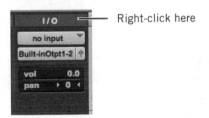
Right-click here

Figure 8.3 Right-click the name of a visible view to show or hide views

To show (or hide) inserts in Mix window, do one of the following:

- Select **VIEW > MIX WINDOW VIEWS** and select either **INSERTS A-E** or **INSERTS F-J**.

- Click on the **MIX WINDOW VIEW SELECTOR** and select either **INSERTS A-E** or **INSERTS F-J**.

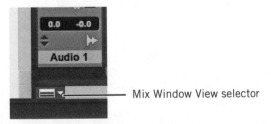
Mix Window View selector

Figure 8.4 The Mix Window View selector, below the tracks display in the Mix window

- **RIGHT-CLICK** on the name of a visible view (such as Instrument or I/O) and select **INSERTS A-E** or **INSERTS F-J** from the pop-up menu.

You'll probably only need to display the first five inserts (Inserts A-E) when you're just getting started. Even for professionals, it's pretty rare for a track to have more than five inserts.

Inserting Plug-Ins on Tracks

We've already looked at several ways to insert plug-ins (including virtual instruments) on tracks in Pro Tools | First. But let's do a quick recap before moving on to using plug-ins to process audio.

To insert a plug-in on a track:

1. Using one of the techniques described above, make sure that the desired Inserts view is visible (**INSERTS A-E** and/or **INSERTS F-J**).

2. Click on the **INSERT SELECTOR** for the desired insert position.

3. Select the desired plug-in from the pop-up menu. The plug-in will be applied at the selected position and the plug-in window will open.

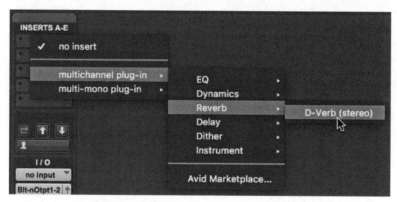

Figure 8.5 Assigning the D-Verb plug-in to an insert

To remove a plug-in from a track:

1. Click on the Insert selector (round dot) to the left of the plug-in you would like to remove.

 Do not click on the main insert button, as that will open the plug-in window.

2. Choose **NO INSERT** from the pop-up menu.

Moving and Duplicating Plug-Ins

After you've begun working with plug-ins on tracks in a project, you may find that you need to move a plug-in to a different insert position or to a different track entirely. You may also want to create a duplicate of the plug-in elsewhere in the project. These tasks are easily accomplished in Pro Tools|First.

To move a plug-in, do the following:

■ Click on the plug-in insert button and drag it to a new insert position on the same track or to an available insert position on another track.

To duplicate a plug-in, do the following:

■ OPTION-CLICK (Mac) or ALT-CLICK (Windows) on the plug-in insert button and drag it to the desired location (on the same track or on another track).

Displaying Plug-In Windows

Before you can adjust the parameters of a plug-in, you'll need to open the plug-in window. Plug-in windows open automatically when you assign a plug-in to a track. You can easily re-open a plug-in window that is not displayed at any time.

To open a plug-in window:

■ Click on the plug-in insert button on the track.

Common Plug-In Controls

Pro Tools plug-ins feature two sets of controls: the standard Pro Tools controls that are common to all plug-ins, and the process-specific controls that are unique to each plug-in. Let's take a look at the common controls first. We'll look at process-specific controls later in this chapter.

Figure 8.6 The plug-in controls shared by all AAX plug-ins in Pro Tools|First

Track Controls

On the left side of the common controls, you can see the Track control area. This area features three selectors: the Track selector, the Insert Position selector, and the Plug-In selector.

Figure 8.7 The plug-in Track controls

Plug-in Track controls include the following:

- **Track selector**—Use this to switch the plug-in view to a different track in the project.

- **Insert Position selector**—Use this to switch the view to a different insert position on the track.

- **Plug-In Selector**—Use this to assign a plug-in or change the current plug-in assignment.

Preset Controls

To the right of the Track controls are the Preset controls. These controls are used to select and manage presets for the plug-in. This area features a number of items: the Plug-In Settings menu, the Plug-In Librarian menu, the Compare button, the Next and Previous settings buttons, and the Settings Select button.

Figure 8.8 The plug-in Preset controls

Plug-in Preset controls include the following:

- **Plug-In Settings menu**—Use this circle with a down-pointing arrow to save settings or to copy, paste, and import settings.

- **Plug-In Librarian menu**—Use this selector, displaying <factory default>, to load an existing preset.

- **Compare button**—Use this button to toggle between the most recently loaded preset and any subsequent modifications that you've made. This is often referred to as an "A/B" comparison.

- **Next and Previous settings buttons**—Use these plus and minus buttons to quickly select the next or previous preset.

- **Settings Select button**—Use this button showing rectangle icons to open the Plug-In Settings dialog box, displaying a large list of available settings presets.

Automation Controls

To the right of the Preset controls are the Automation (or "Auto") controls. These controls can be used to enable and disable parameters and to protect (or "safe") a plug-in against automation.

Figure 8.9 The plug-in Automation controls

Plug-in Automation controls:

- **Auto button**—Use this to enable or disable plug-in parameters for automation. All plug-in parameters are enabled for automation by default in Pro Tools|First.

- **Safe button**—Use this to prevent automation from being written for the plug-in.

 The plug-in automation features in Pro Tools|First are not covered in this book. See the Pro Tools Reference Guide for information about plug-in automation.

Bypass Control

To the right of the Automation controls is the Plug-In Bypass button.

Figure 8.10 Plug-in bypass control

Use this button to disable the currently displayed plug-in so that it will not affect the track's audio signal. This allows you to perform an "A/B" comparison of the affected and unaffected signal.

Adjusting Plug-In Parameters

Once you have a plug-in inserted on a track with the plug-in window visible, you're ready to start adjusting the plug-in's parameters. This is where the fun begins! Pro Tools|First provides a number of ways to adjust plug-in parameters, including the obvious (using the mouse), and the not-so-obvious (using the computer keyboard). Let's take a closer look.

Adjusting Plug-In Parameters with the Mouse

The most straightforward way to adjust plug-in parameters is to use the mouse. For fader–style controls, simply click and drag up to increase the value of the control or drag down to decrease the value. To adjust knob-style plug-in parameter controls, click and drag horizontally or vertically. Clicking and dragging up or to the right will increase the value of a knob-style control, whereas clicking and dragging down or to the left will decrease the value.

 Unlike plug-ins developed by some other companies, Avid's plug-ins do not respond to clicking at the location where you'd like the knob to go. You must click and drag to change the knob's position.

You can modify the way that plug-in controls respond to the mouse using keyboard modifiers.

For fine adjustments:

■   Hold **COMMAND** (Mac) or **CTRL** (Windows) while moving the control.

To return a control to its default value:

■   **OPTION-CLICK** (Mac) or **ALT-CLICK** (Windows) on the control.

Adjusting Plug-In Parameters with the Computer Keyboard

It's actually a little-known fact that you can also use the computer alphanumeric keyboard (or "QWERTY" keyboard) to adjust plug-in parameter controls in Pro Tools.

To change the value of plug-in parameter controls using the computer keyboard:

1.   Click in the text field next to the control that you'd like to adjust. (Once you're in a text field, you can use **TAB** or **SHIFT+TAB** to move to the next or previous text field, respectively.)

2.   Do one of the following to change the control's value:

   •   Press the **UP ARROW** to increase the value

   •   Press the **DOWN ARROW** to decrease the value

   •   Type in a numeric value

3.   To confirm the value press **RETURN** (Mac) or **ENTER** (Windows).

EQ Processing

EQ (short for equalization) is probably the most commonly used processor in the audio universe. In the consumer electronics world, EQ can be found just about anywhere that an audio signal is present; even the most humble car stereo usually has basic low, mid, and high EQ controls.

In the realm of audio production, EQ is an absolutely essential tool for getting individual instruments to sound their best, and for getting a multi-track mix to sound great.

Types of EQ

In the simplest terms, EQ is used to manipulate the frequency component of an audio signal. However, EQ processors themselves come in a variety of flavors that offer different numbers of EQ bands, and different configurations within those bands.

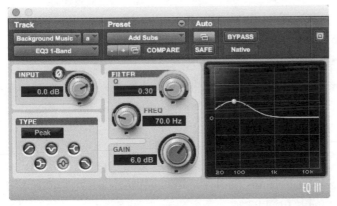

Figure 8.11 The EQ3 1-Band plug-in in Pro Tools | First

Some types of EQ bands include:

- **Parametric**—This is the most common type of EQ band. A parametric band is fully adjustable in terms of the frequency, gain, and Q (width) parameters.

- **High- and Low-Pass Filters**—These constitute another common type of EQ band, and are often abbreviated HPF and LPF, respectively. These filters permit signal to "pass" only above (HPF) or below (LPF) the selected frequency. High-pass filters are commonly used to eliminate low-frequency rumble, while low-pass filters can be employed to remove high-frequency hiss.

- **Shelf**—The shelf is similar to the high- and low-pass filter, but it is used to boost or cut the signal above (high-shelf) or below (low-shelf) the selected frequency by a specified amount.

- **Notch**—A notch filter is essentially a parametric band that has the gain setting fixed at the maximum negative value (approximately -18 dB in Pro Tools | First). This type of filter is used to "notch" out an offending frequency to make it inaudible.

Basic EQ Parameters

You'll find a number of standard EQ parameters on most software and hardware EQ processors. These will vary somewhat based on the type of EQ band.

Common EQ parameters include the following:

- **Frequency**—The Frequency parameter determines the target frequency for an EQ band. Every type of EQ band will have a frequency parameter, although some may be fixed at a specific frequency.

- **Gain**—The Gain parameter is used to boost or cut the volume of the associated EQ band. A gain control is typically found on parametric and shelf bands.

- **Q**—This is probably the most confusing EQ parameter for those who are new to audio production. The Q control is used to adjust the shape (slope or width) of an EQ curve. It behaves somewhat differently depending on the type of EQ band being used (parametric, shelf, filter).

- **In**—The In parameter can be used to enable or disable an EQ band, thus controlling whether that particular band is having an audible effect on the signal. This can be useful for doing an A/B comparison of the signal with and without an individual EQ band.

- **Input/Output** – The Input and Output gain controls can be used to boost or cut the signal at the input (before the EQ has been applied) or output (after the EQ has been applied).

EQ Plug-Ins in Pro Tools | First

Pro Tools | First offers two types of EQ plug-ins: the EQ3 7-Band and the EQ3 1-Band. The EQ3 7-Band is a high-quality 7-band EQ that offers five fully parametric bands (with the low and high bands switchable to shelves), and high- and low-pass filters (both switchable to notch).

The EQ3 1-Band is essentially a single band from the EQ3 7-band, which can be switched between low-pass filter, low shelf, notch, peak, high shelf, and high-pass filter.

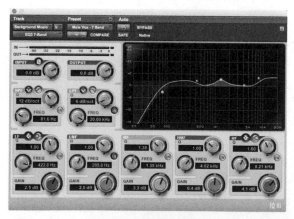

Figure 8.12 The EQ3 7-Band plug-in in Pro Tools | First

Strategies for Using EQ

Different types of material will require different approaches to EQ. But the basic techniques for finding good EQ settings are similar from track to track. Following are some tips for using EQ3 and its bands.

To use an EQ3 7-band on a track:

- Enable the **HIGH PASS FILTER** and increase the frequency enough to eliminate any unwanted noises at the extreme low frequencies, but not so much that the track loses too much low end.

  On some tracks, such as drum overheads, you may want to eliminate almost all of the bass to make room for the kick drum track and other low-frequency instruments.

- Use the **LOW-MID**, **MID**, and/or **HIGH-MID** band to emphasize desirable qualities of a particular track.

  A common approach used to identify a target frequency is to boost the gain substantially (+12 dB or more) and slowly sweep the frequency control back and forth during playback. Listen carefully to the track while adjusting the frequency. Stop sweeping when you hear something you like, tone-wise. Then reduce the gain until the frequency is only slightly pronounced, compared to the original.

- Use the **LOW-MID**, **MID**, and/or **HIGH-MID** band to reduce undesirable qualities of a particular track.

  A similar technique to the above can be used to identify target frequencies to cut. Simply stop sweeping when you hear something in the tone that sounds bad, intrusive, or unwanted. Then adjust the gain to a negative value that effectively reduces the prominence of the frequency, compared to the original.

> (i) Shift-clicking on a Gain control will toggle between positive and negative values. This provides a quick way to compare between boosting and cutting a frequency.

- If necessary, use a **HIGH** or **LOW SHELF** to add some high-end sizzle to cymbals or low-end thump to a bass guitar (respectively).

- Frequently **BYPASS** the plug-in to make sure that the changes you're making are actually improving the sound of the track and helping it to sit better in the overall mix!

Dynamics Processing

Like EQ, dynamics processing is an essential part of the audio production workflow. Unlike EQ, dynamics processing is not particularly well known outside of audio production. It is fair to say that working with dynamics processors is a bit more complex than using EQ to boost the bass or cut the treble on your car stereo. But the basics of dynamic processing are pretty straightforward, and if you use your ears to dial in just the right settings you'll be working like a pro in no time!

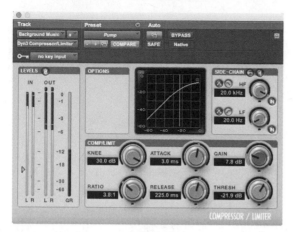

Figure 8.13 The Dyn3 Compressor/Limiter in Pro Tools|First

Types of Dynamics Processors

Dynamics processing refers to the manipulation of the volume (or amplitude) of an audio signal. Many instruments benefit from dynamics processing including vocals, guitar, bass guitar, and drums. Depending on the situation, dynamics processors can be used to control a signal level that is varying dramatically, or to isolate just the loudest part of a signal while reducing or eliminating the quiet parts.

Some types of dynamics processors include:

- **Compressors**—The compressor is the most common type of dynamics processor. It is used to reduce the loudest part of an audio signal, resulting in a more predictable dynamic range. Once the loudest parts have been reigned in, it becomes possible to boost the entire signal without fear of clipping.

- **Limiters**—A limiter is essentially a compressor with a very high ratio setting (see the "Basic Dynamics Parameters" section below). As result, the incoming audio signal is completely "capped" at a specified level that prevents clipping. Limiters are an essential part of the music production workflow and are often used to make an overall mix seem louder.

- **De-Essers**—A de-esser is a compressor that operates at a specific frequency. Its primary use is to reduce excessive "s" sounds in a recording, a phenomenon known as *sibilance*. This type of processor can also be used to eliminate other undesirable high-frequency sounds such as the breath noise in a flute recording.

- **Expanders**—An expander is a dynamics processor that can be used to reduce the level of a signal when it falls below a certain level. Expanders work something like a compressor in reverse. A gentle amount of expansion can help to reduce some of the ambient noise that gets picked up in an audio recording.

- **Gates**—A gate (often called a "noise gate") is a type of expander that will completely silence a signal when it falls below a certain level. Gates are frequently used to eliminate the "bleed" that occurs when a microphone picks up signal from an "off-mike" sound source, such as a snare drum being picked up by a kick drum mike. Gates are also useful to eliminate background noise in a recording, such as the buzz of a guitar amp that can be heard in "silent" parts of the performance. The purpose of a gate is to clean up the sound of a recording by helping to isolate the desired parts of the audio signal and eliminate the unwanted parts.

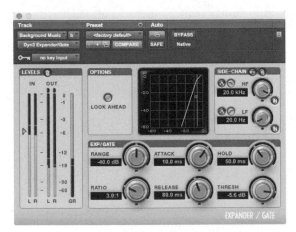

Figure 8.14 The Dyn3 Expander/Gate in Pro Tools|First

Basic Dynamics Parameters

Just like EQ processors, dynamic processors make use of a standard set of controls. These will vary somewhat based on the type of dynamics processor being used.

Common dynamics parameters include the following:

- **Threshold**—The threshold parameter sets the level that the input signal must reach in order to trigger the processor. Note that compressors and limiters are triggered when the signal exceeds the threshold, whereas expanders and gates are triggered when the signal drops below the threshold.

- **Ratio**—The ratio parameter determines the amount of signal reduction that occurs once the threshold has been reached. For example, when using a compressor with the ratio set to 2:1, the signal must exceed the threshold by 2 dB to result in an output increase of 1 dB. A limiter typically features a compression ratio of 100:1.

- **Knee**—The knee parameter determines how suddenly or gradually gain reduction is introduced in a compressor as the signal level approaches the threshold.

- **Gain**—The gain parameter is used to add a level increase (known as "makeup gain") to a signal that has been reduced in volume by a dynamics processor.

- **Attack/Release**—The attack parameter determines how quickly the dynamics processor will act once the audio signal has reached the threshold. The release parameter determines how quickly the dynamics processor will disengage once the threshold is no longer met.

Dynamics Plug-Ins in Pro Tools|First

Pro Tools|First offers three types of dynamics plug-ins: the Dyn3 Compressor/Limiter, the Dyn3 De-Esser, and Dyn3 Expander/Gate. The Dyn3 Compressor/Limiter is a transparent compressor that can also be used as a limiter by setting the ratio very high. The Dyn3 De-Esser makes it easy to eliminate sibilance from vocal tracks and spoken audio. The Dyn3 Expander/Gate can be used to gently reduce quiet sounds such as signal bleed or room noise, or to cut them out entirely.

Figure 8.15 The Dyn3 De-Esser in Pro Tools|First

Applying dynamics processing to tracks can seem confusing at first. But, just like when working with EQ, there are some common strategies to help you find the right settings.

Strategies for Using Compression

To add compression to a track in Pro Tools|First, you can add the Dyn3 Compressor/Limiter plug-in to an insert on the target track.

To use a Dyn3 Compressor/Limiter on a track:

1. Set the **KNEE** to about 10dB, the **ATTACK** to about 10ms, and the **RELEASE** to about 100ms.

2. Start off with a **RATIO** of about 3.0:1. (You may need a higher ratio if the track has a wide dynamic range.)

3. Reduce the **THRESHOLD** setting until you start seeing a small amount of compression registering in the gain reduction (GR) meter. A good starting point is to target around 3 to 6 dB of gain reduction.

(i) You can use the small yellow arrow to the left of the input gain meter to adjust the threshold while viewing the incoming signal level.

4. Adjust the **GAIN** control to increase the overall level of the track.

Make sure that you don't increase the gain so much that the plug-in's output begins clipping. If you're having trouble finding the perfect gain setting, you may need to increase the ratio or lower the threshold.

Strategies for Using a De-Esser

A de-esser is an essential tool when working with vocals. Even a great singer can have problems with sibilance in the studio. Fortunately, de-esser plug-ins have a small number of controls that you can easily learn to use effectively.

 For best results, insert the De-Esser after any compressor plug-ins on the track.

To use a Dyn3 De-Esser on a vocal track:

1. Enable the **HF ONLY** button to limit the effect to only the high frequencies.

2. Enable the plug-in's **LISTEN** button and play back a sibilant portion of the track.

 The Listen button lets you isolate the sibilance targeted by the Frequency control. This lets you hear the sibilant peaks that will be reduced by the plug-in.

3. Adjust the **FREQUENCY** control while listening carefully; try to zero in on just the harsh sibilant frequencies.

 Sibilant sounds typically occur in the 4 to 10 kHz range. Most singers will require de-essing in the 6 to 7 kHz range.

4. Once you've found the target frequency, stop playback and disable the **LISTEN** button.

5. Set the **RANGE** control to -0.0 dB and begin playback across the sibilant section again. Watch the gain reduction (GR) meter to help identify when de-essing is being applied.

6. Slowly lower the Range value, as needed, to set the level at which de-essing is triggered.

    *   While setting the Range, toggle the **BYPASS** control frequently to compare to the original vocal.

    *   Unsolo the track from time to time to hear how the de-essed vocal sounds in the overall mix. You don't want to go too far! A little de-essing goes a long way.

Reverb and Delay Effects

Reverb and delay effects are indispensable tools for creating a sense of space. Collectively known as "time-based effects," reverb and delay can be used to create a wide range of sounds. This range spans the gamut from providing tasteful spatialization of audio, to adding a subtle spaciousness to a track, to creating dramatic effects that completely alter the sound of a voice or instrument.

What Is Reverb?

Reverb effects are used to create the sound of a real or imaginary space. Reverb algorithms can be used to recreate the sound of small spaces (rooms, cars, phone booths) or large spaces (concert halls, parking garages). A number of types of reverbs are available in both hardware and software formats. Some use a series of delays (see "What Is Delay?" below) to create smooth, musical sounding results. Other reverbs use a technique called "convolution," which actually uses samples of real-world acoustic spaces to create incredible realism.

Figure 8.16 The D-Verb plug-in in Pro Tools | First

Reverb in Pro Tools|First

Pro Tools|First offers a basic reverb called D-Verb. D-Verb offers a simplified set of controls that are an excellent introduction into the world of reverb.

Controls in D-Verb include the following:

- **Gain**—D-Verb's gain slider can be used to adjust the signal level at the plug-in's input.

- **Algorithm**—The algorithm control at the top of the plug-in interface offers a number of options including Hall, Church, Plate, Room 1, Room 2, Ambient, and Non-Lin. These algorithms fundamentally change the nature of the reverb.

- **Size**—The size control is used to choose the Small, Medium, or Large variation of the currently selected algorithm.

- **Decay**—The decay control determines how long it will take for the reverb to "fade out" after a sound has been processed.

- **Pre-Delay**—The pre-delay control adjusts the amount of time that the reverb "waits" after receiving an input signal before it begins to create reverb.

- **Diffusion**—When set to a high value, the diffusion control will emphasize the initial build-up of echoes. Low values will reduce the initial build-up, which can result in better clarity.

- **HF Cut**—The high-frequency cut control can be used to reduce the decay time for high frequencies.

- **LP Filter**—Just like the LPF control on an EQ, this control can be used to eliminate content above the specified frequency.

- **Mix**—The Mix control can be used to adjust the wet/dry balance of the plug-in's output. (See "Wet Versus Dry Signals" below.)

Applications for Reverb Processors

There are many creative ways to use reverb in a project. Whether adding a subtle sense of space to a vocal or completely washing out a guitar to create an ambient bed, reverb can truly bring a track to life.

Suggestions and scenarios for reverb usage:

- Add some character to a snare track by inserting a room reverb directly on the track. Then adjust the wet/dry control to get the proper balance.

- Give a vocal track a vintage sound by using a medium plate reverb.

- Create a distant, washed-out guitar sound by using a large church reverb and setting the wet/dry control to 100% wet.

- Add a medium hall reverb in a send-and-return configuration to apply reverb to a number of tracks in a session including vocals, acoustic guitars, keyboards, and more. This can help "gel" the mix by putting all of the components into the same acoustic space.

What Is Delay?

Delay is the term that audio engineers use for a processor that creates an echo. Delay is a simple effect in concept, but over the years both hardware and software delays have evolved into extremely complex processors.

Delay plug-ins provide dozens of different approaches to delay, from digital models of vintage tape-style echos to modern granular pitch-shifted delays. And almost all modern delays have the ability to synchronize their individual echoes to the tempo of a song.

Figure 8.17 The Mod Delay III plug-in in Pro Tools | First

Delay in Pro Tools | First

Pro Tools | First offers a delay plug-in called Mod Delay III. Mod Delay III is a simple but powerful delay plug-in that can generate anything from single echoes to beat-synchronized ping-pong delays that bounce back and forth between the left and right channels. Mod Delay III includes a pitch modulator option that can be applied to the delayed signal.

Controls in Mod Delay III include the following:

- **Delay Time**—The large knob at the top is used to set the plug-in delay time, with a range from 0 ms to 5,000 ms (five seconds).

- **FBK**—The FBK (feedback) control determines how much of the plug-in's output will be "fed back" into the input. The feedback setting ultimately controls the number of echoes that will occur.

- **LPF**—Like on an EQ, the LPF (low-pass filter) control can be used to eliminate content above the specified frequency.

- **Sync**—When enabled, the Sync control will cause the delay time to follow the session tempo.

- **Meter**—The meter control can be used to manually set the time signature for the delay. (This control is disabled when Sync is enabled.)

- **Tempo**—The tempo control can be used to manually set the tempo for the delay in beats per minute. (This control is disabled when Sync is enabled.)

- **Duration**—The duration controls (note buttons) allow the user to set the delay time based on a note value that ranges from whole notes to 1/16 notes. These also include buttons to set triplet and dotted values.

■ **Groove**—The groove control can be used to adjust the delay slightly off the beat, making it possible to create a "swing" feel.

■ **Rate**—The rate control can be used to set a rate (speed) for pitch modulation, from 0 Hz to 20 Hz.

■ **Depth**—The depth control determines the amount of pitch modulation that will be applied to the delayed signal, in a range from 0% to 100%.

■ **Mix**—The Mix control can be used to adjust the wet/dry balance of the plug-in's output. (See "Wet Versus Dry Signals" below.)

Applications for Delay Processors

A little delay can help add excitement to your mix. This is a great way to propel a track forward and add rhythmic variety.

Suggestions and scenarios for delay usage:

■ Use an AudioSuite delay to quickly apply delay to just the last word of a vocal phrase.

  • Select the target word and a little extra time afterwards.

  • Open the AudioSuite Mod Delay III plug-in (**AUDIOSUITE > DELAY > MOD DELAY III**) and configure the parameters.

  • Audition the processing by clicking the **PREVIEW** button (speaker icon) in the lower left corner of the plug-in window and experiment with the wet/dry control to get the proper balance.

  • Then apply the AudioSuite plug-in by clicking the **RENDER** button.

■ Add some width to a mono acoustic guitar track by applying a mono-to-stereo delay plug-in with slightly different delay times for the left and right channels.

■ Apply a simple quarter-note delay in a send-and-return configuration to add sustain, rhythmic emphasis, and interest to a variety of track types including vocals and guitar solos.

■ Get an Edge-like guitar sound (U2) by running a simple guitar part into a dotted-eighth-note delay synced to the song's tempo. Set the feedback setting high enough to give at least 2 to 3 repeats of each note.

Wet Versus Dry Signals

When working with time-based effects such as reverb and delay, you will need to balance the original signal with the processed signal. Audio producers refer to the original signal as the "dry" signal and the reverberated or delayed signal as the "wet" signal. Let's take a look at some common ways to adjust the wet/dry balance.

Using Time-Based Effects as Inserts on Tracks

Although time-based effects are typically applied using a send-and-return configuration (see below), at times you may use a reverb or delay as an insert directly on the source track. For example, you may want to add reverb to a snare track to give it a unique sound, or you may want to create a swirling guitar wash, where the signal is 100% wet. In these scenarios, you can place the desired plug-in directly on the target track.

When applying a time-based effect directly to a track, the only way to adjust the wet/dry balance is to use the plug-in's controls. The location and labeling of these controls can vary from plug-in to plug-in. D-Verb and Mod Delay III use a slider control labeled "Mix."

Figure 8.18 D-Verb's wet/dry balance is adjusted using a slider in the Mix control area.

The Mix control can be adjusted from left to right to make the plug-in's output more wet or more dry. You can also type directly into the number field at the top of the control and manually enter a numerical value from 0% (completely dry) to 100% (completely wet). In addition, you can click on DRY or WET to instantly set the lowest or highest value.

 As a general rule, you'll want to set the plug-in to a relatively dry setting to emulate "natural" reverb or delay characteristics. Start with a low setting, such as 20% and adjust from there as needed.

Using Send-and-Return Configurations

Configuring your time-based effects using a send and return is typically preferable, for a variety of reasons. First, you'll often want to apply the same reverb settings to many tracks in your project, so using a single plug-in is much faster to set up and adjust.

Second, because time-based effects can use significant CPU power, using a send and return will save on CPU processing. You can create one instance of a reverb or delay on an Aux Input track and then use as many sends to the track as necessary to apply the effect for multiple tracks.

And third, each source track's direct output will remain completely dry, while the send level can be used to adjust the wet signal. This makes it quick and easy to modify the wet/dry balance for a whole bunch of tracks in your project without needing to change the settings of the plug-in itself.

Although advanced send-and-return configurations are beyond the scope of this book, you can configure a basic setup with a few simple steps. Use the techniques outlined below to get started with a reverb send.

 The same techniques can be used to create a delay send. Simply modify the name you apply to the Aux Input track and the plug-in you assign to the track.

To set up a reverb send across multiple tracks:

1. In the Mix window, select all of the tracks that you'd like to send to the reverb by clicking on their track nameplates.

2. Hold **OPTION+SHIFT** (Mac) or **ALT+SHIFT** (Windows) and click on an empty send on one of the selected tracks.

 The Option/Alt+Shift key combination provides Do-To-Selected functionality in all Pro Tools products. Any action you take on one track while holding these modifiers will apply to all selected tracks.

3. Select an available option from the list of busses. (For example, choose **BUS 1-2**.) A send to the selected bus will be created across all of the selected tracks.

To create the reverb return:

1. Select **TRACK > NEW**. The New Tracks dialog box will appear.

2. Configure the dialog box for a single stereo Aux Input track and click **CREATE** to create the new track.

3. Rename the new track to something meaningful, like **Reverb**.

4. Set the track's input to the same bus you used before (such as **BUS 1-2**) using the top selector in the **I/O** section.

5. Assign a **D-VERB** plug-in on one of the inserts on the Aux Input track.

To set the send levels:

1. For each of the tracks you used in step one, click on the send button to display the send window.

2. Bring up the send fader as needed to introduce reverb for that track.

Review/Discussion Questions

1. What are three ways that you can show/hide the inserts view in the Edit window? (See "Plug-In Basics" beginning on page 192.)

2. What are three ways that you can show/hide the inserts view in the Mix window? (See "Plug-In Basics" beginning on page 192.)

3. How can you insert a plug-in on a track? How can you remove an inserted plug-in? (See "Inserting Plug-Ins on Tracks" beginning on page 194.)

4. How can you move an insert from one track to another track? How can you duplicate an insert? (See "Moving and Duplicating Plug-Ins" beginning on page 195.)

5. Is it possible to change the insert location that you are viewing in the currently open plug-in window? How might you accomplish this? (See "Common Plug-In Controls" beginning on page 195.)

6. How can you change the track that you are viewing in the currently open plug-in window? (See "Common Plug-In Controls" beginning on page 195.)

7. What is the purpose of the next (+) and previous (–) buttons in the plug-in controls? (See "Common Plug-In Controls" beginning on page 195.)

8. Which keyboard modifier can you use to make fine adjustments on plug-in controls? (See "Adjusting Plug-In Parameters" beginning on page 197.)

9. Which keyboard modifier can you use to reset a plug-in control to its default value? (See "Adjusting Plug-In Parameters" beginning on page 197.)

10. In what ways can plug-in parameters be adjusted using the computer keyboard? (See "Adjusting Plug-In Parameters" beginning on page 197.)

11. What are the four common types of EQ bands? (See "Types of EQ" beginning on page 199.)

12. What two EQ plug-in options are included with Pro Tools|First? (See "EQ Plug-Ins in Pro Tools|First" beginning on page 200.)

13. What three types of dynamics plug-ins are found in Pro Tools|First? (See "Dynamics Plug-Ins in Pro Tools|First" beginning on page 204.)

14. What is the difference between reverb and delay? What category of effects do both of these processes belong to? (See "Reverb and Delay Effects" beginning on page 205.)

15. What are some scenarios in which you might place a time-based effect directly on a track? (See "Using Time-Based Effects as Inserts on Tracks" beginning on page 210.)

16. What are some advantages to using a send-and-return configuration for time-based effects? (See "Using Send-and-Return Configurations" beginning on page 210.)

Optimizing Tracks with Signal Processing

🎧 Activity

In this exercise, you will learn how to use plug-ins to optimize tracks in Pro Tools|First. You'll begin by looking at some practical applications for equalization (EQ). Then, you'll explore some options for controlling dynamics. Finally, you'll create a send-and-return configuration to apply reverb for multiple tracks.

🕐 Duration

This exercise should take approximately 20 minutes to complete.

⊕ Goals/Targets

- Use the EQ3 plug-in to cut bass frequencies and boost high frequencies

- Use the Dyn3 plug-in to reduce variations in peak volume levels

- Set up a send to an Aux Input track

- Apply reverb processing using the D-Verb plug-in

- Save your work for use in Exercise 9

Getting Started

To get started, you will open your completed project from Exercise 7. This will serve as the starting point for this exercise.

Open your existing Lights project:

1. Select **FILE > OPEN PROJECT** or press **COMMAND+O** (Mac) or **CTRL+O** (Windows). The Dashboard will open.

2. If necessary, click **OPEN** on the left side of the Dashboard.

3. Select your Lights-xxx project from the list of available projects.

4. Click **OPEN**. The project will open as it was when last saved. If needed, reopen the Mix window (**WINDOW > MIX**).

5. Open the Memory Locations window, if not already displayed (choose **WINDOW > MEMORY LOCATIONS**). Click on the listed locations in this window as you work, to jump to different song sections.

Applying EQ and Dynamics to Tracks

To get an idea of where EQ processing might be useful, you should take a moment to listen to the project in its current state. Pay particular attention to any areas where frequencies are clashing between multiple tracks. Also listen for tracks that could benefit from more controlled dynamics.

Evaluate the tracks:

1. Press the **SPACEBAR** to begin playback.

2. Listen for tracks that compete for space in the same frequency range, such as the Kick track and the Synth Bass track. Try to formulate some ideas about how to give each track its own space in the frequency spectrum.

3. Also, listen for tracks with dynamics that might cause problems. Listen for consistency in the volume of notes for tracks that should serve as a steady backbone, such as the bass guitar during the choruses.

4. Feel free to solo and mute tracks to isolate certain elements. And move the faders to see if you can find a good balance of tracks, or if certain tracks present unique problems.

   • Is it hard to separate certain tracks from one another without causing one to obscure the other in a given frequency range?

   • Is it hard to find a level for certain tracks that allows all of the notes to be heard without causing certain notes to get too loud?

Adding EQ Processing

When using EQ, you may find yourself wanting to boost frequencies to emphasize the best parts of a track. However, it is equally important to cut frequencies to create room for other tracks to be heard. In this section of the exercise, you will use EQ to reduce the bass frequencies in the Synth Bass track while slightly boosting the high frequencies in order to separate it from competing bass frequencies in the Kick track.

Insert an EQ plug-in on the Synth Bass track:

1. Locate the Inserts section on the Synth Bass track.

2. Click on the first insert position and select **Multichannel Plug-in > EQ > EQ3 7-Band (Stereo)**. The EQ3 plug-in interface will display.

Adjust the EQ settings:

1. Turn on the EQ bands that you expect to use. The default settings have all bands enabled except for the High- and Low-Pass Filters (**HPF** and **LPF**, respectively).

   - Enable the **HPF** band by clicking on the **IN** button for the band so that it becomes lit in blue.

Figure 8.19 Clicking on the IN button for the High-Pass Filter band (shown inactive)

2. Set the parameters for each EQ band:

   - **HPF:** set the Q to **24 dB/oct** (maximum) and the Frequency around **65.0 Hz**.

   - **LF:** set the Q to **1.00** (default), the Frequency to **200.0 Hz**, and the Gain to around **-3.0 dB**.

   - **MF:** set the Q to **1.25**, the Frequency to **800.0 Hz**, and the Gain to around **-2.0 dB**.

   - **HF:** set the Q to **0.50**, the Frequency to **5.00 kHz**, and the Gain to around **2.0 dB**.

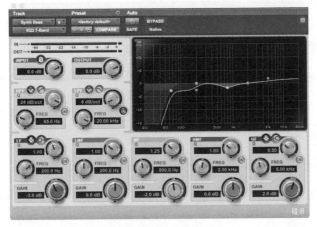

Figure 8.20 The EQ3 7-Band settings for the Synth Bass track

3. Close the EQ3 plug-in window when finished.

Adding Dynamics Processing

Next you'll apply dynamics processing to help control the signal levels. The **Bass Gtr** track has a slightly wider dynamic range than ideal, making it harder to position in the mix without constantly adjusting the volume fader. Here you will rein in the dynamic variation using a compressor.

 A great way to learn to use plug-ins such as EQ and Dynamics is to start from a relevant factory preset.

Insert a Compressor on the Bass Gtr track:

1. Locate the Inserts section on the **Bass Gtr** track.

2. Click on the first insert and select **MULTICHANNEL PLUG-IN > DYNAMICS > DYN3 COMPRESSOR/ LIMITER (STEREO)**. The Dyn3 Compressor/Limiter plug-in interface will display.

Use a factory preset to compress the Bass Gtr track:

1. From the Librarian menu (displaying <factory default>), choose the **Bass Guitar** preset.

Figure 8.21 The Dyn3 Compressor/Limiter settings for the Bass Guitar preset

2. Click on Marker 5 (chorus 1) in the Memory Location window to jump to the first chorus.

3. Play through the first chorus of the song and listen to the **Bass Gtr** track. The dynamic variation should be dramatically reduced.

4. Adjust the **GAIN** control on the Dyn3 Compressor/Limiter to find a good volume level for the track. (Try around **10.0 dB** as a starting point.)

5. Close the Dyn3 Compressor/Limiter plug-in window when finished.

Using a Send-And-Return Configuration for Reverb

In this section, you'll add some reverb to help smooth out the strings and make them sound more natural. You'll set up a send-and-return configuration that can be used by multiple tracks in the project.

Create a new Aux Input track:

1. Choose **TRACK > NEW** or press **COMMAND+SHIFT+N** (Mac) or **CTRL+SHIFT+N** (Windows). The New Tracks dialog box will appear.

2. Configure the settings for one new stereo Aux Input track.

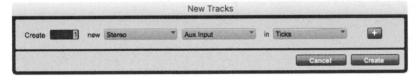

Figure 8.22 The New Tracks dialog box with the correct settings for a stereo Aux Input track

3. Click **CREATE** to create the track.

4. Double-click the track's nameplate and rename the track as Reverb.

5. If needed, drag the track to the right in the Mix window to position it adjacent to the Master Fader.

ⓘ Pro Tools operators often put effects returns just before the Master Fader to make them easy to locate in a session or project.

6. Locate the I/O section on the Reverb track.

7. Click on the track's Input Path selector and select **BUS > BUS 1-2 (STEREO)**.

Assign a reverb plug-in to the Aux Input track:

1. Locate the Inserts section on the Reverb track.

2. Click on the first insert and select **MULTICHANNEL PLUG-IN > REVERB > D-VERB (STEREO)**. The D-Verb plug-in interface will display.

3. From the Librarian menu (displaying <factory default>), choose the Large Hall preset.

4. Set the input gain on the left edge of the plug-in all the way up to -0.0 dB. (See Figure 8.23.)

5. Close the plug-in window when finished.

6. As a final step, **COMMAND-CLICK** (Mac) or **CTRL-CLICK** (Windows) on the Reverb track's Solo button to enable solo-safe mode. This will prevent the track from muting when a source track is soloed.

Figure 8.23 The D-Verb plug-in with the suggested settings

Send audio from Strings track to the Reverb track:

1.   Locate the Sends section on the **Strings** track.

2.   Click on the first send position and select **Bus > Bus 1-2 (Stereo)**. A send to Bus 1-2 will be created, and the associated Send window will display.

3.   Increase the level of the send to about **-3 dB**. You should now be able to hear the reverberated strings when you play the second chorus of the project. Close the send window when finished.

Figure 8.24 The send controls for the reverb send on the Strings track

Finishing Up

To complete this exercise, you will need to save your work and close the project. You will be reusing this project in Exercise 9, so it's important to save and retain the work you've done.

Before you wrap up, you can also listen to the project to hear the processing changes you've made.

Finish your work:

1. Choose **FILE > SAVE** to save the project.

2. Press **RETURN** (Mac) or **ENTER** (Windows) to position the Edit cursor at the beginning of the project.

3. (Optional) Press the **SPACEBAR** to begin playback and listen through the project. Press the **SPACEBAR** a second time when finished to stop playback.

4. Choose **FILE > CLOSE PROJECT** to close the project and return to the Dashboard. If you are notified that tracks with changes have not been uploaded to the cloud, simply click **CLOSE** or **SAVE** to proceed.

(i)   **You do not need to upload track changes unless you are using the Cloud Collaboration features in Pro Tools|First.**

That completes this exercise.

Chapter 9

Finishing a Project

...What You Need to Do to Create a Stereo Mixdown...

This chapter introduces you to the processes of adding automation and creating a stereo mixdown of your Pro Tools|First project. We cover the five automation modes in Pro Tools|First, what their differences are, and how to use them. We also cover a variety of editing techniques that you can use to create or fine-tune the automation on your tracks. We then cover uses for limiters and dither plug-ins on the master bus before wrapping up with a discussion on exporting your mix as a stereo file.

◈ Learning Targets for This Chapter

- Understand what settings will and will not be recalled with a project

- Learn how to select the appropriate automation mode for a desired result

- Learn how to write automation changes in Touch and Latch mode

- Understand how to display and edit automation graphs

- Add appropriate processing to a Master Fader

- Use the Export command to create a stereo mix of a project

After you have finished balancing your tracks, adding processing to the tracks, and adding any desired effects for the mix, it's time to start thinking about finishing up the project and creating a stereo mixdown. As you put the finishing touches on your mix, you can use automation to create and save dynamic changes. Then you can export your mix as a stereo file, configuring the file parameters as needed.

Recalling a Saved Mix

When you open a project that you've previously worked on, all of the Pro Tools|First mixer settings are recalled with the file, including the following:

- **Track layouts and views**—The track order, track heights, and zoom settings that were in place when the project was last saved will all be recalled.

- **Mix attributes, settings, and automation**—The settings for volume faders and pan controls will be recalled for each track, along with any automation you previously created.

- **Track and send routing**—Any routing you've used for submixes, effects sends, and similar configurations will be recalled, along with the send levels and send pan settings.

- **Plug-in assignments**—Plug-in assignments and parameter settings will be recalled for each track.

Occasionally, however, conditions may exist that will prevent a project from recalling exactly as it was when last saved. These conditions can include the following:

- **External effects processors**—As discussed in Chapter 7, if you've used external gear for your mix, you will need to reconnect the gear and reconfigure all the hardware settings whenever you return to the project.

- **Unavailable plug-ins**—If you open the project from a system that does not have the same plug-ins installed as the system where you created the project, any unavailable plug-ins in the project will gray out on screen and will not provide processing.

- **Unavailable media**—Any audio or MIDI data that was added to the project while working offline (without an Internet connection) will be missing when opening the project from a different system.

- **Non-uploaded changes**—Any changes that have not been transferred to the cloud will not be represented when opening the project from a different system.

(i) All project changes are saved in a local cache whenever you use the Save command. The local cache ensures that saved updates will be available to the local system in the future, regardless of whether they are stored in the cloud.

Changes will not be included in the cloud project if your local system does not have an active Internet connection when you save. Changes that are not stored in the cloud will not be available to other systems. Audio may also be unavailable if the audio files do not finish transferring to the cloud when the project is closed.

Using Automation

On a simple project, you may be able to set the volume faders, pan controls, and other parameters on tracks to a static position and leave them unchanged from the start of the mix to the end. But often a mix will require dynamic changes during the course of playback. This is where track automation can be useful.

Pro Tools | First allows you to record changes you make during playback as automation on your tracks. Automatable parameters include track volume, pan, and mute controls; send controls; and plug-in controls.

Selecting an Automation Mode

Pro Tools | First provides five automation modes. The currently active automation mode on each track determines how automation will function for the track. You can set the automation mode for each track independently, using the track's Automation Mode selector.

Figure 9.1 Automation Mode selector in the Mix window

The automation modes available in Pro Tools | First include the following:

- **Off mode**—This mode turns off automation altogether. Pro Tools | First ignores any existing automation on the track, and you cannot write new automation. Use this mode when you want a track to play back without following automation you've previously written for the track.

- **Read mode** (default)—This mode plays back existing automation on the track but will not write any new automation. Use this mode when you want a track to play back automation you have previously recorded for the track, but you do not want to record new changes as automation.

- **Write mode**—This mode writes automation for all parameters whenever the transport is rolling. Use this mode if you want to write real-time automation on a track and lock in the volume, pan, send, and plug-in settings.

- **Latch mode**—This mode writes automation only on parameters that you change during the automation pass. Use this mode to write automation selectively for some track settings without locking in other settings.

- **Touch mode**—This mode writes automation only on parameters that you change, and only while you are actively modifying those parameters. Use this mode to change certain track settings only in specific areas of the track.

To select an automation mode, do the following:

1. Click on the Automation Mode selector in the Mix or Edit window.

2. Select the desired mode from the pop-up menu.

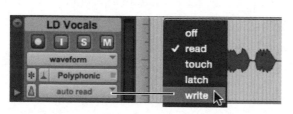 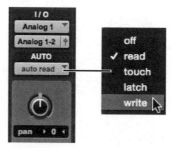

Figure 9.2 Selecting an automation mode: Edit window (left) and Mix window (right)

Writing Real-Time Automation

When writing real-time automation, you will commonly use Latch mode for basic settings on your initial automation passes. This can be useful when writing automation across long sections.

 By way of example, you might use Latch mode to automate changes for different sections of a song, such as to increase the level of the lead vocals during the choruses and return to a lower level during the verses.

To automate basic settings, do the following:

1. Put the target track(s) into Latch mode.

2. Begin playback. Automation will not be writing at this point.

3.   When you reach the location where you need to make a change, adjust the volume, pan, or other settings on the target track(s). The changes will begin writing as new automation and will continue until you make the next change.

4.   Continue playback through the project, adjusting the settings during each section as needed.

5.   Return the track(s) to Read mode when finished (for playback purposes).

With your initial track settings and automation in place, you can use Touch mode to refine the mix in specific areas. This can be useful to touch up existing automation or to make dynamic changes that affect only small areas of the project.

 By way of example, you can use Touch mode to increase the send levels for reverb or delay at the ends of certain vocal lines, while automatically returning to previous levels in between the changes.

To add or modify automation in specific areas, do the following:

1.   Put the target track(s) into Touch mode.

2.   Begin playback. Automation will not be writing at this point.

3.   When you reach the location where you need to make a change, adjust the volume, pan, or other settings on the target track(s). New automation will be written and will continue while you hold the control in place.

4.   Release the control to return the parameter to its previous setting.

5.   Continue playback through the project, making additional changes in selected areas as needed.

6.   Return the track(s) to Read mode when finished (for playback purposes).

Viewing Automation Graphs

Each automatable parameter on a track has an associated automation graph. The automation graph can be displayed in the Edit window, allowing you to see a visual representation of the automation changes.

To display an automation graph, do the following:

1.   Display the Edit window, if not already showing, by choosing **WINDOW > EDIT** or by pressing **COMMAND+=** (Mac) or **CTRL+=** (Windows).

2.   Click on the **TRACK VIEW SELECTOR** at the head of the track in the Edit window. (See Figure 9.3.)

Figure 9.3 Clicking the Track View selector in the Edit window

3. Select the type of automation that you want to display from the pop-up menu. The automation graph will be displayed as a black line, superimposed on the track.

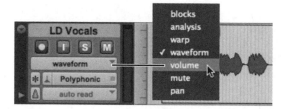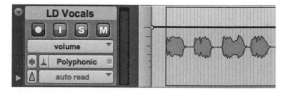

Figure 9.4 Selecting the Volume automation view (left); the Volume automation graph displayed (right)

As an alternative, you can display an automation graph beneath a track using the **SHOW/HIDE AUTOMATION LANES** button (triangle) at the head of a track. On Audio tracks the Volume automation lane will appear by default. Additional automation lanes can be displayed by clicking on the plus sign (**+**) within the displayed lane.

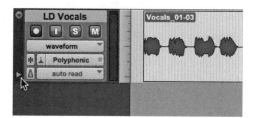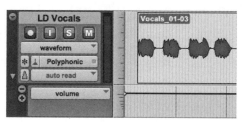

Figure 9.5 Clicking the Show/Hide Automation Lanes button (left); Volume automation lane displayed (right)

Editing Automation Breakpoints

With an automation graph displayed, you can edit the automation using breakpoint–editing techniques. Breakpoints are points on the automation graph where the automation line changes slope or direction.

Using the Grabber Tool for Automation

You can edit the automation graph by adding, moving, or deleting breakpoints using the Grabber tool. To edit automation with the Grabber tool, do any of the following:

- Click on the automation graph line to add a breakpoint.

- Click and drag an existing breakpoint to adjust its position.

■   **OPTION-CLICK** (Mac) or **ALT-CLICK** (Windows) on an existing breakpoint to remove it.

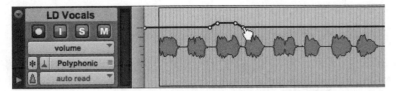

Figure 9.6 Editing the Volume playlist using the Grabber tool

Automation playlists can also be edited using other Edit tools, such as the Pencil tool.

Using the Pencil Tool for Automation

The Pencil tool can be useful for drawing automation changes on an automation graph. The Pencil tool's different drawing modes can be used to create a variety of automation shapes.

To draw a freehand automation shape, do the following:

1.   Click and hold the **PENCIL** tool icon; in the Pencil tool pop-up menu, verify that the **FREE HAND PENCIL** mode is active.

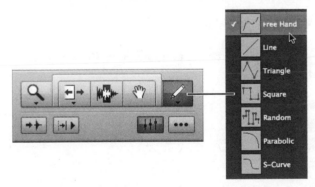

Figure 9.7 Selecting the Free Hand Pencil tool

2.   Click and drag on an automation graph to draw a new shape or automation curve.

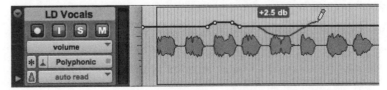

Figure 9.8 Drawing freeform automation with the Pencil tool

A series of new automation breakpoints will be created, matching the shape you draw.

To draw a smooth ramp, do the following:

1. Click and hold the **PENCIL** tool icon and choose the **LINE PENCIL** from the pop-up menu.

2. Click and drag on an automation graph to draw a new line segment.

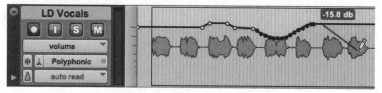

Figure 9.9 Drawing a line segment with the Pencil tool

3. Release the mouse at the point where you want the ramp to end.

To create automation ramps that alternate between opposite settings, you can use the Triangle mode of the Pencil tool. When used on a Pan graph, for example, the Triangle Pencil mode lets you draw panning changes that sweep back and forth from left to right.

The Triangle Pencil tool uses the current Grid setting as the basis for its modulation rate.

To use the Pencil tool to create a sweeping pan effect, do the following:

1. Set the Grid value to the increment that you want to use for the pan rate. This should generally be set to a quarter note value or larger for smooth panning.

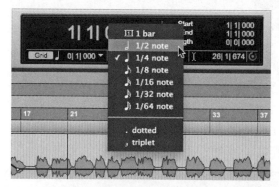

Figure 9.10 Selecting a Grid value for pan sweeps

2. Click on the **TRACK VIEW SELECTOR** at the head of the track in the Edit window and select **PAN** from the pop-up menu.

3. Click and hold the **PENCIL** tool icon and choose the **TRIANGLE PENCIL** from the pop-up menu.

4. Click and drag on the pan automation graph, dragging both horizontally and vertically. The vertical starting position and vertical distance that you drag determines the pan position and variation.

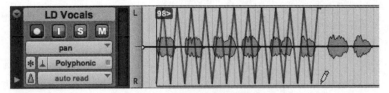

Figure 9.11 Drawing an alternating pan sweep

 Any Pencil tool mode can be used for drawing automation except for the Parabolic or S-Curve modes.

Creating a Mixdown

Mixing down is the process of recording the output from multiple tracks to a stereo file. This process is also commonly referred to as *bouncing* the project. Mixing down is often the last phase of audio production, although you can create a bounce at any time to create a complete mix as a stereo file.

Adding Processing on the Master Fader

Prior to creating a final mix, you may want to consider using some final dynamics processing on the entire mix to optimize your output levels. You can also add a dither plug-in to preserve the low-level dynamics in your mix during a bit-depth reduction.

Adding a Limiter to Optimize Output Levels

As discussed in Chapter 8, a limiter is a dynamics processor that caps the audio signal at a specified level. A limiter can be used on the Master Fader to protect against clipping. Using a limiter can also help make the overall mix seem louder. Here, we will use the Dyn3 processor to function as a brickwall limiter.

 Commercial versions of Pro Tools include the Maxim plug-in for this purpose. Maxim is an ultra-maximizer plug-in and has a similar effect to the brickwall limiter function described here.

To use a limiter on your mix in Pro Tools | First, do the following:

1. Add a stereo Master Fader to the project, if you don't already have one.

2. Click on an insert position (such as Insert A) and select **MULTICHANNEL PLUG-IN > DYNAMICS > DYN3 COMPRESSOR/LIMITER (STEREO)**. (See Figure 9.12.)

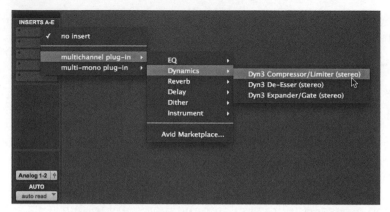

Figure 9.12 Selecting a limiter plug-in for the Master Fader track

The Dyn3 Compressor/Limiter plug-in window will open.

3. Rotate the **RATIO** control fully clockwise to set the ratio at 100:1.

4. Play through the project, taking note of the peak readings displayed on the **IN** meter.

5. Adjust the **THRESHOLD** control to a few dB above the peak meter readings for the project. For example, if your project is showing peak readings around -6 dB, try setting the Threshold at **-3.5 dB** or so. This will prevent the signal from exceeding -3.5 dB during any instantaneous peaks.

6. Set the **ATTACK** and **RELEASE** to their minimum values (**10.0 µs** and **5.0 ms**, respectively) to provide a quick response for the momentary peaks you are targeting with this type of limiter.

7. Adjust the **GAIN** control to add make up gain to the signal. Set this value slightly less than the amount of reduction provided by the Threshold setting. If your Threshold is set to **-3.5 dB**, for example, you might set the Gain to **3.0 dB**. This will increase the overall loudness of the mix while keeping the peak levels a half dB below clipping.

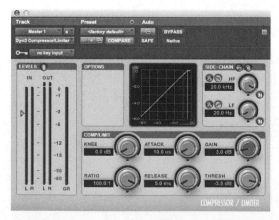

Figure 9.13 The Dyn3 Compressor/Limiter with the Ratio, Threshold, and Gain control set

Creating a CD-Ready Mix

To create a CD-ready mixdown from Pro Tools | First, you will need to perform a bit-depth reduction: your mixdown file will need to use 16-bit audio in order to be burned onto a CD, whereas Pro Tools | First uses 32-bit floating point audio files by default.

 The Red Book audio CD standard requires audio files that are encoded with a sample rate of 44.1 kHz and a word length of 16 bits.

As discussed in Chapter 3, lower bit-depth audio also exhibits a reduced dynamic range. To help preserve the dynamic range when reducing bit depth, you can add *dither* to your project. Dither is a form of randomized noise used to minimize signal loss when audio is near the low end of its dynamic range, such as during a quiet passage or fade-out.

Adding Dither to a Mix

Proper use of dithering allows you to squeeze better subjective performance out of 16-bit audio.

The most common application of dithering is on a Master Fader, as the last processor in the signal path. To create a mix for CD, you would add the dither plug-in as an insert to optimize the final 16-bit output.

 If you will be keeping your mixed file at 24-bit or 32-bit floating-point resolution, you should NOT use dither. Doing so will needlessly add noise to the mix.

To add dither to the Master Fader, do the following:

1. Click on an insert position below any other processors on the Master Fader (such as Insert B) and select MULTICHANNEL PLUG-IN > DITHER > POW-r DITHER (STEREO).

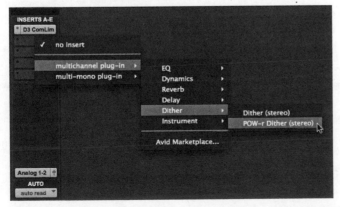

Figure 9.14 Selecting the POW-r Dither plug-in for the Master Fader track

The POW-r Dither plug-in window will open.

(i)   **The dither plug-in should be the last processor on your Master Fader track.**

2.   Choose the type of noise shaping to use for your mix.

Figure 9.15 Selecting Noise Shaping Type 2 in the POW-r Dither plug-in

---

POW-r Dither Noise Shaping Options

Noise shaping is a method of improving the signal-to-noise ratio of dither. POW-r Dither noise shaping improves audio performance and reduces the perceptible noise in the dither by shifting it into a less audible range.

Type 1: Features the flattest frequency spectrum, designed for less-stereophonic material with a fairly narrow dynamic range; recommended for solo instrument recordings and spoken-word recordings.

Type 2: Features psychoacoustically-optimized noise-shaping over a wide frequency range; recommended for material with moderate stereophonic complexity including rock and pop music.

Type 3: Features psychoacoustically-optimized noise-shaping designed for full-spectrum, wide-stereo field material; recommended for material with a broad dynamic range, such as classical and orchestral music; can also be effective for rock and pop music.

Considerations for Bouncing Audio

When exporting a mix from Pro Tools|First, the bounced file will capture all audible information in your mix just as you hear it during playback.

The following principles apply to the mixdown file:

- **The file will include only audible tracks.** What you hear during playback is exactly what will be included in the mix. Any tracks that are muted will not be included. Similarly, if any tracks are soloed, they will be the *only* tracks included.

- **The file will be a rendered version of your project.** Inserts, sends, and external effects will be applied permanently. Listen closely to your entire project prior to exporting the mix to ensure that everything sounds as it should. Pay close attention to levels, being sure to avoid clipping.

- **The file will be created based on the Timeline selection.** If you have an active selection when you export your mix, the mix file will last for the length of the selection only. If you do not have a selection, Pro Tools|First will create a bounce from the start of the project to the end of the longest track.

Exporting an Audio Mix

When you are ready to create your mixdown in Pro Tools|First, you can use the **EXPORT > AUDIO MIX** command from the **FILE** menu. This provides a fast and easy way to create a bounce to a stereo file, requiring little to no setup.

 The Export > Audio Mix command in Pro Tools|First is the equivalent of the Bounce > To Disk command in commercial versions of Pro Tools.

Selecting Export Options

The Export Audio Mix command combines the outputs of all currently audible tracks to create a new audio file on your hard drive. You can select options for the exported file using the Export Audio Mix dialog box.

To bounce all currently audible tracks and select the export options, do the following:

1. Verify that the project plays back as desired. (Check levels, processing, and mute/solo states for tracks).

2. Choose **FILE > EXPORT > AUDIO MIX**. The Export Audio Mix dialog box will appear.

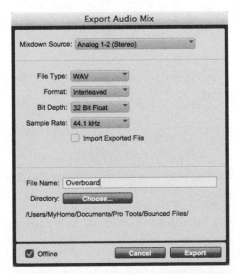

Figure 9.16 The Export Audio Mix dialog box

3.   Verify the path used in the **MIXDOWN SOURCE** drop-down list. This option will default to the main stereo outputs.

4.   Choose the desired file type for your bounce file from the **FILE TYPE** pop-up menu: WAV or AIFF.

5.   Choose the file format for your stereo bounce from the **FORMAT** pop-up menu.

   • **Interleaved**—Creates a single file containing both channels of a stereo mix. Interleaved files are compatible with most online services and music applications, including SoundCloud and iTunes.

   • **Multiple Mono**—Creates two separate mono files for a stereo mix: one for the left channel and another for the right channel. This file format is required by certain media applications.

   • **Mono (Summed)**—Creates a single audio file as a summed mono mix of the bus path. Use this option if you need to create a composite mix of mono tracks. All pan information will be disregarded.

6.   Choose the desired bit depth for the bounced file(s) from the **BIT DEPTH** pop-up menu.

   • Choose **16 Bit** if you plan to burn your bounce to CD without further processing.

   • Choose **24 Bit** when you want to create a final mix that will be mastered separately.

   • Choose **32 Bit Float** for high-resolution files that will undergo further processing or editing.

7.   Choose the desired sample rate for the bounce files from the **SAMPLE RATE** pop-up menu. Higher sampling rates will provide better audio fidelity but will also increase the size of the resulting file(s).

(i)   If you plan to burn your bounced audio directly to CD without further processing, choose 44.1 kHz as the sample rate for the bounce.

8.   If desired, enable the **IMPORT EXPORTED FILE** checkbox. This option will import the bounced file as a new track in your project.

(i)   The Import Exported File option is available only if the target sample rate for the bounce file matches the sample rate of your session.

9.   Optionally specify a different file name and location for your bounced file(s) using **FILE NAME** field and the Directory: **CHOOSE** button.

   By default, the bounced file will be named after the session and placed in the **BOUNCED FILES** folder inside the **DOCUMENTS > PRO TOOLS** folder for your user account.

10.   For a faster-than-real-time bounce (default), leave the **OFFLINE** checkbox enabled. Alternatively, you can disable this option to bounce in real time, while listening to the mix.

11.   After confirming your settings, click the **EXPORT** button.

Monitoring Bounce Progress

When performing an offline bounce, Pro Tools processes the bounce without audio playback. A progress window will appear, displaying the Timeline processed amount, the total Timeline duration, and the bounce speed as a multiple of the real-time duration.

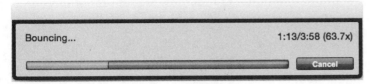

Figure 9.17 The offline bounce progress window

If you perform a real-time bounce instead, a countdown window will appear, displaying the time remaining for your bounce to complete.

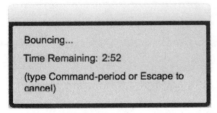

Figure 9.18 The real-time bounce countdown window

Locating the Exported File

After the bounce completes, you can retrieve your mix file from within the **BOUNCED FILES** folder in your local project cache (or another location you selected in the **EXPORT AUDIO MIX** dialog box).

To locate your bounced mix, do the following:

1. Using the Application Switcher, the Dock, the taskbar, or the Start menu, switch from Pro Tools | First to the Finder (Mac) or File Explorer (Windows).

 The Application Switcher lets you toggle through open applications by pressing COMMAND+TAB on a Mac or ALT+TAB on Windows.

2. Navigate to the Bounced Files folder in your Pro Tools folder:

    On the Mac:

    *   Choose **GO > DOCUMENTS** to open the Documents folder for your user account.
    *   Double-click on the Pro Tools folder to open it; then double-click on the Bounced Files folder.

On Windows:

- Press the **START** key (or **WINDOWS** key) and begin typing "Bounced Files." The **Bounced Files** folder will appear in the search results.

- Click on the displayed result to open the **Bounced Files** folder.

Your bounced mix file will be included in the **Bounced Files** folder, along with any other mixes you've bounced from Pro Tools | First.

Review/Discussion Questions

1. What are some mix attributes that are recalled with a project in Pro Tools|First? What are some items that may not be recalled? (See "Recalling a Saved Mix" beginning on page 224.)

2. How many automation modes are available in Pro Tools|First? What is the difference between Off mode and Read mode? (See "Selecting an Automation Mode" beginning on page 225.)

3. Which automation mode is useful for writing automation to selected parameters across long sections of your mix? Which mode is useful for touching up automation and making changes that affect only small areas? (See "Writing Real-Time Automation" beginning on page 226.)

4. What is the purpose of displaying an automation graph? What does an automation graph look like? (See "Viewing Automation Graphs" beginning on page 227.)

5. What are some ways of editing an automation graph with the Grabber tool? (See "Using the Grabber Tool for Automation" beginning on page 228.)

6. What Pencil tool option can you use to create a pan effect that sweeps back and forth from left to right? How can you control the speed (or rate) of the pan effect? (See "Using the Pencil Tool for Automation" beginning on page 229.)

7. What is meant by the term *mixing down*? What other term is commonly used to describe this process? (See "Creating a Mixdown" beginning on page 231.)

8. What process can you use to optimize the output levels for your mix? What plug-in can you use in Pro Tools|First for this purpose? (See "Adding a Limiter to Optimize Output Levels" beginning on page 231.)

9. What is the purpose of adding dither to the Master Fader? When would you not want to use dither? (See "Adding Dither to a Mix" beginning on page 233.)

10. What are some things to consider when preparing to create a bounce of your mix? How will the bounce be affected by soloed or muted tracks? (See "Considerations for Bouncing Audio" beginning on page 234.)

11. What sample rate and bit depth should you use when exporting a mix for use on an audio CD? (See "Selecting Export Options" beginning on page 235.)

12. Where will your exported file be located after completing the Export > Audio Mix command? (See "Locating the Exported File" beginning on page 237.)

Preparing the Final Mix

🎧 Activity

In this exercise, you will perform the steps necessary to create a final mix for your project in Pro Tools|First. You'll begin by adding processing to the Master Fader to optimize levels and prepare for exporting the mix. Then, you'll create a fadeout at the end of the song using real-time automation.

🕐 Duration

This exercise should take approximately 20 minutes to complete.

⊕ Goals/Targets

- Add a limiter to the Master Fader
- Add dither to the Master Fader
- Work with Latch automation
- Save your work for use in Exercise 10

Getting Started

To get started, you will open your completed project from Exercise 8. This will serve as the starting point for this exercise.

Open your existing Lights project:

1. Select **FILE > OPEN PROJECT** or press **COMMAND+O** (Mac) or **CTRL+O** (Windows). The Dashboard will open.

2. If necessary, click **OPEN** on the left side of the Dashboard.

3. Select your Lights-xxx project from the list of available projects.

4. Click **OPEN**. The project will open as it was when last saved. If needed, reopen the Mix window (**WINDOW > MIX**).

5. Choose **WINDOW > MEMORY LOCATIONS** to open the Memory Locations window, if not already displayed. You'll use this window for navigating through the song sections as you work.

Adding Processing to the Master Fader

In this section of the exercise, you will add some processing to the Master Fader track. First, you'll add a limiter to the track to optimize the output levels. Then you'll add dither to preserve the best possible sound quality when outputting the mix at 16-bit resolution.

Add a limiter to the Master Fader track:

1. Click on the first insert on the Stereo Mix track (Master Fader) and select **MULTICHANNEL PLUG-IN > DYNAMICS > DYN3 COMPRESSOR/LIMITER (STEREO)**. The plug-in window will display.

2. Adjust the Dyn3 Compressor/Limiter settings as follows:

   • Knee: 0.0 dB

   • Attack: 10.0 μs (minimum setting)

   • Gain: 3.0 dB

   • Ratio: 100:1 (maximum setting)

   • Release: 5.0 ms (minimum setting)

   • Threshold: -6.0 dB

Figure 9.19 The Dyn3 Compressor/Limiter with the suggested settings

3. Press the **SPACEBAR** to begin playback.

4. Click on Marker 4 (**verse 1b**) in the Memory Locations window to jump to that section of the song.

5. Watch the Gain Reduction meter (**GR**) to see where the limiter is being activated. Allow playback to continue through the first half of the verse.

6. Reset the **Stereo Mix** track to its default level by **OPTION-CLICKING** (Mac) or **ALT-CLICKING** (Windows) on the volume fader. You should now see more gain reduction occurring in the plug-in but no clip indication happening on the track's meters.

7. Continue monitoring playback through the first chorus to observe the results during the loudest sections and verify that the mix is not clipping.

8. Close the plug-in window and stop playback when finished.

Add dither to the Master Fader track:

1. Click on the last insert on the Master Fader track and select **MULTICHANNEL PLUG-IN > DITHER > POW-R DITHER (STEREO).**

2. Set the destination bit depth to **16 BIT.**

3. Set the Noise Shaping to **NOISE SHAPING TYPE 2**. This setting is ideal for rock and pop mixes.

Figure 9.20 The POW-r Dither plug-in with the suggested settings

Writing Automation

The music for this song has a sudden and unnatural cutoff at the end. You can address the problem by adding a final fadeout at the end of the song. Here, you'll use Latch automation mode to write a fadeout in real time using the volume fader on the Master Fader track.

Enable automation on the Master Fader track:

1. Click on Marker 9 (**outro**) in the Memory Locations window to jump to that section of the song.

2. Click on the Automation Mode selector for the **Stereo Mix** track and choose **LATCH** automation mode. (See Figure 9.21.)

Figure 9.21 Enabling Latch mode on the Master Fader track

3. Choose **WINDOW > TRANSPORT** to display the Transport window, if not already shown.

Automate a fadeout on the Master Fader track:

1. Press the **SPACEBAR** to begin playback.

2. Click on the volume fader for the **Stereo Mix** track and slowly move the fader all the way down to minus infinity (-∞). You'll have about 10 to 15 seconds to complete the fadeout.

3. Keep an eye on the Counters in the Transport window during your fadeout. Be sure to complete the fadeout before you reach Bar 101. Once you have faded all the way down, you can release the fader and it will stay in position.

4. Stop playback once automation has been written a few bars past the end of the song.

5. Press the **SPACEBAR** to listen to the fadeout and verify the automation.

6. If you're not satisfied with the result, try another pass of writing the automation. It frequently takes several attempts to get the timing of a fadeout just right!

7. Once you're happy with the fadeout, set the automation mode on the **Stereo Mix** track back to **READ** mode.

View the volume automation on the Master Fader track:

1. Choose **WINDOW > EDIT** or press **COMMAND+=** (Mac) or **CTRL+=** (Windows) to display the Edit window and make it active.

2. If needed, scroll the **Stereo Mix** track into view. The automation graph will show the results of the fadeout you wrote for the track.

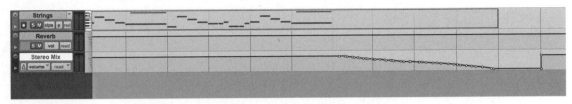

Figure 9.22 The volume automation graph on the Master Fader track showing the final fadeout

Finishing Up

To complete this exercise, you will need to save your work and close the project. You will be reusing this project in Exercise 10, so it's important to save and retain the work you've done.

Finish your work:

1. Press **RETURN** (Mac) or **ENTER** (Windows) to position the Edit cursor at the beginning of the project.

2. Choose **FILE > SAVE** to save the project.

3. Choose **FILE > CLOSE PROJECT** to close the project and return to the Dashboard. If you are notified that tracks with changes have not been uploaded to the cloud, simply click **CLOSE** or **SAVE** to proceed.

That completes this exercise.

Chapter 10

Beyond the Basics

...*What to Explore to Become a Power User*...

In this chapter, we take a brief look at various advanced features in Pro Tools|First. We begin with a quick overview of using Elastic Audio to manipulate the rhythmic attributes of audio clips. Then we explore some fundamental MIDI editing techniques that can be used to create and modify MIDI data. Next we discuss how you can simplify project management with submixing. The chapter concludes with a sample of some keyboard shortcuts that you can use to dramatically accelerate your editing workflow.

◈ Learning Targets for This Chapter

- Understand the basics of Elastic Audio

- Explore fundamental MIDI editing techniques

- Gain familiarity with submixing techniques

- Learn essential keyboard shortcuts

For those who are new to the world of DAWs, or simply new to Pro Tools, the information required to produce a finished project can seem a bit overwhelming. Learning the fundamentals should obviously be the first goal, so that you'll have a strong foundation. But it's also helpful to learn some advanced features so you'll be able to work quickly and effectively.

The goal of this chapter is to present some key features in Pro Tools|First that you can get started using right away. Many of the topics we touch on here are easily deep enough to warrant an entire chapter in an advanced course. However, here we address just the basic functionality so that you'll be able to put these features to use quickly. Once you've gained a bit of experience with Pro Tools, you can come back to these topics at a later date and learn them comprehensively.

Elastic Audio

Elastic Audio is the name of the Pro Tools feature that allows you to manipulate the timing of audio. Elastic Audio is enabled for all Audio tracks in Pro Tools|First by default. You can remove or change the Elastic Audio processing on individual tracks in your project at any time.

With Elastic Audio enabled, you have a number of options available to alter the timing of your tracks (commonly called *warping* the audio).

Enabling Elastic Audio

Elastic Audio is enabled on an Audio track using an Elastic Audio processor, assigned from the **ELASTIC AUDIO PLUG-IN** selector at the head of the track in the Edit window. Pro Tools provides five types of Elastic Audio processors. Each type of processor is optimized for a specific kind of audio content.

 In Pro Tools|First, the Polyphonic Elastic Audio processor is used on all Audio tracks by default. But you can change the active Elastic Audio processor as needed for optimal results.

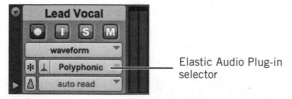

Elastic Audio Plug-in selector

Figure 10.1 The Elastic Audio plug-in selector in the Edit window

 Unlike other plug-ins used in Pro Tools|First, Elastic Audio plug-ins are assigned in the Edit window. These are not available as inserts in the Mix window.

The available Elastic Audio processors include the following:

- **Polyphonic**—This is an all-purpose algorithm that works well on complex material. (Enabled on all Audio tracks in Pro Tools|First by default.)

- **Rhythmic**—This processor is the best choice for material that includes drums or other percussive elements.

- **Monophonic**—This processor is ideally suited to monophonic material such as vocals or bass guitar.

- **Varispeed**—This processor links time and pitch changes to create tape speed effects.

- **X-Form** (Rendered Only) —This is an extremely high-quality algorithm. Due to its complexity, X-Form cannot be run in real-time and must be rendered instead.

(i) **Rendered processing writes the results to new files on disk. This process must be completed prior to being able to play back any changes.**

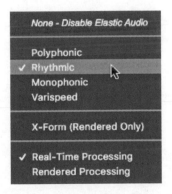

Figure 10.2 The Elastic Audio plug-in options in Pro Tools|First

Warping Audio

Once you've enabled Elastic Audio on a track, you can begin to manipulate the timing of the audio on that track. Pro Tools|First provides a number of options for warping with Elastic Audio.

Warping Audio Using Quantization

The fastest way to tighten the rhythm of an audio performance is to use standard Pro Tools quantize features. This uses the same dialog box that is commonly used to alter MIDI performances. The Quantize dialog box can be used to warp audio data as long as it resides on an Elastic Audio–enabled track.

What Is Quantization?

Quantization is the process of aligning musical events to an underlying rhythmic pattern. Quantization is commonly used to clean up the timing of MIDI performances by moving individual MIDI notes closer to the Bars|Beats grid. This results in more precise timing and a tighter rhythmic feel.

Extreme quantization can make a performance sound "mechanical," which can be desirable for certain genres of music such as EDM. For a more "human" feel, you can apply a more subtle amount of quantization and include a degree of randomization, swing, or other characteristics.

To quantize audio using the Quantize dialog box:

1. Verify that Elastic Audio is enabled on the target track.

2. Select the audio clip or clips that you would like to quantize.

3. Do one of the following to open the Quantize dialog box:

   • Select **EVENT > EVENT OPERATIONS > QUANTIZE**.

   • Press **OPTION+0** [zero] (Mac) or **ALT+0** [zero] (Windows).

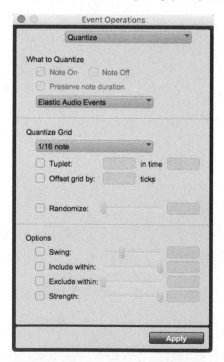

Figure 10.3 The Quantize dialog box

4. In the What to Quantize section of the dialog box, select ELASTIC AUDIO EVENTS from the pop-up menu, if it is not already active.

5. Configure the Quantize Grid settings as desired. (Typically, the default 1/16 note grid is a good choice.)

 You can use a larger setting, such as 1/8 note, for material that doesn't include 1/16 note timing, or to focus only on the main beats/sub-beats without "correcting" the timing of smaller sub-divisions of the beat.

6. Click APPLY. The transient peaks in the audio waveforms will be quantized based on the settings you have specified.

Warping Audio Using the Edit Tools

If you need to change the timing of your tracks without quantizing to a grid, you have the option of manually warping the audio using the regular Edit tools that you already know. Pro Tools provides a number of ways to manually warp audio on Elastic Audio enabled tracks. The most common method uses a technique called range warping.

 Other Elastic Audio editing techniques include Telescoping Warp and Accordion Warp. Please refer to the "Working with Elastic Audio" chapter of the Pro Tools 110 course book to learn more.

 Elastic Audio topics are also covered extensively in the Pro Tools 12 Essential Training: 110 course on Lynda.com.

To use range warp to change the timing of audio:

1. Verify that the Edit mode is set to Slip or Grid, depending on your needs. Typically you'll want to use Slip mode for performing small changes, or Grid mode for conforming audio to the beat.

2. Click on the Track View selector and set the track view to WARP. You will see all of the Event markers that Pro Tools|First created for the audio (vertical gray lines).

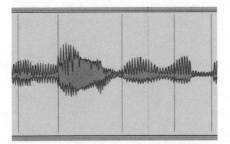

Figure 10.4 Warp view with Event markers visible

Pro Tools' Elastic Audio function adds Event markers automatically at all transient locations and other significant rhythmic events within a clip.

3. Use the **ZOOMER** tool to zoom in on the section that you're planning to edit.

4. Switch to the **GRABBER** tool.

5. If no Event Marker exists at the location that you'd like to warp, create one by **CONTROL-CLICKING** (Mac) or **START-CLICKING** (Windows) at the desired location.

6. **SHIFT-CLICK** on the Event marker to prepare to range warp. The Event marker will automatically be converted to a Warp marker, as will the Event markers immediately to the left and right. This will protect the audio on either side of the section you will be warping.

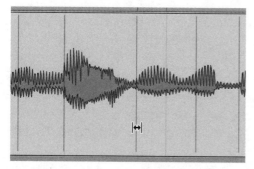

Figure 10.5 The Range Warp cursor that appears when the Shift modifier is held

  Warp markers anchor the audio at a given point on the timeline. Warp markers are recognizable in Warp view by a blue triangle at their base and their solid black color.

7. Now you can use the **GRABBER** tool to reposition the Warp marker in the center to adjust the timing of the underlying audio event relative to the events on either side.

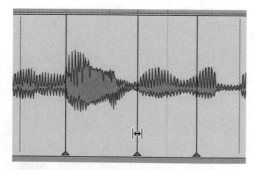

Figure 10.6 Warp view after the Event markers have been converted to Warp markers

If the entire clip is selected, you will not be able to move the individual markers. Click somewhere off the clip to deselect the clip before warping the audio.

Automatically Warping Audio with Tempo Changes

With any of the Elastic Audio plug-ins enabled on an Audio track, the track will automatically follow tempo changes in the project, as long as the track is using tick-based timing. Tracks using sample-based timing will not follow tempo changes. All tracks in Pro Tools | First use tick-based timing by default.

The track timebase can be changed at any time using the Timebase selector on the track. The Timebase selector will display a green metronome icon when the track is using tick-based timing and a blue clock icon when using sample-based timing.

 ——— Track Timebase selector

Figure 10.7 The Timebase selector on an Audio track

 Commercial versions of Pro Tools software use sample-based timing on all tracks except MIDI and Instrument tracks.

 If you have Elastic Audio–enabled tracks that you do not want to respond to tempo changes, you can set the timebase of those tracks to sample-based. Sample-based tracks are not affected by tempo changes created in the project.

MIDI Editing Techniques

MIDI editing is another topic worthy of its own chapter (or several chapters). But as with Elastic Audio, a little knowledge is all you need to get started. Understanding the fundamentals of MIDI editing is absolutely essential in the modern studio. Whether your goal is to add a few MIDI instruments to a song or to compose a virtual orchestral masterpiece, you'll need to know how to edit MIDI data quickly and accurately.

MIDI Track Views

The three primary track views that you'll use with MIDI-capable tracks are Clips view, Notes view, and Velocity view. You can select from these view options for any MIDI or Instrument track using the Track View selector at the head of the track in the Edit window. (See Figure 10.8.)

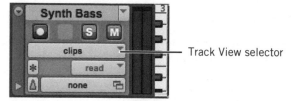

Track View selector

Figure 10.8 Track View selector on an Instrument track

Clips View

On MIDI-capable tracks, Clips view is used to edit and arrange MIDI clips. In this view, you can perform the same basic editing techniques that you use in Waveform view on an Audio track:

- Cut, Copy, Paste, and Clear selections or clips

- Duplicate and Repeat selections or clips

- Trim clips

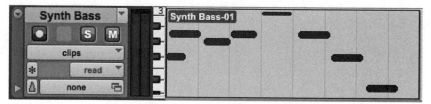

Figure 10.9 Clips view on an Instrument track

Duplicate and Repeat Commands

The Duplicate and Repeat commands provide ways to quickly create multiple instances of a clip or selection. Duplicate is the best option when you only need to make one or two copies. If you need to make multiple copies, it can be faster to use the Repeat command instead.

To use the Duplicate command, select a clip or a portion of a track. Then choose **EDIT > DUPLICATE** or press **COMMAND+D** on the Mac (**CTRL+D** on Windows). To use the Repeat command instead, choose **EDIT > REPEAT** or press **OPTION+R** on the Mac (**ALT+R** on Windows).

Notes View

Notes view is where you'll do most of your work on MIDI-capable tracks. You can perform a wide range of tasks using this view, including the following:

- Adding and deleting notes

- Selecting notes

- Transposing notes (changing a note's pitch)

- Moving notes (changing a note's timing)

- Trimming the note start and end (changing a note's duration)

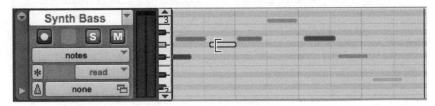

Figure 10.10 Trimming a MIDI note using Notes view on an Instrument track

Velocity View

Velocity view can be used to edit the velocity data associated with individual MIDI notes. A note's velocity is a measurement of how hard the note has been "struck." This characteristic can substantially change the sound of a virtual instrument.

Velocity values are displayed using vertical indicators known as *velocity stalks*. You can edit velocity values by raising or lowering velocity stalks in Velocity view. This can be done in any of the following ways:

- Adjusting the velocity of single notes with the Grabber tool

- Scaling velocity values of multiple selected notes up or down with the Grabber tool

- Scaling velocity values up or down for an entire clip with the Trim tool

- Drawing gradual changes in velocity (crescendo/decrescendo) with the Pencil tool

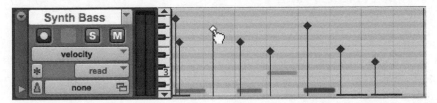

Figure 10.11 Adjusting the velocity value of a note in Velocity view on an Instrument track

Editing MIDI Data

Pro Tools|First offers the same powerful MIDI editing toolset that you'll find in commercial versions of Pro Tools. These tools can be used to create and edit MIDI performances, regardless of whether or not you own a MIDI controller such as a keyboard.

Let's take a closer look at some options for creating and working with MIDI data in Pro Tools|First.

The Smart Pencil Tool

While it is possible to use other tools to edit MIDI data, one of the best and most powerful options is to use the Pencil tool. The Pencil is essentially a Smart Tool for editing MIDI because it can perform edit functions that would typically require a number of different tools. These edit functions include creating, deleting, moving, transposing, and trimming MIDI notes.

Creating MIDI Notes

Manually entering MIDI note data may seem like a slow method of creating a performance, compared to playing the performance on a MIDI controller. But in fact, many music producers prefer to manually enter note data for certain types of tracks (such as drums, percussion, and bass). With a little practice, you can manually create MIDI note data very quickly and accurately.

To manually create a MIDI note:

1. In the Edit window, set the Edit mode to **GRID**, and set the Main timescale to **BARS|BEATS**.

2. Set the Grid value to the desired rhythmic interval. (A 1/16-note interval is commonly used when programming drums and musical instruments.)

3. Create or locate an Instrument or MIDI track.

4. Change the track display to **NOTES** view.

   (i) While in Clips view, clicking anywhere in a track's playlist with the Pencil tool will automatically change the track to Notes view.

5. Set the Pencil tool to **FREE HAND** mode.

6. Click and hold with the Pencil at the location (in both pitch and time) where you would like to enter a note. You can adjust the note's pitch and duration by dragging up/down and forward/backward until you release the mouse button. (See Figure 10.13.)

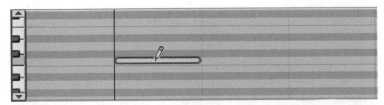

Figure 10.12 Manually entering a MIDI note with the Pencil tool

To manually create a sequence of MIDI notes at the same pitch:

1.   Follow steps 1-4 above.

2.   Set the Pencil tool to **LINE** mode.

3.   Click and hold with the Pencil at the location where you would like the sequence of notes to begin. Do not release the mouse button.

4.   While still holding the mouse button, drag the Pencil to the right or left to create a string of notes at the same pitch.

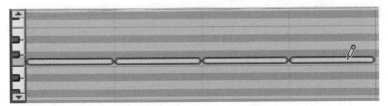

Figure 10.13 Manually entering a sequence of MIDI notes at the same pitch

5.   Once you have created the desired number of notes, release the mouse button.

Selecting MIDI Notes

Another essential part of working with MIDI data involves selecting notes. Understanding how to quickly select single notes and groups of notes is critical to the MIDI editing workflow. You can use the following techniques to select notes on a MIDI or Instrument track in Notes view.

To select an individual note, do one of the following:

■   Using the Grabber tool, click anywhere on a note.

■   Using the Pencil tool, click in the center of a note. (The Pencil tool becomes a Note Grabber when positioned over the center of a MIDI note.)

To select groups of notes, do one of the following:

■   Using the Pencil tool or Grabber tool, shift-click on each of the desired notes.

- Using the Grabber tool, click in an empty space on the playlist and draw a rectangle around the desired notes.

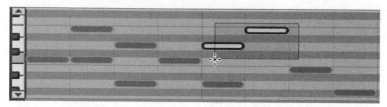

Figure 10.14 Selecting a group of MIDI notes with the Grabber tool

- Using the Selector tool, click on the playlist and drag to the left or right to select all notes within the selected time range on the playlist.

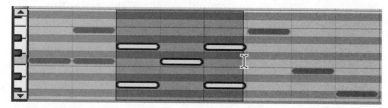

Figure 10.15 Selecting a group of notes with the Selector tool

Editing MIDI Notes

With basic note creation and selection techniques in hand, a whole range of MIDI editing functions are available to you. Let's look at some essential MIDI editing techniques that you'll need to know.

Deleting MIDI Notes

To delete an individual note, do one of the following:

- Using the Pencil tool, **OPTION-CLICK** (Mac) or **ALT-CLICK** (Windows) on a note.

- Using the Grabber or Pencil tool, **DOUBLE-CLICK** on a note.

To delete a group of notes:

- Select the notes and press **DELETE** (Mac) or **BACKSPACE** (Windows).

Moving MIDI Notes

To move a note to a new location, do one of the following:

- Using the Grabber tool, click on the note and drag left or right.

- Using the Pencil tool, click on the middle of the note and drag left or right.

To move a group of notes to a new location, do the following:

1. Select the target notes.

2. Using the Grabber or Pencil tool, drag any one of the notes left or right. All of the selected notes will move together.

(i) **When working in Grid mode, hold Command (Mac) or Ctrl (Windows) to temporarily suspend the grid.**

Transposing MIDI Notes

To change a note's pitch, do one of the following:

■   Using the Grabber tool, click on the note and drag up or down.

■   Using the Pencil tool, click on the middle of the note and drag up or down.

To change the pitch of a group of notes, do the following:

1. Select the target notes.

2. Using the Grabber or Pencil tool, drag one of the notes up or down. All of the selected notes will transpose together.

(i) **When moving or transposing notes, you can hold Option (Mac) or Alt (Windows) to copy the notes. This is a quick way to create harmonies or chords for melodic instruments.**

Trimming MIDI Notes

To trim a note, do the following:

1. Using the Trim tool or the Pencil tool, position the cursor near the beginning or end of the note.

2. Click and drag left or right to trim the note start or end point.

To trim a group of notes, do the following:

1. Select the target notes.

2. Using the Trim tool or the Pencil tool, position the cursor near the beginning or end of any one of the selected notes.

3. Click and drag left or right to trim the start or end point of all of the selected notes.

Working with Velocity

Most modern MIDI controllers are "velocity sensitive," meaning that they automatically detect how hard a key or pad is struck. The velocity data is transmitted and recorded as a characteristic of the MIDI note. However, when notes are manually entered (with the Pencil tool, for example), they will all share a default velocity value. This can lead to very stiff, robotic–sounding performances. Modifying and manipulating velocity data is essential to creating great sounding MIDI parts.

We've already covered how to edit velocity using Velocity view. Another, often simpler option is to use the velocity lane below a MIDI or Instrument track.

To display the velocity lane beneath a MIDI-capable track:

■ Click on the Show/Hide automation lanes control (triangle at the head of the track).

   The Velocity lane will display beneath the main track playlist.

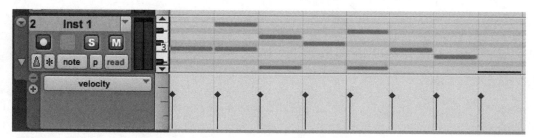

Figure 10.16 The Velocity lane displayed below an Instrument track

To edit MIDI velocity data for a single note:

■ Use the Grabber or Pencil tool to click and drag the diamond at the top of a velocity stalk.

To edit MIDI velocity data for a group of notes:

1. Select the group of notes.

2. Use the Grabber or Pencil tool to click and drag the diamond at the top of one of the velocity stalks. The velocity of all of the selected notes will be adjusted together.

Real-Time Properties

During the music production process, you'll frequently want to make adjustments to MIDI data. One available option is to use the Event Operations dialog box to transpose, quantize, and otherwise fine-tune your MIDI performances (EVENT > EVENT OPERATIONS > EVENT OPERATIONS WINDOW). This dialog box gives you many choices and extensive control over the changes you apply to MIDI data.

However, when you're right in the middle the creative flow and you want to perform a simple quantize operation, it's not always convenient to stop and look at a complex dialog box. In these instances, you'll want to take advantage of the Real-Time Properties view in Pro Tools|First.

Figure 10.17 The Real-Time Properties view on an Instrument track

The Real-Time Properties view can be used to quickly apply the following modifications to the clips on a MIDI-capable track:

- **Quantization:** Select a quantize grid value and swing amount.

- **Duration:** Shorten or lengthen notes or set them equal to a specific length.

- **Delay:** Adjust the timing of notes to start earlier or later.

- **Velocity:** Scale the velocity of notes up or down or change the range of velocities by percentage.

- **Transpose:** Transpose notes up or down by a specified number of octaves and/or semitones.

A powerful advantage of using Real-Time Properties over the Event Operations dialog box is that you can quickly toggle each of the properties on and off at any time. And you can modify the settings at any time without having to undo a previous change, as you typically do with Event Operations.

To enable or disable a real-time property:

- Click the button with the abbreviated name of the property. The button will display in green when enabled and will be grey when disabled.

Once enabled, the available parameter controls for the property will appear. You can use these controls to quickly adjust the parameter settings. Once a value has been changed from its default, all of the clips on the track will show a small "T" in the upper right corner. (See the example in Figure 10.18 above.)

 For more information on MIDI Real-Time Properties, see the chapter on "Editing and Fine-Tuning a Performance" in the Pro Tools 110 course book.

MIDI Real-Time Properties are also covered extensively in the Pro Tools 12 Essential Training: 110 course on Lynda.com.

Using the MIDI Editor

If you're looking for a more powerful view for editing MIDI data, you'll definitely want to check out the MIDI Editor in Pro Tools | First. The MIDI Editor is a dedicated panel for viewing and editing MIDI data across a single track or multiple tracks.

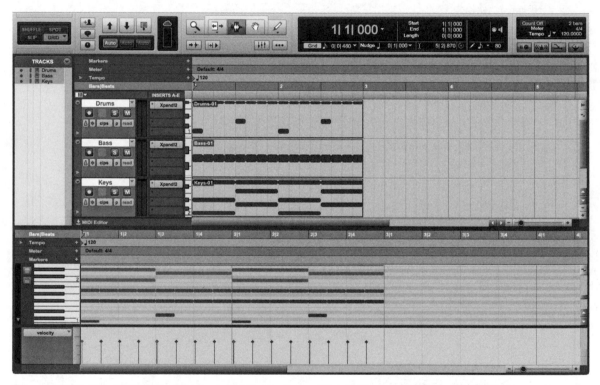

Figure 10.18 The MIDI Editor displayed at the bottom of the Edit window in Pro Tools | First

Opening the MIDI Editor

Pro Tools | First provides several ways to open the MIDI Editor.

To open the MIDI Editor, do one of the following:

■ Click the MIDI Editor show/hide control at bottom left of the Edit window. (See Figure 10.20.)

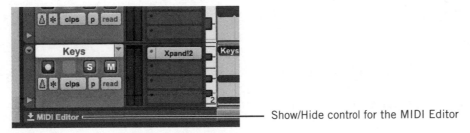

Show/Hide control for the MIDI Editor

Figure 10.19 Control for showing and hiding the MIDI Editor at the bottom of the Edit window

- Choose **VIEW** > **MIDI EDITOR**.

- Press **CONTROL+=** (Mac) or **START+=** (Windows).

Focusing Tracks in the MIDI Editor

Once the MIDI Editor is visible, there are a number of ways to focus one or more tracks.

To focus a single track in the MIDI Editor, do one of the following:

- Using the Grabber tool, **DOUBLE-CLICK** on a MIDI clip on the track.

- Right-click on a MIDI clip on the track and choose **OPEN IN MIDI EDITOR**.

- Right-click on the track nameplate (or the track name in the Track List) and choose **OPEN IN MIDI EDITOR**.

To focus multiple tracks in the MIDI editor, do one of the following:

- Shift-click on the track nameplates with the MIDI Editor open.

- Select one or more MIDI clips on each track's playlist with the MIDI Editor open.

Displaying Controller and Automation Data

The MIDI Editor offers a single automation lane that can be used to edit continuous control and automation data. This lane displays at the bottom of the MIDI Editor by default.

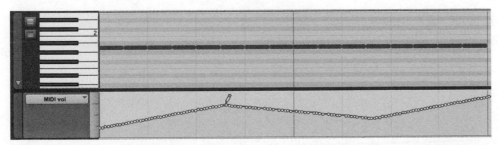

Figure 10.20 Editing MIDI volume data using the automation lane in the MIDI Editor

To show/hide the automation lane:

■ Click the Show/Hide automation lanes control at the bottom left of the MIDI Editor.

To change the parameter that is currently visible in the automation control lane:

■ Click on the Lane view selector and select the parameter that you wish to display.

The MIDI Editor available in Pro Tools|First is known in commercial versions of Pro Tools as the Docked MIDI Editor. Commercial versions also provide full-sized MIDI Editor windows with additional functionality.

Submixing

Submixing is a technique whereby multiple tracks are summed to a common destination track (typically an Aux Input) to simplify certain mixing tasks. While submixing is most useful in sessions with a large number of tracks, there are advantages to using submixes in smaller projects as well.

Simplifying a Mix

Submixing is frequently used to help simplify the mixing process. By submixing a group of related tracks, you can more easily apply effects across the whole group. You can also automate the summed levels of the group using a single fader.

Submixing is an essential technique for managing drum recordings, which typically span across a number of tracks. By routing the drums to a common Aux Input, you can apply compression or limiting to the group (for example) using a single plug-in. Then, you can quickly set the level for the entire drum kit using a single fader, while maintaining the relative levels of the individual tracks, as set by their own faders.

But submixing isn't just for drums. It's always a great way to manage any related group of tracks such as background vocals, guitars, and keyboards.

To create a submix, follow these steps:

1. If necessary, create a new Aux Input track.

2. Click on the Input selector of the Aux Input track and select an unused bus (such as **Bus 1-2**).

3. Select all of the tracks that you wish to include in the submix.

4. Hold **OPTION+SHIFT** (Mac) or **ALT+SHIFT** (Windows) and click on the Output selector for any one of the selected tracks.

5. Choose the same bus that you selected in step two above. You should now be able to hear all of the submixed tracks passing through the Aux Input during playback.

Figure 10.21 A drum submix with the source tracks (blue) routed to an Aux Input track (green).

6. As a final step, **COMMAND-CLICK** (Mac) or **CTRL-CLICK** (Windows) on the Aux Input's Solo button to enable solo-safe mode. This will prevent the Aux from muting when other tracks are soloed.

Once you've routed the source tracks to the submix destination, you can easily insert plug-ins on the Aux Input to have them apply to the submix. You can also adjust the volume and panning on the Aux Input to modify the submix level and position in the larger mix.

Creating Stems

Another important use for submixes is to aid in the creation of *stems*. Stems are mixed-down versions of your submixes that can be useful when mixing or remixing a project in a different DAW. Stems can also be used to supplement a live performance.

Once you've routed all of your tracks to submixes, it is very easy to create stems in Pro Tools|First.

 Commercial versions of Pro Tools allow users to create stems for all of their submixes in a single pass. This is not possible in Pro Tools|First.

To create stems from submixed tracks, do the following:

1. Make a selection that spans the section of the song that you would like to export as stems. This might be the entire song, or it might be one section of the song like a verse or chorus.

2. Locate the first submix track that you would like to export as a stem.

3. Select all of the tracks feeding the submix, along with the submix Aux Input track.

4. Hold **OPTION+SHIFT** (Mac) or **ALT+SHIFT** (Windows) and click the **SOLO** button on one of the tracks. All of the tracks in the submix will solo.

5. Play the session for a bit to verify that no other tracks are currently audible.

(i)   If your submix tracks include sends to a reverb or delay, make sure that the reverb or delay Aux Input is also soloed.

6. If you are using any plug-ins (such as a limiter) on the Master Fader track, bypass or remove them.

(i)   In general, when you move submix tracks to another DAW, you will want to reapply master bus processing in the destination DAW for maximum control. If this will not be the case, consider keeping the processing in place on the Master Fader in Pro Tools|First during stem creation.

7. Choose **FILE > EXPORT > AUDIO MIX** or press **OPTION+COMMAND+B** (Mac) or **CTRL+ALT+B** (Windows). The Export Audio Mix dialog box will appear.

8. Choose the desired settings from the Export Audio Mix dialog, and then click Export. The submix will be exported as an audio file.

9. Repeat the process for each of the submixes in your project.

When you are finished, you will have an audio stem file for each of the submixes. These files can then be aligned in another Pro Tools project, or in a different DAW. Using these stems, you should be able to recreate the original mix with no more than a few small tweaks.

Keyboard Shortcuts

In closing, we'll cover some keyboard shortcuts that will dramatically accelerate your work in Pro Tools|First. Learning even a handful of essential shortcuts can elevate your status from prospect to pro user in no time.

Function Keys

The following tables show uses for the Function keys in Pro Tools and Pro Tools|First. These are the keys labeled **F1** through **F12** at the top of a standard alpha-numeric keyboard.

Edit Modes

Key	Function
F1	Shuffle mode
F2	Slip mode
F3	Spot mode
F4	Grid mode

Edit Tools

Key	Function
F5	Zoomer tool
F6	Trim tool
F7	Selector tool
F8	Grabber tool
F10	Pencil tool

Commands Keyboard Focus Keys

The following tables show uses for Commands Keyboard Focus keys in Pro Tools and Pro Tools|First. These are single-key shortcuts that activate commands in Pro Tools|First when pressed.

 Commercial versions of Pro Tools have multiple keyboard focus modes. To use the shortcuts listed here, Commands Keyboard Focus mode must be active.

Zoom Functions

Key	Function
E	Zoom Toggle
R	Zoom Out
T	Zoom In

Trim Functions

Key	Function
A	Trim Clip Start to the Cursor Location
S	Trim Clip End to the Cursor Location

Fade Functions

Key	Function
D	Fade In to the Cursor Location
F	Apply a Crossfade
G	Fade Out from the Cursor Location

Edit Functions

Key	Function
Z	Undo
X	Cut
C	Copy
V	Paste
B	Separate Clip at the Cursor Location

Track Commands

The following table shows keyboard shortcuts that can be used on tracks that contain the Edit cursor (or an Edit selection) in Pro Tools | First.

Key	Function
SHIFT+R	Record Enable the Track
SHIFT+S	Solo the Track
SHIFT+M	Mute the Track

Review/Discussion Questions

1. What type(s) of tracks use Elastic Audio in Pro Tools|First? (See "Elastic Audio" beginning on page 248.)

2. Which Elastic Audio processor uses all-purpose algorithm that works best on complex material? (See "Elastic Audio" beginning on page 248.)

3. Which processor is the best for vocal tracks? (See "Elastic Audio" beginning on page 248.)

4. Is it possible to use quantization on an Elastic Audio-enabled track? (See "Warping Audio" beginning on page 249.)

5. How can you quickly create a Range Warp on an Elastic Audio-enabled track? (See "Warping Audio" beginning on page 249.)

6. Which track views are commonly used to edit MIDI data? (See "MIDI Track Views" beginning on page 254.)

7. Which tool is the most efficient for creating and editing MIDI data? (See "Creating MIDI Notes" beginning on page 256.)

8. How can new MIDI notes be manually created on a track? (See "Creating MIDI Notes" beginning on page 256.)

9. What are some common techniques for editing MIDI notes? (See "Editing MIDI Notes" beginning on page 258.)

10. What is MIDI velocity? What are some ways that velocity data can be viewed and edited in Pro Tools|First? (See "Working with Velocity" beginning on page 260.)

11. Which properties can be modified using the Real-Time Properties view? (See "Real-Time Properties" beginning on page 260.)

12. Is it possible to view MIDI data from multiple tracks simultaneously using the MIDI Editor? (See "Using the MIDI Editor" beginning on page 262.)

13. What parts of the music production process can be simplified using submixes? (See "Submixing" beginning on page 264.)

14. Why is it helpful to create stems when exporting your Pro Tools | First project to be imported into a different DAW? (See "Creating Stems" beginning on page 265.)

Finalizing a Project

🎧 Activity

In this exercise, you will perform the final steps necessary to finish a project in Pro Tools|First. You'll begin by creating a drums submix. Then, you'll duplicate and transpose the **Strings** track to achieve a bigger string sound. Finally, you'll export your mix to a stereo audio file.

🕐 Duration

This exercise should take approximately 20 minutes to complete.

✪ Goals/Targets

- Submix multiple tracks to a stereo Aux Input track

- Duplicate an Instrument track to create a variation on an existing MIDI performance

- Use MIDI Real-Time Properties to transpose MIDI data to a different octave

- Export the final mix as a stereo file

Getting Started

To get started, you will open your completed project from Exercise 9. This will serve as the starting point for this exercise.

Open your existing Lights project:

1. Select **FILE > OPEN PROJECT** or press **COMMAND+O** (Mac) or **CTRL+O** (Windows). The Dashboard will display.

2. If necessary, click **OPEN** on the left side of the Dashboard.

3. Select your Lights-xxx project from the list of available projects.

4. Click OPEN. The project will open as it was when last saved. If needed, reopen the Mix window (WINDOW > MIX).

5. Choose WINDOW > MEMORY LOCATIONS to open the Memory Locations window, if not already displayed. You'll use this window for navigating through the song sections as you work.

Creating a Drum Submix

You'll begin by creating a submix of all the drum tracks by routing them to a single Aux Input track. You will then be able to use the Aux Input track to set the volume for the drums as a whole without having to adjust the faders on all of the individual tracks.

Create a new Aux Input track:

1. Choose TRACK > NEW or press COMMAND+SHIFT+N (Mac) or CTRL+SHIFT+N (Windows). The New Tracks dialog box will appear

2. Configure the settings for a new stereo Aux Input track.

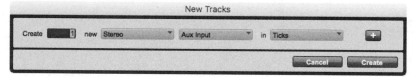

Figure 10.22 The New Tracks dialog box with the correct settings for the Aux Input track

3. Click CREATE. A new Aux Input track will be added to the project.

4. Rename the new Aux Input track Drum Submix.

Route the drums to the submix track using a bus:

1. Locate the I/O section on the Drum Submix track.

2. Set the track's input to BUS 3-4 (STEREO).

3. Hold COMMAND (Mac) or CTRL (Windows) and click on each of your drum tracks (Kick, Snare, Hi Hat, and Claps) to select them all.

4. Hold OPTION+SHIFT (Mac) or ALT+SHIFT (Windows) and click on the Output Path selector on the Kick track.

5. Select BUS 3-4 (STEREO) from the Output Path selector. The same output will be assigned across all of your selected drum tracks. (See Figure 10.23.)

Figure 10.23 The drum tracks submixed into the Drum Submix track using Bus 3-4

You can now take a moment to adjust the level of the drums relative to other tracks in the mix using the volume fader on the Drum Submix track. Try pushing the Drum Submix up a few dB to see how it changes the mix.

Adding a Second Strings Track

The Strings track is sounding pretty good, but you may find that it sounds a little thin. In this section, you will help the strings sound more like a real orchestra by adding a second track and transposing that track down an octave.

Duplicate the Strings track:

1. Click on the nameplate of the Strings track and verify that it is the only track selected.

2. Do one of the following to duplicate the track:

   - Select TRACK > DUPLICATE.

   - Right-click on the track name and choose DUPLICATE.

   - Press OPTION+SHIFT+D (Mac) or ALT+SHIFT+D (Windows).

3. The Duplicate Tracks dialog box will appear. Enable all of the options in the dialog box, as shown in Figure 10.24 below.

Figure 10.24 The proper settings to duplicate the Strings track and all of its settings

4. Click **OK** to create the duplicate track.

5. Rename the new track **Strings Low** and rename the original track **Strings Hi**.

6. Pan the **Strings Low** track to the right a bit by setting the left pan control to center (0). This will be a nice complement to the panning you did in Exercise 7 on the **Strings Hi** track.

In the next series of step, you'll transpose the duplicated notes to double the strings an octave lower.

Transpose the Strings Low track using Real-Time Properties:

1. Press **COMMAND+=** (Mac) or **CTRL+=** (Windows) to toggle to the Edit window.

2. Do one of the following to display the Real-Time Properties view:

    *   Select **VIEW > EDIT WINDOW VIEWS > REAL-TIME PROPERTIES**.

    *   Click on the **EDIT WINDOW VIEW SELECTOR** and enable the Real-Time Properties view.

3. In the Real-Time Properties view on the **Strings Low** track, click the **TRN** button to enable transposition.

4. Enter **-1** into the **OCT** field. This will transpose the MIDI part on the **Strings Low** track down by one octave.

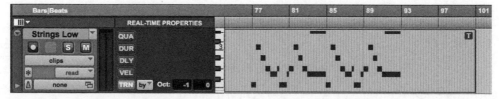

Figure 10.25 The Strings Low track with the suggested Real-Time Properties transposition

Exporting an Audio Mix

In this section of the exercise, you will export the final audio mix of your project. Exporting a mix is a necessary step whenever you want to burn a song to CD, post it to a music-sharing site like SoundCloud, or sell it on services like iTunes or Band Camp. For this project, you'll create a 16-Bit, 44.1 kHz WAV file. Selecting these parameters will ensure that the resulting file is compatible with all of the common distribution options.

Export your final mix:

1. Set the edit mode for the project to **SLIP** mode.

2. Place the Edit cursor on the **Stereo Mix** Master Fader track, just past the end of the final fadeout that you created in Exercise 9.

3. Press **SHIFT+RETURN** (Mac) or **SHIFT+ENTER** (Windows) to select from the cursor position back to the beginning of the project. This will set a timeline range for your export.

> (i) If you don't make a selection before exporting your mix, Pro Tools|First will make certain assumptions about where your project ends, which may not be accurate. It's generally a good idea to set the range yourself to control the exact length.

4. Select **FILE > EXPORT > AUDIO MIX** or press **OPTION+COMMAND+B** (Mac) or **CTRL+ALT+B** (Windows). The Export Audio Mix dialog box will display.

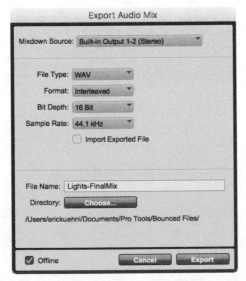

Figure 10.26 The Export Audio Mix dialog box

5. In the Export Audio Mix dialog box, select the following settings:

   - File Type: WAV

   - Format: Interleaved

   - Bit Depth: 16 Bit

   - Sample Rate: 44.1 kHz

6. Specify the filename for your mix near the bottom of the dialog box.

7. If desired, click the CHOOSE button to select a destination (folder location) for the exported mix.

> **ⓘ** **If you do not specify a different destination, your mix will be exported to the Bounced Files folder located in the Documents > Pro Tools folder.**

8. To listen to the mix as the project is being exported, uncheck the OFFLINE checkbox. This will create a real-time export. Otherwise, leave the box checked for a faster-than-real-time export.

9. When ready, click the EXPORT button to begin exporting your mix. Depending on the option you selected, you will see a countdown or a progress bar as the export completes.

Finishing Up

Congratulations! You've completed all of the required audio production work for a Pro Tools | First project, including:

- Importing audio and MIDI files

- Editing clips and assigning virtual instrument

- Mixing and balancing tracks

- Adding EQ, dynamics, and effects processing

- Creating automation

- Submixing tracks

- Applying MIDI Real-Time Properties

- Exporting the final mix as a stereo file

To wrap up, you'll need to locate the file you exported and verify the results. You may also want to remove the project from your Avid Cloud Account to make room for your next Pro Tools | First endeavor.

Locate your exported stereo mix file:

1.   Switch from Pro Tools|First to the Mac Finder or Window File Explorer.

2.   If you kept the default export location in the Export Audio Mix dialog box, do the following:

   •   Click on the Documents location in the sidebar/Navigation pane to open your Documents folder.

   •   Open the Pro Tools folder and then open the Bounce Files folder within it. Your mix file should be within this folder.

   Otherwise, navigate to the folder location you selected for your export.

3.   Select your mix file and do one of the following to listen to the results of your exported mix:

   •   On a Mac-based system, press the **SPACEBAR** to begin playback using the QuickLook feature.

   •   On a Windows-based system, right-click on the file and select **PLAY WITH WINDOWS MEDIA PLAYER**.

4.   Listen through the entire mix to verify that the results are as you expected/intended.

Be sure to listen to the mixed files that you create with Pro Tools|First before sharing them with others. If an unintended condition has affected the export, you may not have realized it, especially if you used the Offline option.

5.   If you hear any problem with the file (such as missing parts, wrong file duration, etc.), return to Pro Tools|First to correct the issue. Look for soloed or muted tracks, a selection that is too long or too short, and so forth. Once corrected, play back the project to verify that it sounds correct and repeat the export process.

Once you have created and verified your final mix, you can optionally delete the project and all of its associated audio files to make room in your cloud storage for your next project.

Deleting a project is an irreversible action. This will permanently delete the Pro Tools|First document and all of the associated media. Use this operation with caution.

Delete your unneeded project file(s):

1.   Return to Pro Tools|First and close the project, if you haven't already done so. The Dashboard will display automatically.

   With the **OPEN** action selected in the left side panel, the Dashboard will display your available projects and allow you to delete any projects you no longer need.

2. Click on the down arrow next to the name of a project you wish to discard and select **DELETE** from the pop-up menu.

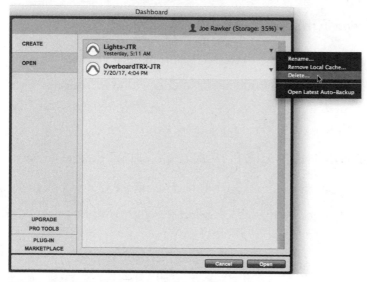

Figure 10.27 Deleting the Lights project

A confirmation dialog box will appear, verifying your intent to remove all copies of the project.

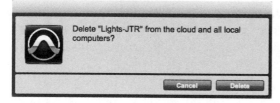

Figure 10.28 Confirmation dialog box for deleting a project

3. Click **DELETE** to proceed or **CANCEL** to return to the Dashboard without deleting the project.

4. Repeat this process for any other projects you no longer need.

That completes this exercise.

Index

About the Authors

This book was written and developed by Frank D. Cook and Eric Kuehnl and published by NextPoint Training, Inc. in partnership with Hal Leonard.

Frank D. Cook is a bass guitarist and longtime Pro Tools user. The president of NextPoint Training, Inc., he has worked in the technical publications and education industries for more than twenty years. As a writer, editor, technical publications manager, and business owner, Cook has authored, edited, and contributed to hundreds of guides, manuals, reports, textbooks, and other publications for clients in a wide variety of industries.

Cook has been a consultant for Avid Technology for over twelve years, helping to define the strategy and develop curricula for Avid's official Pro Tools training and certification programs. He is the author of the acclaimed Pro Tools 101 course book, along with four additional book titles in the Avid Learning Series. Cook teaches Pro Tools as an adjunct professor at American River College and Sacramento City College in Sacramento, California. He is the author of two Pro Tools courses for Lynda.com and is an Avid Master Instructor.

Eric Kuehnl is a composer, sound designer, and educator. He is the Director of Partner Programs at NextPoint Training, Inc. Kuehnl is also the Co-Director of the Music Technology Program at Foothill College in Los Altos Hills, California. He is an Avid Master Instructor for both Pro Tools and the S6 control surface and is the author of the Pro Tools for Game Audio course book published by Avid Technology.

Previously, Kuehnl was an Audio Training Strategist in the Avid Education Department and a Senior House Engineer for Sony Computer Entertainment America. He holds a Master's degree from California Institute of the Arts, a Bachelor's degree from Oberlin Conservatory, and has studied composition at the Centre Iannis Xenakis in Paris.